Death in Hollywood

By Willard C Phillips

* **Bobby Driscoll** (March 3, 1937 –

(March, 1968) American child actor

Robert Cletus Driscoll was born in Cedar Rapids, Iowa in 1937. Bobby was the only child of an insulation salesman, and a schoolteacher. Soon after his birth, his family moved to Des Moines where they lived until 1943. When a doctor advised Bobby's father to relocate to California due to lung problems resulting from handling asbestos, the family moved to Los Angeles. Bobby's barber's son, an actor, got him an audition at MGM for a part in the 1943 movie, Lost Angel, which starred Margaret O'Brien.

Bobby next played the part of Al Sullivan, the youngest of the five Sullivan brothers, in the 1944 film The Fighting Sullivans. He then appeared in Sunday Dinner for a Soldier (1944), The Big Bonanza (1944), and So Goes My Love (1946). He had a role in Identity

Unknown in 1945, and O.S.S. with Alan Ladd, which was released in 1946.

At just nine, Bobby became the first actor Walt Disney put under contract His first Disney movie was1946's Song of the South. The film turned Driscoll into a child star. Driscoll starred in So Dear to My Heart, opposite Burl Ives, but Howard Hughes, who had bought RKO the previous year, considered the film unworthy of release. When it was finally shown to the public in 1949, it was a hit. Then Bobby played Jim Hawkins in the Walt Disney production of Treasure Island, with Robert Newton as Long John Silver. Treasure Island was an international hit

Driscoll's last major success, Peter Pan, an animated film, was produced between 1949 and mid-1951. Driscoll was used as the reference model for the close-ups and provided Peter Pan's voice.

Perceived as a child actor, Bobby was unable to get serious character movie roles. Beginning in 1953 and for most of the next three years, most of his work was on television, in shows such as Fireside Theatre, Studio One, Dragnet, Medic, and Dick Powell's Zane Grey Theater.

Between 1948 and 1957, he performed in many radio productions, including Treasure Island in January 1951 and Peter Pan in December 1953.

After Bobby left the Disney studios, his parents sent him to Westwood University High School. There his grades dropped substantially and he began to experiment with drugs. In an interview years later, he stated, "I was 17 when I first experimented with the stuff. In no time I was using whatever was available, mostly heroin, because I had the money to pay for it." In 1956, age 19, he was arrested for the first time for possession of marijuana.

In December 1956, Driscoll and his girlfriend eloped to Mexico trying to avoid their parents' objections to their marriage. They had three children, but the relationship didn't last; they separated, and then divorced in 1960.

Bobbie's final screen roles were the 1955 release, The Scarlet Coat, and The Party Crashers in 1958.

He was charged with disturbing the peace and assault with a deadly weapon after hitting a heckler with a pistol. The man made insulting remarks while Bobby was washing a girlfriend's car. The charges were dropped. Late in 1961, at age 24, he was sentenced and imprisoned at the Narcotic Rehabilitation Center of the California Institution for Men in Chino, California.

When Driscoll left Chino in early 1962, he was unable to find work as an actor. Embittered, he said, "I have found that memories are not very useful. I was carried on a silver platter ... and then dumped into the garbage."

In 1965, a year after his parole expired, he moved to New York, hoping to work on the Broadway stage. Unsuccessful, he became part of Andy Warhol's Greenwich Village art community known as The Factory. The Factory was the hip hangout for artsy types, and drug users. It was famed for its groundbreaking parties. It is noteworthy that the first works that Warhol submitted to a fine art gallery, homoerotic drawings of male nudes, were rejected for being too openly gay

Bobby left The Factory in late 1967, penniless, and he disappeared into Manhattan's underground. On March 30, 1968, about three weeks after his 31st birthday, two boys playing in a deserted East Village tenement at 371 East 10th St found his dead body. The medical examination determined that he had died from heart failure caused by an advanced hardening of the arteries due to longtime drug abuse. There was no ID on the body, and photos taken of it and shown around the neighborhood yielded no identification. When Driscoll's body went unclaimed, he was buried in an unmarked pauper's grave in New York City's Potter's Field on Hart Island.

Late in 1969, about nineteen months after his death, Driscoll's mother sought the help of officials at the Disney studios in her attempt to contact him. This resulted in a fingerprint match at NYPD. His burial site on Hart Island is where his remains still remain.

Preface

Like moths attracted to a flame they are drawn to Hollywood; the talented and not so talented; the beautiful, the characters, and the weird. Like moths they are consumed, not by the flame of success but by the frailty of their own character. Many, perhaps thousands, remain unknown and uncounted because they never got past that hell pit known as the streets of Los Angeles.

Some claw their way to the pinnacle only to be dashed down by a fickle public and a cold-hearted system that has mercy only for the money-makers. Others, like Pinocchio on Pleasure Island, succumb to the easy access to drugs and decadent sex. The saddest of all perhaps, are those that waste the years of their short lives clinging desperately to hope and then in a moment of despair simply give up. Death in Hollywood is a biographical register of those poor fools; a short account of their lives; perhaps, in a few cases, the culmination of their dream of fame.

Following are more than one hundred forty stories much like Bobby Driscoll's; a list of those who have committed suicide or been murdered in Hollywood or after exposure to the movie industry. The list grows daily.

Dorothy

Abbott (December 16, 1920 –December 15, 1968)
American film actress and showgirl.

Born in Kansas City, Missouri, Abbott appeared
in many films between the 1940s and 1960s as an extra
(Road to Rio, The Razor's Edge, Little Women, etc). In
Las Vegas she was a showgirl at the Flamingo Hotel
and she appeared in roles on The Ford Television
Theatre, Leave It to Beaver, and Dragnet.

Depressed about the end of her marriage (her
husband, an L.A. police officer was having an affair
with Ann Southern), Abbott committed suicide in Los
Angeles on December 15, 1968, a day before her 48th
birthday.

Stanley Adams

(April 7, 1915 – April 27, 1977) American film actor.

Born in New York City, Adams had his first film role in 1952, when he played the bartender in the movie version of Death of a Salesman. He is well known for playing Cyrano Jones in the Star Trek: The Original Series episode "The Trouble with Tribbles".

Adams played Otis Campbell's brother on an episode of The Andy Griffith Show, and his other roles on TV shows include a time travelling scientist and a bartender on The Twilight Zone, "King Kaliwani" in the finale episode of Gilligan's Island and "Tybo" the carrot leader of the vegetable rebellion on Lost in Space. He played Rusty Trawler, "the 9th richest man in America under 50" in the Audrey Hepburn film 'Breakfast at Tiffany's'.

Evidently despondent over a failing career He shot himself in the head in 1977 at the age of 62.

Nick Adams (July 10, 1931 – February 7, 1968) American film and television actor.

Born Nicholas Aloysius Adamshock in Nanticoke, Pennsylvania. In 1948, while visiting New York City, 17-year-old Adamshock wandered into an audition for a play called The Silver Tassie and met Jack Palance, who was understudying for Marlon Brando in A Streetcar Named Desire at the time. When Palance asked Adamshock why he wanted to act, Adams replied, "For the money." Palance introduced Adamshock to the director of The Silver Tassie as Nick Adams. After the director declined to hire him as an extra, Palance sent Adams to a nearby junior theater group where he got his first acting job playing the role of Muff Potter in Tom Sawyer. While trying to get a role in the play Mister Roberts Adams had a brief encounter with Henry Fonda who advised him to get some training as an actor.

Adams' friends teased him about his acting ambitions. "Everybody thought I was crazy", he recalled. "My father said, 'Nick, get a trade, be a barber or something.' I said, 'But Pop, I want to do something where I can make lots of money. You can't make lots of money with just a trade.'"

After a year of unpaid acting in New York, Adams hitchhiked to Los Angeles where he landed a small role (as Chick) in Rebel Without a Cause in 1955; also that year Adams played the role of "Bomber" the paper boy in the widely popular film adaptation of Picnic.

In 1959 Adams starred in the television series The Rebel playing the character Johnny Yuma. From that point on his career was downhill.

After finishing Los Asesinos (1968) in Mexico, Adams bought a plane ticket with his own money and flew to Rome to co-star with Aldo Ray in a SciFi horror movie called Murder in the Third Dimension, but when he got there, he found the project had been dropped. Susan Strasberg, who had worked with him 13 years earlier on the hit film Picnic and was living in Italy, recalls encountering a thoroughly demoralized Adams in a Rome bar. On the night of February 7, 1968 his lawyer and friend drove to the actor's home in Beverly Hills to check on him after a missed dinner appointment. They discovered Adams in his upstairs bedroom, slumped dead against a wall.

During the autopsy Dr. Thomas Noguchi found enough paraldehyde, sedatives and other drugs in the body "to cause instant unconsciousness and death.

Adams' highly publicized life and death at a young age made his private life the subject of many writers who have claimed Adams was either gay or bisexual and may have had relationships with both James Dean and Elvis Presley. One of the earliest mentions on this topic was made by gossip columnist Rona Barrett, in which she said Adams "had become the companion to a group of salacious homosexuals" who flattered the actor, which affected his judgment. Mike Connolly (a gay gossip columnist for the Hollywood Reporter from 1951 to 1966) was said to put the make on the most prominent young actors, including Robert Francis, Guy Madison, Anthony Perkins, Nick Adams, and James Dean. According to American Film (1986), "Nick Adams, who was ... gay, was the butt of anti-gay humor in Pillow Talk.

* **Ross Alexander**

(July 27, 1907 – January 2, 1937)   American stage and film actor.

Born Alexander Ross Smith in Brooklyn, New York, Alexander began his acting career in Broadway productions during the 1920s. He was signed to a film contract by Paramount Pictures but his film debut in The Wiser Sex (1932) was not a success, so he returned to Broadway. In 1934 he was signed to another film contract, this time by Warner Bros.

Alexander was better suited to the Warner Bros. style of film. His biggest successes of the period were A Midsummer Night's Dream and Captain Blood (1935). He married actress Aleta Freel in 1934. The marriage ended the following year when Freel committed suicide on December 7, 1935.

Alexander soon after married another actress, Anne Nagel with whom he had appeared in the films China Clipper and Here Comes Carter (1936). In 1936 he starred in Hot Money. Warner Bros. had decided by this time that Alexander's potential as an actor was limited, and that his personal problems did not allow him to focus completely on his career. Although they continued casting him in films, the importance of his roles was greatly diminished.

With his professional and personal lives in disarray, and deeply in debt, Alexander shot himself in the head in the barn behind his home. Alexander used the same gun his wife Aleta Freel shot herself with two years earlier. His final film, Ready, Willing and Able, was released posthumously.

Lou Cannon wrote in his book 'Governor Reagan: His Rise to Power' that a young Ronald Reagan, then working as a radio broadcaster in Iowa, was hired in part by Warner Brothers to replace the recently deceased Alexander.

Pier Angeli (19 June 1932 – 10 September 1971) Italian-born television and film actress. Her American cinematographic debut was in the starring role of the 1951 film 'Teresa'.

She was born Anna Maria Pierangeli in Cagliari, Sardinia, Italy. Her twin sister is the actress Marisa Pavan. Working for MGM throughout the 1950s, she appeared in a series of films, including The Light Touch with Stewart Granger.

She would have had the role of Anna Magnani's daughter in The Rose Tattoo for Paramount, but because motherhood interfered, the role went to her twin sister, Marisa Pavan, who was nominated for an Academy Award for Best Supporting Actress for the role. Angeli was lent out to Columbia, for Port Afrique (1956) and then returned to MGM for Somebody Up There Likes Me as Paul Newman's long-suffering wife. Next she appeared in The Vintage (1957) with Mel Ferrer and John Kerr, and finished her contract in Merry Andrew, starring Danny Kaye.

At the age of 39, despondent and lonely, Angeli was found dead of a barbiturate overdose.

*

Matthew Ansara

(August 29, 1965 – June 25, 2001)

He was an actor and bodybuilder, the only son of Barbara Eden and her then husband Michael Ansara. His first acting job at age 15 was in the pilot episode of Harper Valley PTA. His credits include Your Mother Wears Combat Boots, To Protect and Serve, and Con Games.

On June 25, 2001, Ansara was found dead in his pickup truck. It later became apparent that Ansara had died of an accidental heroin overdose two months before his 36th birthday.

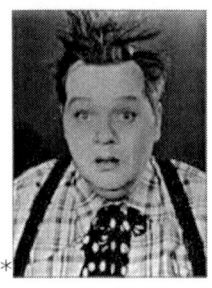

Roscoe "Fatty" Arbuckle

(March 24, 1887 – June 29, 1933) was an American illustrated song slide "model," silent film actor, comedian, director, and screenwriter. Starting at the Selig Polyscope Company he eventually moved to Keystone Studios where he worked with Mabel Normand and Harold Lloyd. He mentored Charlie Chaplin and discovered Buster Keaton and Bob Hope. He was one of the most popular silent stars of the 1910s, and soon became one of the highest paid actors in Hollywood, signing a contract to make $1 million a year in 1918. In 1921, Arbuckle threw a party at San Francisco's St Francis hotel during the Labor Day weekend. Bit player Virginia Rappe became ill at the party and died a few days later. Arbuckle was accused of raping and accidentally killing Rappe, and endured three widely publicized trials for manslaughter. His films were subsequently banned and he was publicly ostracized. Though he was acquitted by a jury and received a written apology, the trial's scandal overshadowed his legacy as a pioneering comedian. Arbuckle worked sparingly through the 1920s. He tried returning to filmmaking, but industry resistance to distributing his pictures continued. He retreated into alcoholism. In the words of his first wife, "Roscoe only seemed to find solace and comfort in a bottle".

After a small one-year anniversary party with his wife on June 29, 1933, Arbuckle went to bed and suffered a fatal heart attack in his sleep. Alcoholism is said to have been the cause. He was 46 years old.

 **James Arness**

His daughter Jenny Lee Aurness (May 23, 1950 - May 12, 1975) committed suicide.

* **Don (Red) Barry**

(January 11, 1912 – July 17, 1980) was an American film actor who got his nickname "Red" after appearing as the first Red Ryder in the highly successful 1940 film Adventures of Red Ryder.

By the 1950s, Barry had fallen to supporting actor in 'B' westerns. One more or less typical example of his work was as a black-clad gunfighter in a 1961 episode of the western television series Maverick with Jack Kelly and Buddy Ebsen called "Last Stop: Oblivion." On January 13, 1965, he appeared in the final episode of the short-lived 'Mickey' sitcom starring Mickey Rooney. Barry was cast as a free-loading friend who had saved Mickey's life in World War II. Barry played a supporting role in Shalako in 1968 with Sean Connery. He appeared 8 times on the long running series The Virginian in the 1960s. He also appeared in at least two episodes of Michael Landon's Little House on the Prairie. In one episode, he was tried for burning down the Garvey's barn and for assaulting Andy Garvey.

On July 17, 1980, he shot himself in the head with a pistol.

* **Nikki Bacharach**

July 12, 1966 - January 04, 2007 daughter of Angie Dickenson and Burt Bacharach.

Angie Dickinson married Burt Bacharach in 1965. Following the birth of their daughter in 1966, Dickinson temporarily put her career on hold, although she did appear in the occasional picture, such as the western The Last Challenge (1967) with Glenn Ford and the comedy Some Kind of Nut (1969).Their daughter, Lea Nikki, known as Nikki, arrived a year after they were married. Born three months prematurely, Nikki suffered from chronic health problems, including visual impairment. She was later diagnosed with Asperger syndrome. Angie declined many roles to focus on caring for her daughter. Nikki's parents eventually placed her at the Wilson Center, a psychiatric residential treatment facility for adolescents located in Faribault, Minnesota. Nikki remained there for nine years. Later, Nikki studied geology at California Lutheran University, but her poor eyesight prevented her from pursuing a career in that field. Burt penned the song Nikki for their fragile young daughter.On January 4, 2007, Nikki committed suicide in her apartment in the Los Angeles suburb of Thousand Oaks. She was 40. In a joint statement, Dickinson and Bacharach said: "She quietly and peacefully committed suicide to escape the ravages to her brain brought on by Asperger's... She loved kitties, and earthquakes, glacial calving, meteor showers, science, blue skies and sunsets, and Tahiti. She was one of the most beautiful creatures created on this earth, and she is now in the white light, at peace."

* **Diana Barrymore**

(March 3, 1921 – January 25, 1960) Film and stage actress

She was the aunt of actress Drew Barrymore.

Born Diana Blanche Barrymore New York City, New York, she was the daughter of John Barrymore and his second wife, poet Blanche Oelrichs

Her parents' tumultuous marriage lasted only a few years and they divorced when she was four. Educated in Paris, France and at schools in New York City, she had little contact with her father.

At age 19, Barrymore made her Broadway debut and the following year made her first appearance in motion pictures with a small role in a Warner Bros. production. Alcohol and drug problems soon emerged, and negative publicity cost her work. After less than three years in Hollywood, and five significant film roles, Barrymore's personal problems ended her film career.

Barrymore's life became a series of alcohol and drug related disasters marked by bouts of severe depression that resulted in several suicide attempts. She squandered her movie earnings and her inheritance from her father's estate, and when her mother died in 1950 she was left penniless.

Barrymore died from an overdose of alcohol and sleeping pills on January 25, 1960.

John Barrymore

(February 15, 1882 – May 29, 1942) American stage and screen actor

John Barrymore is mostly known for his roles in movies like Dr Jekyll & Mr Hyde (1920), Grand Hotel (1932), Dinner at Eight (1933), Twentieth Century (1934), and Don Juan (1926). He was the brother of Lionel Barrymore and Ethel Barrymore, and the paternal grandfather of Drew Barrymore.

Barrymore was born in Philadelphia. Barrymore fondly recalled the summer of 1896 which he spent on his father's estate on Long Island when he and his brother Lionel lived a Robinson Crusoe-like existence, attended by a black servant named Edward. John was expelled from Georgetown Preparatory School in 1898 (age 16) after being caught in a bordello.

He made his stage debut in 1903 and first appeared on the London stage 2 years later.

While still a teenager, he courted showgirl Evelyn Nesbit in 1901 and 1902. For years, rumors swirled that Nesbit had become pregnant and that Barrymore had arranged an abortion, disguised as an operation for "appendicitis". In 1906, another Nesbit lover, famed architect Stanford White, was murdered by Nesbit's husband, Pittsburgh millionaire Harry K. Thaw. Barrymore was subpoenaed to testify at Thaw's trial in defense hopes of showing that Nesbit had a history of "immorality." Both Barrymore and Nesbit denied the abortion story under oath.

Barrymore was staying at the St. Francis Hotel in San Francisco when the 1906 earthquake struck. He spent the next few days drinking at the home of a friend on Van Ness Avenue. During this drinking spell, he worked out a plan to exploit the earthquake for his own purposes. He presented himself as an on-the-scene "reporter", making up everything he claimed to have witnessed

Barrymore collapsed on his boat, The Mariner, in 1929 off the coast of Mexico while on honeymoon with wife Dolores. Much of his health problems stemmed from his consumption of bad and sometimes nearly poisonous illegal alcohol during the period of Prohibition in the United States. In the late 1930s, Barrymore began to lose his ability to remember his lines. From then on, he insisted on reading his dialogue from cue cards. He continued to give fair performances in lesser pictures, such as Inspector Nielson in some of Paramount Pictures' Bulldog Drummond mysteries, and he offered one last appearance in RKO's 1939 feature The Great Man Votes. During his last years, he married his fourth and last wife, Elaine Barrie, a union that turned out to be disastrous.

Barrymore collapsed while appearing on Rudy Vallee's radio show and died in his hospital room, May 29, 1942. His dying words were "Die? I should say not, dear fellow. No Barrymore would allow such a conventional thing to happen to him." Alcoholism is blamed for his early death.

Scotty Beckett

(October 4, 1929 – May 10, 1968) was an American child actor

Born in Oakland, California, Beckett got his start in show business at age 3 when the family moved to Los Angeles and a casting director heard him singing. Beckett landed a part in Gallant Lady (1933). His father died that same year. In 1934, Beckett joined the Our Gang series.

Beckett appeared as a regular in the Our Gang movies in 1934 and 1935. His role was taken over by Carl "Alfalfa" Switzer in 1935, and Beckett left the series to do features.

Beckett was a prolific child and young adult actor from the late 1930s to the early 1950s. He appeared as one of the unborn children in Shirley Temple's The Blue Bird (1940). He also played Al Jolson as a teenager in The Jolson Story (1946).

Although he was working steadily at MGM, his life grew increasingly difficult in the late 1940s and early 1950s. In 1948 he was arrested on suspicion of drunk driving. The following year he eloped with Beverly Baker, a tennis star, but their marriage dissolved within a period of months. In 1954, he ran afoul of the law again, once for passing a bad check and once for carrying a concealed weapon.

That same year Beckett's career took an upward turn when he was cast as Winky, the comic sidekick in the popular TV show Rocky Jones, Space Ranger. This was his last major role. He made a few subsequent TV and film appearances, and then left show business forever.

The last ten years of Beckett's life were filled with divorce, violence, drugs and arrests. On May 8, 1968, he checked into a Hollywood nursing home, needing medical attention after suffering a serious beating. He died two days later at the age of 38.

Although pills and a note were found, no conclusion was made by the coroner as to the exact cause of death; however, some speculate he overdosed on barbiturates or alcohol.

John Belushi

(January 24, 1949 – March 5, 1982) was an American comedian, actor, and musician

Belushi was born in Chicago, Illinois. His first big break as a comedian occurred in 1971, when he joined The Second City comedy troupe in Chicago. In 1973, Belushi moved to New York where he was a regular on The National Lampoon Radio Hour, a half-hour comedy program.

Belushi was famous for his work on Saturday Night Live, which he joined as an original cast member in 1975. One of his best-known movies, Animal House was made between SNL seasons. On John's 30th birthday in 1979, he had the number one film in the U.S., Animal House, the number one album in the U.S., The Blues Brothers, and was on the highest-rated late night television program.

Belushi left Saturday Night Live in 1979 to pursue a film career. He made four more movies; three of them, 1941, Neighbors, and most notably The Blues Brothers were made with fellow SNL alumnus Dan Aykroyd.

On March 5, 1982, Belushi was found dead in his room at Bungalow number 3 of the Chateau Marmont on Sunset Boulevard in West Hollywood, California. The cause of death was a speedball; the combined injection of cocaine and heroin. On the night of his death, he was visited by friends Robin Williams and Robert De Niro.

Brenda   Benet

(August 14, 1945 – April 7, 1982) American actress

Benet was born Brenda Ann Nelson in Hollywood, Los Angeles, California. Her first acting roles were in 1964, with appearances on Shindig! and The Young Marrieds. She became a popular in prime time television in the 1960s and 1970s, with roles including I Dream of Jeannie, Mannix, My Three Sons, Hogan's Heroes, Love, American Style, and The

Courtship of Eddie's Father. She also had a major feature role in the film Walking Tall (1973).

She became best known for her role as scheming villainess Lee Dumonde on the daytime serial Days of our Lives, a role she played from 1979 until her death in 1982.

Benet's first marriage was to The Donna Reed Show actor Paul Petersen in 1967. In 1969, Benet left Petersen for actor Bill Bixby.

Benet's son Christopher died in 1981. While on a skiing vacation, he went into cardiac arrest. Benet was devastated by her son's death and sank into a severe depression. On April 7, 1982, Benet took her own life by a self-inflicted gunshot wound. She was 36.

John Berg (April 5, 1949 – December 15, 2007) American actor

He appeared in several television roles, including Law & Order, The Practice, Passions, The Bold and the Beautiful, House, Boston Legal, NCIS, Monk and others. He had only one film credit, however, playing a Romulan senator in Star Trek Nemesis.

Berg committed suicide in his home by turning on a hibachi grill in his bedroom and succumbing to its carbon monoxide fumes. He was 58 years old.

Mary Kay Bergman (June 5, 1961 – November 11, 1999) American voice artist.

Bergman was born in Los Angeles. At an early age, she found herself drawn to fantasy entertainment ranging from science fiction to Disney. Bergman was known for voicing most of the female characters in animated series such as Fox Kids, The Secret Files of the Spy Dogs, in which she played a dog named Mitzy and also a number of other characters. She also voiced characters for South Park and the 1999 feature film South Park: Bigger, Longer & Uncut. Her characters included Liana Cartman, Sheila Broflovski, Sharon Marsh, Mrs. McCormick and Wendy Testaburger. Originally, Bergman was credited on South Park under the name Shannon Cassidy because she was also serving as Disney's official Snow White voice.

After suffering from manic depression and generalized anxiety disorder, Bergman committed suicide in her West Los Angeles, California apartment at the age of 38.

Bonnie Lee Bakley

Blake (June 7, 1956 – May 4, 2001) was the wife of actor Robert Blake.

Bonny Lee Bakley was born in Morristown, New Jersey. She was raised by her grandmother in Glen Gardner, NJ. She dropped out of high school at age 16 and went to New York City to pursue a career in modeling. She was married at 21 to her first cousin Paul Gawron and had three children with him: Glenn, Holly and Jeri.

She was convicted in Little Rock, Arkansas for possessing false identifications. In 1989, she was convicted of drug possession in Memphis, Tennessee she was allegedly holding drugs for rocker Jerry Lee Lewis. Later in 1995, she was convicted of passing bad checks. Bonny earned living sending nude pictures of women to men, with the promise of visiting them if they sent her money.

Bakley also had a history of pursuing celebrities. Her friends and relatives described her as "celebrity-obsessed". She had an affair with rock legend Jerry Lee Lewis and claimed to have had his daughter in 1993. However, DNA tests later disproved her claim. Lewis has denied ever having a baby with Bakley. Her photo business however, continued to be lucrative. Eventually she obtained enough money to buy several houses in Memphis and a house outside of Los Angeles. She was unsuccessful in her Hollywood career as a singer and actor under the stage name Lee Bonny.

In 1999, Bonnie Lee Bakley met Robert Blake at Chuck McCann's birthday party. At the time she was seeing Christian Brando. Blake slept with Bakley and later claimed that she had assured him that she was taking birth control pills. Friends of Bakley later said that she was, rather, taking fertility pills at the time. She was soon pregnant with what would be her fourth child. Initially, Bakley believed that Christian Brando was the father, but later told Blake she wasn't sure, and that it might be his. When a DNA test determined that it was Blake, not Brando, who was the father of Bakley's youngest child, Blake agreed to marry her. It was his second marriage, and her tenth. Although they were married, Bakley lived in a small guest house beside her husband's house in the Studio City area of the San Fernando Valley. It is rumored that Blake only married her to eventually get custody of their child, whom Blake wanted his childless daughter to raise.

On May 4, 2001 Blake took Bakley to an Italian dinner at Vitello's Restaurant on Tujunga Avenue in Studio City. Bakley was killed by a gunshot to the head while sitting in the car, which was parked on a side street around the corner from the restaurant. Blake claimed that he had returned to the restaurant to collect a gun which he had left there, and was not present when the shooting occurred. That gun had not fired the fatal shots.

Blake, was arrested April 18, 2002 for murder, soliciting murder, conspiracy to commit murder, and laying in wait for the murder of his wife. On April 22, 2002, he pleaded not guilty to one count of murder and two counts of solicitation of murder. April 29, 2002, Bakley's four children filed a wrongful-death lawsuit against Blake and his former handyman/bodyguard, Earle Caldwell.

July 25, 2002, Blake's adult daughter, Delinah Blake, gained custody of Rosie.

After Blake posted $1.5 million bail he was released from jail on March 14, 2003 and placed under house arrest. December 20, 2004, opening statements began in the criminal trial. The defense hoped to deflect suspicion from Blake by pointing the finger at Christian Brando, but that tactic failed due to a lack of evidence. Blake, his fans, and the media smeared the reputation of Bonny, the victim, his wife, and the mother of his child. Ronald "Duffy" Hambleton, and Gary McLarty, both former stuntmen, testified that Blake told them he was looking for someone to hire to kill Bonny. On March 4, 2005, jurors began deliberations. March 16, 2005, Blake was acquitted of first-degree murder, one count of solicitation of murder, and deadlocked on a second solicitation charge after jurors were split 11-1 in favor of acquittal. September 1, 2005 opening statements began in the civil trial. On October 25, 2005, Christian Brando invoked the Fifth Amendment when he took the witness stand.

After closing arguments on November 3, 2005, jurors began deliberations. On November 18, 2005, jurors found Blake "intentionally caused the death" of Bonny by a 10-2 vote and he was ordered to pay Bonny's children $30 million in damages. They voted against implicating Caldwell.

Clara Blandick

(June 4, 1880 – April 15, 1962) American actress.

She was born Clara Dickey, aboard the Willard Mudgett, an American ship captained by her father, docked in Hong Kong harbor at the time. Her parents settled in Quincy, Massachusetts, soon thereafter.

She grew up in Boston, and appeared in a production of the play Richard Lovelace. She moved from Boston to New York City, and began pursuing acting as a career. Her first professional appearance came in 1901, when she was cast as Jehanneton in the play If I Were King. Blandick finally broke onto Broadway in 1912, when she was cast as Dolores Pennington in Widow by Proxy. By 1914 she was reappearing on the silver screen, this time as Emily Mason in the film Mrs. Black is Back.

During World War I, Blandick did overseas volunteer work for the American Expeditionary Force in France. She also continued to act on stage and occasionally in silent pictures.

In 1929, Blandish moved to Hollywood. By the 1930s, she was well-known in theatrical and film circles as an established supporting actress. Though she landed roles like Aunt Polly in the 1930 film Tom Sawyer (a role she reprised in the 1931 film Huckleberry Finn), she spent much of the decade as a character actor.

In 1939, Blandick landed her most memorable minor role, Auntie Em in The Wizard of Oz. She retired from acting at the age of 69 and went into seclusion at the Hollywood Roosevelt Hotel.

Throughout the 1950s, Blandick's health steadily failed. She was losing her sight and suffering from severe arthritis. On April 15, 1962, she returned home from Palm Sunday services at her church. She began rearranging her room, placing her favorite photos and memorabilia in prominent places. She laid out her resume and a collection of press clippings from her lengthy career. She dressed immaculately, in an elegant royal blue dressing gown. Then, with her hair properly styled, she took an overdose of sleeping pills. She lay down on a couch, covered herself with a gold blanket over her shoulders, and tied a plastic bag over her head. Clara left the following note: "I am now about to make the great adventure. I cannot endure this agonizing pain any longer. It is all over my body. Neither can I face the impending blindness. I pray the Lord my soul to take. Amen."

Michael Blosil The 18-year-old adopted son of singer Marie Osmond leapt to his death from his Los Angeles apartment. Entertainment Tonight Online reported that Blosil left a suicide note saying his severe depression made him feel like he didn't fit in.

Charles Boyer (28 August 1899 – 26 August 1978) French/American actor

Born in Figeac, Lot, Midi-Pyrénées, France, Charles was a shy, small-town boy who discovered the movies and theatre at the age of eleven. Boyer performed comic sketches for soldiers while working as a hospital orderly during World War I. He began studies briefly at the Sorbonne, and was waiting for a chance to study acting at the Paris Conservatory. In 1920, his quick memory won him a chance to replace the leading man in a stage production, and he scored an immediate hit. MGM signed Boyer to a contract, and he loved life in the United States, but nothing much came of his first Hollywood stay from 1929 to 1931. At first, he performed film roles only for the money and found that supporting roles were unsatisfying. However, with the coming of sound, his deep voice made him a romantic star.

His first break came with a very small role in Jean Harlow's Red-Headed Woman (1932). After starring in a French adaptation of Liliom (1934), he began to receive public favor.

Boyer landed his first leading Hollywood role in the romantic musical Caravan (1934). French expatriate Claudette Colbert requested him in the psychiatric drama Private Worlds (1935).

The offscreen Boyer was bookish and private, far removed from the Hollywood high life. But onscreen he made audiences swoon as he romanced Marlene Dietrich in The Garden of Allah (1936), Jean Arthur in History Is Made at Night (1937), Greta Garbo in Conquest (1937), and Irene Dunne in Love Affair (1939).

In 1938, he landed his famous role as Pepe le Moko, the thief on the run in Algiers. Although he never invited costar Hedy Lamarr to "Come with me to the Casbah" in the movie, this line was in the movie trailer.

In contrast to his glamorous image, Boyer began losing his hair early, had a pronounced paunch, and was noticeably shorter than leading ladies. When Bette Davis first saw him on the set of All This, and Heaven Too, she did not recognize him and tried to have him removed.

His only marriage was to British actress Pat Paterson, whom he met at a dinner party in 1934. The two became engaged after two weeks of courtship and were married three months later. They moved from Hollywood to Paradise Valley, Arizona. The marriage lasted 44 years.

On 26 August, 1978, two days after his wife died from cancer, and two days before his own 79th birthday, Boyer committed suicide with an overdose of Seconal while at a friend's home in Scottsdale. On the night of 10 December, 1964, at his own 21st birthday party in his LA home, their son Michael shot himself. The media reported his death as a deliberate suicide.

Jonathan

Gregory Brandis (April 13, 1976 – November

12, 2003) American actor, director, and screenwriter.

Brandis was born in Connecticut, the only child of Mary, a teacher and personal manager, and Gregory Brandis, a food distributor and firefighter. He began his career as a child model and began acting in television commercials. Brandis landed a recurring role on One Life to Live when he was six years old. He moved to Los Angeles with his family at age nine, and made guest appearances on shows such as L.A. Law, Who's the Boss?, Murder, She Wrote, The Wonder Years, Full House and Kate & Allie.

At the age of fourteen, he received his first starring role in The Never Ending Story II: The Next Chapter as Bastian Bux, a young boy who returns to a world of wonder on the wings of his imagination. That same year, Brandis played the young "Stuttering Bill" Denbrough, the main character in the 1990 miniseries Stephen King's It, based on the epic horror novel by Stephen King. Following this, Brandis appeared in Sidekicks co-starring Chuck Norris and Ladybugs with actor/comedian Rodney Dangerfield. Around the age of seventeen, Brandis landed one of his best known roles as scientific prodigy Lucas Wolenczak in Steven Spielberg's futuristic science fiction series SeaQuest DSV. The role propelled him into teen idol status. During the run of SeaQuest DSV, he also voiced Mozenrath, a young evil sorcerer and necromancer in Disney's animated series Aladdin.

In addition to acting, Brandis directed several independent films and authored screenplays. During his stint on SeaQuest DSV, he co-wrote an episode of the series entitled "The Siamese Dream". He produced and directed the short film The Slainville Boys, shortly before his death.

On November 12, 2003, Brandis died at Cedars-Sinai Medical Center in Los Angeles from injuries he suffered after he hanged himself. He was 27 years old

Tarita Cheyenne

Brando (February 20, 1970 – April 16, 1995) was the daughter of Marlon Brando by his third wife, Tarita Teriipia, a Tahitian whom he met while filming Mutiny on the Bounty in 1962.

Born in 1970, Cheyenne was raised by her mother Tarita on the island of Tahiti, south of Papeete. Her parents divorced in 1972.

In 1989, Cheyenne was injured in a car accident when she crashed her boyfriend's jeep after her father refused to allow her to visit him while he was filming The Freshman in Toronto, Canada. The facial injuries she sustained brought an end to her modeling career.

In 1990, Dag Drollet, Cheyenne's boyfriend and father of her unborn child, was shot to death by Cheyenne's elder half-brother, Christian Brando, at their father's Mulholland Drive property in Los Angeles. This occurred after Cheyenne had alleged that Drollet was abusive. Statements Cheyenne made to the police shortly after the shooting led them to believe that the shooting was not an accident. Her mental state at the time was fragile, and she required sedation. Her father sent Cheyenne to a hospital in Tahiti, which prevented U.S. authorities from subpoenaing her to testify at the trial of her half-brother Christian; he later was sentenced to 5 years for the voluntary manslaughter of Dag Drollet.

After arriving in Tahiti, Cheyenne gave birth to a son she named Tuki Brando. Shortly after that Cheyenne tried to take her own life by overdosing on sleeping pills. She was formally diagnosed with schizophrenia, became isolated from her former friends, and lost custody of her son to her mother (who raised him in Tahiti). In 1995, at the age of twenty-five, Cheyenne committed suicide at her mother's house by hanging herself. Neither her father nor her half-brother Christian was able to attend her funeral in Tahiti.

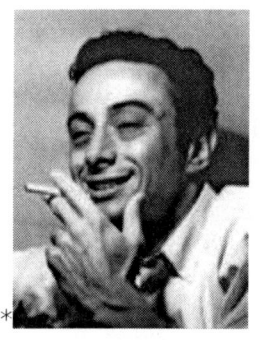

Lenny Bruce

(October 13, 1925 – August 3, 1966), American Comedian

Lenny Bruce was born Leonard Alfred Schneider in Mineola, New York. His parents divorced when he was five years old, and Lenny moved in with various relatives over the next decade. His mother was a stage performer and had a large influence on Bruce's career. Bruce joined the United States Navy at the age of 17 in 1942, and saw active duty in Europe. In May 1945 he reported to his ship's medical officer that he was experiencing homosexual urges. This led to his Undesirable Discharge in July 1945. However, he had not admitted to or been found guilty of any breach of naval regulations and successfully applied to have his discharge changed to "Under Honorable Conditions ... by reason of unsuitability for the naval service".

In 1947, soon after changing his last name to Bruce, he earned $12 and a free spaghetti dinner for his first stand-up performance in Brooklyn, New York. He later was a guest, introduced by his mother, who called herself 'Sally Bruce', on the Arthur Godfrey Talent Scouts show, doing a "Bavarian mimic" of American movie stars (e.g., Humphrey Bogart).

Bruce's early comedy career included writing the screenplays for Dance Hall Racket in 1953, which featured Bruce, his wife, Honey Harlow, and mother, Sally Marr, in roles, Dream Follies in 1954, a low-budget burlesque romp, and a children's film, The Rocket Man, in 1954. He also released four albums of original material on Berkeley-based Fantasy Records, with rants, comic routines, and satirical interviews on the themes that made him famous: jazz, moral philosophy, politics, patriotism, religion, law, race, abortion, drugs, the Ku Klux Klan, and Jews. His growing fame led to appearances on the nationally televised Steve Allen Show.

Bruce met his future wife, Honey Harlow, a stripper from Baltimore, Maryland, in 1951. They were married that same year. The need of money resulted in Bruce pursuing schemes, the most notable of which was the Brother Mathias Foundation scam, which resulted in Bruce being arrested for impersonating a priest. He was found not guilty because of the legality of the New York state-chartered foundation, the actual existence of the Guiana leper colony, and the inability of the local clergy to expose him as an impostor. Later, in his semi-fictional autobiography How to Talk Dirty and Influence People, Bruce revealed that he had made about $8,000 in three weeks, sending $2,500 to the leper colony and keeping the rest.

On October 4, 1961, Bruce was arrested for obscenity at the Jazz Workshop in San Francisco; he had used the word cocksucker and riffed that "to is a preposition, come is a verb", that the sexual context of come is so common that it bears no weight, and that if someone hearing it becomes upset, he "probably can't come". Although the jury acquitted him, other law enforcement agencies began monitoring his appearances, resulting in frequent arrests under charges of obscenity. In April 1964, he appeared twice at the Cafe Au Go Go in Greenwich Village, with undercover police detectives in the audience. On both occasions, he was arrested after leaving the stage, the complaints again pertaining to his use of various obscenities.

A three-judge panel presided over his widely publicized six-month trial, with Bruce and club owner

Howard Solomon both found guilty of obscenity on November 4, 1964. Bruce was sentenced, on December 21, 1964, to four months in a workhouse; he was set free on bail during the appeals process and died before the appeal was decided. Solomon later saw his conviction overturned. Bruce, who died before the decision, never had his conviction stricken. Bruce later received a full posthumous gubernatorial pardon.

On August 3, 1966, Bruce was found dead in the bathroom of his Hollywood Hills home. The official photo, taken at the scene, showed Bruce lying naked on the floor, a syringe and burned bottle cap nearby, along with various other narcotics paraphernalia. The official cause of death was "acute morphine poisoning caused by an accidental overdose."

Julia Bruns

(1895 – December 24, 1927) American stage and silent film actress.

At age 18, Bruns was a passenger in a Baldwin Red Devil flown by Tony Jannus, a contestant in a New York Times air derby, on October 12, 1913 (the Wright brother's first flight was in 1903). The plane ascended nearly 4,000 feet and flew for twenty minutes above the air at Oakwood Heights, Staten Island.

Bruns first acting role was in The American Maid written by John Philip Sousa. For a number of years she appeared on stage in the United States and Europe.

She was among the players in the Willard Mack theatrical drama Her Market Value.

She made three motion pictures in Hollywood, No Place For Father (1913), At First Sight (1917), and Quand on aime (1919). The first movie was directed by Lionel Barrymore. Her final film was made in France and paired her with actor Paul Guide' and director Henry Houry.

In 1926 Bruns wrote a series of articles about her life as a drug addict and her effort to find a cure. She was jailed in Chicago, Illinois for theft of jewels worth $1,000 in September 1925. Bruns admitted stealing the jewels to obtain money to purchase narcotics.

Bruns died of alcohol poisoning in a furnished room in New York City, in 1927.

 **Clyde Bruckman**

(September 20, 1894 – January 4, 1955) American writer and director.

Bruckman may be best known for his collaborations with Buster Keaton. Bruckman co-wrote a number of Keaton's most popular films, including Our Hospitality, Sherlock Jr., The Navigator, Seven Chances, The Cameraman and The General, which Bruckman also co-directed.

Bruckman continued directing comedies during the sound era, his most famous credit being The Fatal Glass of Beer, W. C. Fields' esoteric satire of Yukon melodramas. Unfortunately for his career path, Bruckman's fondness for alcohol caused production delays that cost him directorial assignments. From 1935 forward, Bruckman would be limited to writing scripts.

Bruckman's wealth of silent-comedy experience earned him a steady position in Columbia Pictures' short-subject department, and he was instrumental in Columbia's hiring his old boss Buster Keaton in 1939. Bruckman continued to write new material for The Three Stooges and other comics, but as time went by he resorted to borrowing gags from Harold Lloyd's and Buster Keaton's silent films. After Bruckman lifted the magician's-coat sequence from Lloyd's Movie 'Crazy' for the Three Stooges' 'Loco Boy Makes Good', and the "loosely basted tuxedo" routine from Lloyd's 'The Freshman' for the Stooges' 'Three Smart Saps', Lloyd sued Columbia and won.

Bruckman was hired by Universal Pictures to write comedy scenes for the studio's B musical features. This was a lucrative assignment that paid better than short subjects. He continued recycling gags but on a larger scale, now lifting entire sequences from older films. Bruckman inserted the tuxedo routine into Universal's "B" musical-comedy feature, Her Lucky Night. Bruckman adapted material from Lloyd's, Welcome Danger, into Universal's Joan Davis-Leon Errol comedy She Gets Her Man, and again consulted Movie Crazy for Universal's "B" comedy So's Your Uncle. Lloyd, outraged by three "wholesale infringements" within months, filed suit for $1,700,000. (The court validated Lloyd's claim but not the damages he sought; Lloyd received $40,000.) Bruckman was fired, and never worked on a feature film again.

The desolate Bruckman borrowed a .45-calibre pistol from Buster Keaton, claiming to need it for a hunting trip. On the afternoon of January 4, 1955, Bruckman, a resident of Santa Monica, California, parked his car outside a local restaurant, entered a restroom, and shot himself in the head.

Richard Burton

(10 November 1925 – 5 August 1984) Welsh actor

Richard Burton was born Richard Walter Jenkins in the village of Pontrhydyfen, Neath Port Talbot, Wales. He grew up in a working class, Welsh-speaking household, the twelfth of thirteen children.

Burton was less than two years old in 1927 when his mother, Edith Maude, died at the age of 43 after giving birth to her 13th child. His sister Cecilia and her husband Elfed took him into their Presbyterian mining family in nearby Port Talbot.

Burton early on displayed an excellent speaking and singing voice and won an Eisteddfod prize as a boy soprano.

In 1943, at the age of eighteen, Richard Burton (who had now taken his teacher's surname) served in the RAF (1944–1947) as a navigator. Burton's eyesight was too poor for him to be considered pilot material.

In the 1940s and early 1950s Burton worked on stage and in cinema in the United Kingdom. He had made his professional acting debut in Liverpool and London, appearing in Druid's Rest, but his career was interrupted by conscription in 1944. Early on as an actor, he developed the habit of toting around a book-bag filled with novels, dictionaries, a complete Shakespeare, and books of quotations, history, and biography, and enjoyed solving crossword puzzles. Burton could, given any line from Shakespeare's works, recite from memory the next several minutes of lines

In 1947, after his discharge from the RAF, Burton went to London. His first film was The Last Days of Dolwyn, set in a Welsh village about to be drowned to provide a reservoir. His reviews praised him for his "acting fire, manly bearing, and good looks." Burton met his future wife, the young actress Sybil Williams, on the set, and they married in February 1949. They had two daughters, and divorced in 1963 after Burton's widely reported affair with Elizabeth Taylor. In the years of his marriage to Sybil, Burton appeared in the West End in a highly successful production of The Lady's Not for Burning, alongside Sir John Gielgud and Claire Bloom, in both the London and New York productions. He had small parts in various British films: Now Barabbas Was a Robber; Waterfront (1950) with Robert Newton; The Woman with No Name (1951); and a bigger part as a smuggler in Green Grow the Rushes.

In 1952, Burton successfully made the transition to a Hollywood star; on the recommendation of Daphne du Maurier, he was given the leading role in My Cousin Rachel opposite Olivia de Havilland. In Desert Rats (1953), Burton plays a young English captain in the North African campaign during World War II who takes charge of a hopelessly out-numbered Australian unit against the indomitable Field Marshal Rommel. The following year he created a sensation by starring in The Robe, the first film to premiere in the wide-screen process CinemaScope. In 1954, Burton took his most famous radio role, as the narrator in the original production of Dylan Thomas' Under Milk Wood, a role he would reprise in the film version twenty years later. He was also the narrator, as Winston Churchill, in the highly successful 1960 television documentary series The Valiant Years.

In terms of critical success, Burton's Hollywood roles throughout the 1950s did not live up to the early promise of his debut.

After playing King Arthur in Camelot on Broadway for six months, Burton replaced Stephen Boyd as Mark Antony in the troubled production

Cleopatra (1963). During the filming, Burton met and fell in love with Elizabeth Taylor.

Against his family's advice, Burton married Taylor on Sunday 15 March, 1964 in Montreal. Ever optimistic, Taylor proclaimed, "I'm so happy you can't believe it. This marriage will last forever."

At the time of his death, Burton was preparing to film Wild Geese II, the sequel to The Wild Geese, which was eventually released in 1985.

In a February 1975 interview with his friend David Lewin he said he "tried" homosexuality. He also suggested that perhaps all actors were latent homosexuals, and "we cover it up with drink". In 2000, Ellis Amburn's biography of Elizabeth Taylor suggested that Burton had an affair with Laurence Olivier and tried to seduce Eddie Fisher

He was an insomniac and a notoriously heavy drinker. However, ongoing back pain and a dependence upon pain medications have been suggested as the true cause of his misery. He was also a heavy smoker from the time he was just eight years old; and by his own admission in a December 1977 interview with Sir Ludovic Kennedy, Burton was smoking 60–100 cigarettes per day.

Burton died at age 58 from a brain hemorrhage on 5 August, 1984 at his home in Céligny, Switzerland, and is buried there; although his death was sudden, his health had been declining for several years, and he suffered from a constant and severe pain in the neck. He had been warned that his liver was enlarged as early as March 1970, and had been diagnosed with cirrhosis of the liver and kidneys in April 1981.

* **Donald S**

Cammell (17 January 1934 – 24 April 1996)

Scottish film director

Cammell was born in the Camera Obscura (then known as Outlook Tower) on Castlehill, near the castle in Edinburgh, Scotland, the son of the poet and writer Charles Richard Cammell. Cammell wrote and co-directed 'Performance' with Nicolas Roeg in 1968, and didn't get another film produced until Demon Seed in 1977. Cammell made the horror thriller 'White of the Eye' in 1987. Between and TV directing jobs, Cammell directed music videos for the likes of U2.

When Cammell's 1995 film Wild Side was cancelled by the producer, he committed suicide in Hollywood, California by shooting himself.

*

Max Cantor (May 15, 1959 - October 3, 1991) American journalist and actor

His father was the theatrical producer Arthur Cantor. During Cantor's trips to London with his father, Vidal Sassoon personally cut his hair. He grew up in the Dakota Apartments on West 72nd Street in New York. Cantor attended Collegiate School but graduated from Buxton School in Williamstown, MA. He spent his summers until 14 at Camp Hillcroft in Billings, New York alongside fellow campers such as the children of Albert Shanker and Burt Lancaster. He won top roles in Winnie the Pooh and The Velveteen Rabbit. He was a 1982 graduate of Harvard University, where he lived in Adams House and starred in several productions by the then-student director Peter Sellars. He wrote for The Village Voice on ibogaine as a cure for heroin addiction, and took an interest in the cult surrounding East Village cannibal murderer Daniel Rakowitz.

He became a heroin addict while researching addicts in New York and died from a heroin overdose at the age of 32.

*

Truman Capote

(September 30, 1924 – August 25, 1984) American writer.

Born in New Orleans in 1924, Capote was abandoned by his mother and raised by his elderly aunts and cousins in Monroeville, Alabama. As a child he lived a solitary and lonely existence, turning to writing for occupation.

In his mid-teens, Capote was sent to New York to live with his mother. He dropped out of school, and at age seventeen, got a job with The New Yorker magazine. Within a few years he was writing regularly for various publications. Capote's first book, Other Voices, Other Rooms, was published in 1948. Other Voices, Other Rooms received instant praise for its prose, and its frank discussion of homosexual themes, and, perhaps most of all, for its suggestive cover photograph of Capote himself.

With literary success came social celebrity. The young writer was seen at the best parties, clubs, and restaurants. He answered accusations of not working by claiming he was researching a book. With the publication of Breakfast at Tiffany's and the subsequent hit film, Capote was famous as well as popular, and so he began work on a new experimental project that he imagined would revolutionize the field of journalism.

In 1959, Capote set about creating a new literary genre, the non-fiction novel, In Cold Blood (1966). An instant classic, In Cold Blood brought its author millions of dollars and fame unparalleled by nearly any other literary author since.

Capote began to work on a project exploring the intimate details of his friends. He received a large advance for a book which was to be called Answered Prayers. The publication of the first few chapters in Esquire magazine in 1975 caused a major scandal.

With these first short publications Capote found that many of his close friends and acquaintances shut him off completely. Though he claimed to be working on Answered Prayers (which many imagined would be his greatest work), the shock of the initial negative reactions sent him into a spiral of drug and alcohol use, during which time he wrote very little of any quality. When Capote died in 1984, at the age of fifty-nine, he left behind no evidence of any continued progress on Answered Prayers.

Capote died in Los Angeles on August 25, 1984, aged 59 from liver cancer. According to the coroner's report the cause of death was "liver disease complicated by phlebitis and multiple drug intoxication".

Arthur Edmund Carewe (December 30, 1884 – April 22, 1937)

Armenian/American actor in the silent and early sound film era.

Born Hovsep Hovsepian in Trabzon, Ottoman Empire, Carewe came to the United States on August 7, 1896. He decided upon a stage career and attended the American Academy of Dramatic Arts in New York City. By 1910, he had assumed the stage name of Arthur Carew. He relocated to Chicago sometime before 1915 and operated a furnishing goods business until he moved to Hollywood in 1919. His debut role was in the Constance Talmadge comedy Romance and Arabella.

Carewe became a well respected character actor and was considered for the role of Count Dracula in 1931, which would eventually go to Bela Lugosi. Seen in many classic offerings such as The Phantom of the Opera (1925), Uncle Tom's Cabin (1927), The Cat and the Canary (1927), Trilby (1923), Doctor X (1932), and Mystery of the Wax Museum (1933), Carewe completed nearly 50 films, mostly during the silent film era.

Shortly after completing Charlie Chan's Secret (1936), he suffered a stroke, which ended his acting career. He was found dead in his car in the parking lot of a Santa Monica beach motel, an apparent suicide by a gunshot to the head.

Jack Cassidy

(March 5, 1927 – December 12, 1976) American actor of stage, film and screen.

Cassidy was born in Richmond Hill, New York. He achieved his greatest success as a musical performer on Broadway, appearing in Alive and Kicking, Wish You Were Here, Shangri-La, Maggie Flynn, Fade Out - Fade In, It's a Bird...It's a Plane...It's Superman, and She Loves Me.

On television he became a frequent guest star, appearing in such programs as Bewitched, Get Smart, That Girl, Columbo, Hawaii Five-O, Match Game, and McCloud. Cassidy also co-starred in the movie The Eiger Sanction with Clint Eastwood.

Cassidy was married twice. His first wife was actress Evelyn Ward. They had a son, David Cassidy. After divorcing in 1956, Jack married actress Shirley Jones. David and Shirley later starred together in the sitcom The Partridge Family. Jack and Shirley had three sons, Shaun, Patrick, and Ryan, and divorced in 1974.

In his 1994 autobiography, C'Mon, Get Happy, David wrote that he became increasingly concerned about his father in the last years of his life. He suffered from alcoholism and displayed increasingly erratic behavior. In 1974, his neighbors were shocked to see him watering his front lawn naked in the middle of the afternoon. Shirley Jones described a similar incident when she found him sitting naked in a corner, reading a book. Jones said to Cassidy that they had to get ready to do a show, and he calmly looked up and said, "I know now that I'm Christ". In December 1974, he was hospitalized in a psychiatric facility for 48 hours. At that time, Jones found out that he had been previously diagnosed with bipolar disorder. David wrote about his father's bisexuality in his autobiography, a fact he discovered only after his father's death.

In 1976, Cassidy was living alone in an apartment in West Hollywood, California. Sometime in the early morning hours of December 12, 1976, he lit a cigarette and fell asleep or passed out on a couch, which then caught fire and the flames spread throughout the apartment. His body was found on the floor, as if he had been trying to crawl to the sliding glass doors but was overcome by smoke inhalation.

Capucine (6 January 1933 – 17 March 1990) French actress and fashion model

Capucine was born Germaine Lefebvre in Toulon, France. At 17, while riding in a carriage in Paris, she was noticed by a commercial photographer. She became a model, working for fashion houses Givenchy and Christian Dior.

In 1957, film producer Charles K. Feldman spotted Capucine while she was modeling in New York City. Feldman brought her to Hollywood to learn English and study acting under Gregory Ratoff. She was signed to a contract with Columbia Pictures in 1958 and landed her first English-speaking role in the film Song Without End (1960). For the next few years, Capucine made six more major motion pictures, including North to Alaska (1960) and Walk on the Wild Side (1962).

She met actor William Holden in the early 1960s. They starred in the films The Lion (1962) and The 7th Dawn (1964). Holden was married to Brenda Marshall, but the two began a two-year affair.

On 17 March 1990, Capucine jumped from her eighth-floor apartment in Lausanne, Switzerland.

Ronni Chasen

(October 17, 1946 – November 16, 2010) American publicist.

Chasen was born Veronica Cohen in Kingston, New York in 1946. Chasen began her early career as a publicist for her brother, film director Larry Cohen, who hired her for his 1973 blaxploitation film, Hell Up in Harlem.

Chasen became known in Hollywood for her PR work on such films as On Golden Pond, and the second film in the Oliver Stone/Michael Douglas Wall Street movie franchise, Wall Street 2: Money Never Sleeps.

Chasen was working with Richard D. Zanuck and Lili Zanuck for the Oscar campaign of the 2010 film, Alice in Wonderland, at the time of her death.

Chasen was shot in Beverly Hills on November 16, 2010, at approximately 12:28 a.m. PST, as she was driving home from the Hollywood premiere of the film Burlesque.

Neighbors near the intersection of Whittier Drive and Sunset Boulevard in the city of Beverly Hills originally reported hearing gunshots in front of their homes, but more calls came in to the 911 call center a few moments later stating that a late model, black Mercedes-Benz had run a curb, then hit and toppled a concrete street light. When police crews arrived, they found Chasen slumped in the driver's seat, the steering wheel airbag inflated, with blood emanating from her nose and chest area, in and out of consciousness with the front passenger side window shattered. Chasen was pronounced dead at Cedars-Sinai Medical Center.

Beverly Hills Police Department sources stated that Chasen received approximately five gunshot wounds to the chest, which caused her to lose control of the vehicle just after turning from Sunset Boulevard onto Whittier Drive. Police surmised that Chasen's killer was an expert marksman and likely shot her from an SUV or truck that pulled alongside her car. A leaked coroner's report noted that hollow-point bullets might have been used by the gunman.

On December 1, 2010 the Los Angeles Times reported that a man believed to be involved with Chasen's murder committed suicide after being confronted by police at the Harvey Apartments on Santa Monica Boulevard in East Hollywood and that the suspect in Ronni Chasen's slaying had been under police surveillance before he killed himself. The Los Angeles Times reported the man, a convicted felon named Harold Martin Smith, was approached by police in the apartment lobby, at which point he pulled out a pistol and shot himself in the head. On December 6, 2010 it was reported that the man was no longer considered a person of interest in the murder. However, on December 8, 2010 the Beverly Hills Police Department declared its preliminary conclusion that Chasen's murder had been a random act of violence, a robbery attempt turned violent. According to the police, the gun the suspect used to kill himself was the same one used to murder Chasen. Police said they believed the man acted alone and it was in no way connected with road rage – an operating theory the previous week. The big break in the case was a tip through America's Most Wanted – after the suspect began bragging to neighbors that he shot Chasen and got $10,000 for it. The AMW tipster – who wants to remain anonymous – stands to collect a $125,000 reward.

*

Lana Jean

Clarkson (April 5, 1962 – February 3, 2003)

American actress and fashion model.

Born in Long Beach, California, to Donna and James M. Clarkson, Lana Clarkson was raised in the hills of Napa Valley, California. While living in Northern California, she attended Cloverdale High School and also Pacific Union College Preparatory School. During the Christmas season of 1978 and after her father's death, Clarkson's family moved back to Southern California and settled down in the Los Angeles region of San Fernando Valley, where Lana pursued a career in entertainment industry as a performer and fashion model.

In the early 1980s, Clarkson landed bit parts in film and television. In 1982, she made her screen debut as a cameo character in director Amy Heckerling's coming-of-age comedy based on the Cameron Crowe book, 'Fast Times at Ridgemont High', as the wife of science teacher Mr. Vargas (Vincent Schiavelli). The film was her first speaking role. In 1983, she also peeks into the frame in "Scarface" behind Michelle Pfeiffer dancing the floor of the Babylon Club.

Clarkson's best known films may be her work with Roger Corman, appearing first in his fantasy film Deathstalker. Corman oriented his films towards young male viewers, using a mix of action and female nudity. Clarkson's work in Deathstalker led to her being offered the title role in Corman's next film, Barbarian Queen. The film gained cult status, in part due to an infamous scene where Clarkson is bound topless to a torture rack, interrogated, and raped.

In 1987, Clarkson appeared in the John Landis spoof Amazon Women on the Moon. Following that, Clarkson starred in Roger Corman's Barbarian Queen sequel, Barbarian Queen II: The Empress Strikes Back, though the plots and characters bore no resemblance to the other film. Filmed in Mexico, the movie featured mud-wrestling Amazon women, magic scepters, and (like its predecessor) several lengthy scenes where Clarkson is tortured topless or naked on a stretching rack by a villain. Clarkson received star billing in the film which went directly to video. Although sales of the video were low, Corman did manage to turn a profit.

In 1990, she starred as a supporting character in the period horror film Haunting of Morella as the evil attendant to a young woman played by model/actress Nicole Eggert. In the film, Clarkson played a dominating lesbian character who tries to resurrect the spirit of a witch burned at the stake during the Salem witch trials.

Clarkson's work in the B movie sci-fi genre inspired a cult following, making her a favorite at comic book conventions, where she made some promotional appearances signing autographs for her fans. She appeared in numerous other B movies as well as a range of television spots and appearing in commercials for Mercedes-Benz, Kmart, Nike, Mattel and Anheuser-Busch. Her television appearances include parts on Night Court, Silk Stalkings, Riptide, Three's Company, Knight Rider and Wings, and a guest appearance as a villain on the television adaptation of Roger Corman's film Black Scorpion in what would be her final role.

As she approached her thirties, Clarkson's career began to stall. No longer able to earn a living as an actress, Clarkson sought alternate routes of income, including operating her own website on which she sold autographed DVDs of her films and communicated directly with her fans on her own message board. Although she made a living by playing busty, lusty women, Lana's fondest desire was to be cast as a comic actress or perform as a comedian. On February 3, 2003, Clarkson was shot dead in the mansion of music producer Phil Spector. In the early hours of that morning, she met Spector while working at the House of Blues. Both left the House of Blues later in Spector's limo and drove to his mansion. Spector and Clarkson went inside while his driver waited outside in the car. About an hour later, the driver heard a gunshot before Spector exited his house through the back door with a gun. He was quoted as saying, according to affidavits, "I think I just shot her."

Montgomery

Clift (October 17, 1920 – July 23, 1966) American film and stage actor

Montgomery Clift was born in Omaha, Nebraska and later resided in Jackson Heights, Queens, until he got his break on Broadway. Appearing on Broadway at the age of fifteen, Clift achieved success and performed on stage for ten years before moving to Hollywood.

Clift's first movie was opposite John Wayne in the 1948 film Red River which was shot in 1946 and released in 1948. Clift's second movie was The Search, followed by The Heiress.

Entering the 1950s, Clift was the most sought-after leading man in Hollywood, and his only direct competitor was Marlon Brando. His next movie was A Place in the Sun (1951).

Clift's peak came with the 1953 classic From Here to Eternity. His final completely pre-accident movie was Terminal Station.

Monty drank substantially, several times mentioned as "falling down drunk", but while he was working on a film or play he was very focused on the material and not drunk. In addition he took a quantity of drugs, mostly uppers and tranquilizers.

On May 12, 1956, while filming Raintree County, he smashed his car into a telephone pole after leaving a party at the Beverly Hills home of his Raintree County co-star and close friend Elizabeth Taylor. After a long recovery, he returned to the set to finish the film. The pain of the accident led him to rely on alcohol and pills for relief, as he had done after an earlier bout with dysentery left him with chronic intestinal problems. As a result, Clift's health and looks deteriorated considerably.

Clift continued to work over the next ten years. His next three films were Lonely Hearts (1958), The Young Lions (1958), and Suddenly, Last Summer (1959). In 1958, he turned down what became Dean Martin's role in Rio Bravo, which would have reunited him with John Wayne. Clift starred with Lee Remick in Elia Kazan's Wild River in 1960. He then costarred in John Huston's The Misfits (1961), which was both Marilyn Monroe's and Clark Gable's last film.

By the time Clift was making John Huston's Freud: The Secret Passion (1962), his destructive lifestyle was affecting his health.

On July 22, 1966, Clift spent most of the day in his bedroom in his New York City townhouse. At 1 am, his personal secretary James went up to say goodnight.

At 6 am the next day, James went to wake him but found the bedroom door locked. Unable to break it down, he ran down to the garden and climbed a ladder to the bedroom window. Inside, he found Clift dead: he was undressed, lying on his back in bed, with glasses on and fists clenched. His early death was likely exacerbated by his drinking and drug use.

Montgomery Clift certainly had sexual relationships with both men and women. He has been described as having a very tortured life. Being gay or bisexual in the 1940's and 50's was almost universally viewed by psychiatrists as a mental abnormality. There is scant evidence that he had a sexual relationship with Elizabeth Taylor, but they were very close friends.

*

Kurt Donald Cobain (February 20, 1967 – April 5, 1994)

American singer-songwriter, musician and artist, best known as the lead singer and guitarist of the grunge band Nirvana.

Kurt Donald Cobain was born on February 20, 1967, at Grays Harbor Hospital in Aberdeen, Washington, to Wendy Elizabeth (née Fradenburg), and Donald Leland Cobain. Cobain had one younger sister named Kimberly, born in 1970.

Cobain's family had a musical background. His maternal uncle Chuck Fradenburg starred in a band called The Beachcombers, his Aunt Mari Earle played guitar and performed in bands throughout Grays Harbor County, and his great-uncle Delbert had a career as an Irish tenor; making an appearance in the 1930 film King of Jazz.

At age four, Cobain started playing the piano and singing. When Cobain was seven years old, his parents divorced. Later in his life, he said the divorce had a profound effect on his life. His mother noted that his personality changed dramatically; Cobain became defiant and withdrawn. In a 1993 interview, he elaborated:

"I remember feeling ashamed, for some reason. I was ashamed of my parents. I couldn't face some of my friends at school anymore, because I desperately wanted to have the classic, you know, typical family; Mother, father. I wanted that security, so I resented my parents for quite a few years because of that."

Kurt behaved insolently toward adults. He began bullying another boy at school. On June 28, 1979, Cobain's mother granted full custody of Kurt to his father.

Cobain's teenage rebellion quickly became overwhelming for his father, who placed Kurt in the care of family and friends. While living with the born-again Christian family of his friend Jesse Reed, Cobain became a devout Christian and regularly attended church services. Cobain later renounced Christianity, engaging in what would be described as "anti-God" rants. The song "Lithium" is about his experience while living with the Reed family. Cobain would regard himself as both a Buddhist and a Jain during different points of his life, educating himself about the philosophies through various sources, including watching late night television documentaries on both subjects.

Although not interested in sports, Kurt was enrolled in a junior high school wrestling. Kurt was a skilled wrestler, yet hated the experience. Later, his father enlisted him in a little league baseball team, where Cobain would intentionally strike out to avoid playing on the team.

As a teenager living in Montesano, Cobain eventually found escape through the thriving Pacific Northwest punk scene, going to punk rock shows in Seattle. Cobain soon began frequenting the practice of fellow Montesano musicians the Melvins.

During his sophomore year in high school, Cobain began living with his mother in Aberdeen. Two weeks prior to graduation, he dropped out of Aberdeen High School upon realizing he did not have enough credits to graduate. His mother gave him a choice: find employment or leave. After one week, Cobain found his clothes and other belongings packed away in boxes. Feeling banished from his own mother's home, Cobain stayed with friends, occasionally sneaking back into his mother's basement.

In late 1986, Cobain moved into an apartment, paying his rent by working at a Polynesian coastal resort approximately 20 miles north of Aberdeen. During this period, he was traveling frequently to Olympia,

Washington to go to rock concerts. During his visits to Olympia, Cobain formed a relationship with Tracy Marander. The couple had a close relationship, but one that was often strained with financial difficulties and Cobain's absence when touring. Marander supported the couple by working at the cafeteria of the Seattle–Tacoma International Airport, often stealing food. Cobain spent most his time sleeping into the late evening, watching television and concentrating on art projects. Marander's insistence that he get a job caused arguments that influenced Cobain to write "About a Girl", which was featured on the Nirvana album Bleach. Marander is credited with having taken the cover photo for the album. Marander was not aware that "About a Girl" was written about her until years after Cobain's death.

Soon after Marander separated from him, Cobain began dating Tobi Vail, an influential DIY punk zinester of the riot grrrl band Bikini Kill. After meeting Vail, Cobain vomited as he was so completely overwhelmed with anxiety regarding his infatuation with her. This event would inspire the lyric: "Love you so much it makes me sick," which would appear in the song "Aneurysm". Cobain's relationship with Vail would inspire the lyrical content of many of the songs on Nevermind.

Courtney Love met Cobain on January 12, 1990, in Portland's Satyricon nightclub. Love made advances, but Cobain was evasive. Early in their interactions, Cobain broke off dates and ignored Love's advances because he was unsure he wanted a relationship. Cobain noted, "I was determined to be a bachelor for a few months [...] But I knew that I liked Courtney so much right away that it was a really hard struggle to stay away from her for so many months." Courtney Love first saw Cobain perform in 1989 at a show in Portland, Oregon; they talked briefly after the show and Love developed a crush on him.

Cobain was aware of Love through her role in the 1987 film Straight to Hell. According to journalist Everett True, the pair was formally introduced at an L7 and Butthole Surfers concert in Los Angeles in May 1991. In the weeks that followed, after learning from Dave Grohl that Cobain shared mutual interests with her, Love began pursuing Cobain. In late 1991 the two were often together and bonded through drug use.

Around the time of Nirvana's 1992 performance on Saturday Night Live, Love discovered that she was pregnant with Cobain's child. On February 24, 1992, Cobain and Love were married on Waikiki Beach in Hawaii. In an interview with The Guardian, Love revealed the opposition to their marriage from various people: "Kim Gordon [of Sonic Youth] sits me down and says, 'If you marry him your life is not going to happen, it will destroy your life.' But I said,

'Whatever! I love him, and I want to be with him!'... It wasn't his fault. He wasn't trying to do that."

Following a tour stop at Terminal Eins in Munich, Germany, on March 1, 1994, Cobain was diagnosed with bronchitis and severe laryngitis. He flew to Rome the next day for medical treatment, and was joined there by his wife, Courtney Love, on March 3, 1994. The next morning, Love awoke to find that Cobain had overdosed on a combination of champagne and Rohypnol. Cobain was immediately rushed to the hospital, and spent the rest of the day unconscious. After five days in the hospital, Cobain was released and returned to Seattle. Love later stated that the incident was Cobain's first suicide attempt.

On April 2 and April 3, 1994, Cobain was spotted in various locations around Seattle, although most of his close friends and family were unaware of his whereabouts. He was not seen on April 4, 1994. On April 3, 1994, Love contacted a private investigator, Tom Grant, and hired him to find Cobain. On April 7, 1994, amid rumors of Nirvana breaking up, the band pulled out of that year's Lollapalooza music festival.

On April 8, 1994, Cobain's body was discovered at his Lake Washington home by an electrician who had arrived to install a security system. Apart from a minor amount of blood coming out of Cobain's ear, the electrician reported seeing no visible signs of trauma, and initially believed that Cobain was asleep until he saw the shotgun pointing at his chin. A suicide note was found, addressed to Cobain's childhood imaginary friend "Boddah", that said, paraphrasing, "I haven't felt the excitement of listening to as well as creating music, along with really writing . . . for too many years now". A high concentration of heroin and traces of diazepam were also found in his body. Cobain's body had been lying there for days; the coroner's report estimated Cobain to have died on April 5, 1994.

Donald Cortez "Don" Cornelius (September 27, 1936 – February 1, 2012) American television show host and producer who was best known as the creator of the nationally syndicated dance/music franchise Soul Train, which he hosted from 1971 to 1993.

Don Cornelius was born in Chicago in 1936. Originally a journalist inspired by the civil rights movement, Cornelius recognized that in the late 1960s there was no television venue in the United States for soul music, and so he introduced many African-American musicians to a larger audience through their appearances on Soul Train. As writer, producer, and host of Soul Train, Cornelius was instrumental in offering wide exposure to musicians like James Brown, Aretha Franklin, and Michael Jackson.

Cornelius was best known for the catchphrase that he used to close the show: "... and you can bet your last money, it's all gonna be a stone gas, honey! I'm Don Cornelius, and as always in parting, we wish you love, peace and soul!"

Cornelius last appeared at the 2009 BET Awards to present The O'Jays with the 2009 BET Lifetime Achievement Award.

On October 17, 2008, Cornelius was arrested at his Los Angeles home on Mulholland Drive on a felony domestic violence charge. He was released on bail. Cornelius appeared in court on November 14, 2008 and was charged with spousal abuse and dissuading a witness from filing a police report. Cornelius appeared in court again on December 4, 2008, and pleaded not guilty to spousal abuse and was banned from going anywhere near his estranged wife, Russian model Victoria Avila, who had filed two restraining orders against him. On March 19, 2009 he changed his plea to no contest and was placed on probation.

At around 4 a.m. on February 1, 2012, police officers responding to a report of a shooting found Cornelius at his Mulholland Drive home. Cornelius is reported to have suffered a self-inflicted gunshot to the head. He was declared dead at Cedars-Sinai Medical Center.

Ray Combs

(April 3, 1956 – June 2, 1996)   American comedian, actor, and host of the game show Family Feud

Combs was born in Hamilton, Ohio. He entered the world of comedy after moving to Los Angeles in 1983. He began his career doing audience warm-ups for sitcoms. Johnny Carson noticed this and invited him to perform on The Tonight Show in October 1986.

In 1987, he had a small role as a cop in the comedy film Overboard starring Kurt Russell and Goldie Hawn.

In 1988, game show producers Mark Goodson and Howard Felsher selected Combs to host a new version of Family Feud. Audiences initially accepted

Combs' performance on Family Feud despite the inevitable comparisons to longtime host Richard Dawson.

The taping of his final episode aired in first-run syndication on May 27, 1994.

In July 1994, Combs injured his spinal disc in a car accident which left him in permanent pain. He also went through financial problems with two of his comedy clubs. Combs made several attempts to make it back into television, most notably as the host of the cable TV game show Family Challenge; all failed. About a week prior to his death, he appeared on television for the last time, live on a Memorial Day edition of The Home and Family Show with Cristina Ferrare and Chuck Woolery on May 27, 1996, where he talked about his experiences while hosting Family Challenge.

On June 1, 1996, police were called to Combs' home over reports of a disturbance. Combs had reportedly destroyed the inside of his home and had also been banging his head against the walls. Shortly after police arrived, Combs' estranged wife Debbie arrived and informed police that Combs was suicidal and had spent the previous week in the hospital for a suicide attempt. Combs was then admitted to the psychiatric ward of Glendale Adventist Medical Center and placed on a 72-hour mental observation hold. On Sunday, June 2, 1996, Combs committed suicide by removing the sheets from his bed and using them to hang himself in the closet of his hospital room.

* **Bob Crane** (July 13, 1928 – June 29, 1978) American actor

Bob Crane was born in Waterbury, Connecticut, but he spent his childhood and teenage years in Stamford, Connecticut. On June 21, 1948, Bob enlisted in the National Guard and was honorably discharged on May 1, 1950. In 1949, he married Anne Terzian, and they had three children. Bob and Anne divorced, and he married Patricia Olsen, an actress. They had one son, and adopted a daughter.

In 1950, Crane started his broadcasting career in New York. He then moved to Connecticut. Crane later moved his family to California to host a morning show in Hollywood. It quickly became the number-one rated morning show in the LA area.

Crane began substituting for Johnny Carson on the daytime game show Who Do You Trust? and appeared on The Twilight Zone, Alfred Hitchcock Presents, and General Electric Theater. Carl Reiner gave him a guest shot on The Dick Van Dyke Show, where he was noticed by Donna Reed. She suggested him for the role of neighbor Dr. Dave Kelsey in her sitcom.

In 1965, Crane was offered the starring role in Hogan's Heroes which became a hit and finished in the Top Ten in its first year on the air. The series lasted six seasons.

In 1968, during the run of Hogan's Heroes, Crane appeared with Elke Sommer, in The Wicked Dreams of Paula Schultz.

Hogan's Heroes was cancelled in 1971. Crane later appeared in two Disney films, 1973's Superdad with the title role and Gus (1976).

In 1973, Crane purchased Beginner's Luck, a play that he starred in and directed. The production toured for five years.

During the run of Hogan's Heroes, Richard Dawson introduced Crane to John Henry Carpenter, who had access to video tape recorders. Carpenter photographed Crane's sexual escapades with various women.

On the night of June 28, 1978, Crane is alleged to have called Carpenter to tell him that their friendship was over. The following day, Crane was discovered beaten to death in Scottsdale, Arizona. Robert Graysmith's book The Murder of Bob Crane states that investigators found semen on Crane's dead body, indicating that the murderer may have ejaculated on him after killing him.

According to an episode of A&E's Cold Case Files, police officers who arrived at the scene of the crime noted that Carpenter called the apartment several times that night. The car Carpenter had rented the previous day was impounded, and in it, blood was found that matched Crane's blood type. Due to insufficient evidence, the Maricopa County Attorney declined to file charges.

The case was reopened in 1990. The detectives in charge hoped that additional witnesses would incriminate Carpenter. He was arrested and held for trial after a Superior Court Judge found that the evidence justified a trial by jury.

Carpenter was found not guilty.

* **Patricia Cutts** (20 July 1926 - 6 September 1974) English/American actress

Born in London, Cutts was the daughter of the writer-director Graham Cutts. Her first roles were small parts in American films such as I Was a Male War Bride and The Man Who Loved Redheads and the television shows Alfred Hitchcock Presents and Perry Mason. She made a small appearance in Hitchcock's North by Northwest. She starred alongside Vincent Price in The Tingler. In 1958 she appeared in the film Merry, however in the 1960s, her screen appearances were restricted to guest spots on television shows such as The Lucy Show, Car 54, Where Are You?, Adventures in Paradise, and Playhouse 90.

She accepted the role of Blanche Hunt in Coronation Street in 1974. Producers were shocked when, after appearing in only two episodes, Cutts was found dead at her London flat, aged 48. An inquest into her death produced a verdict of suicide by barbiturate poisoning.

Cass Daley (July 17, 1915 – March 22, 1975) American radio, television and film actress.

Born Catherine Dailey in Philadelphia, Pennsylvania, Daley began singing as a child in front of neighborhood storefronts. In the 1930s, she began a stage career appearing in the 1936-1937 Ziegfeld Follies. In the 1940s, Daley began a movie career, appearing in The Fleet's In (1942), and Crazy House (1943). In 1950, she starred in her own radio show The Cass Daley Show.

With radio in decline, she retired to raise her son in Newport Beach.

She attempted a comeback in the 1970s appearing in small television, film and stage roles.

On March 22, 1975, alone in her apartment, the 59 year-old comedienne apparently fell and landed on her glass coffee table. A shard of glass jammed into her throat and she bled to death before her husband came home and discovered her.

* **Karl Dane** (October 12, 1886 – April 14, 1934) Danish comedian and actor known for his work in American films, mainly of the silent film era. .

Dane was born Rasmus Karl Therkelsen Gottlieb in Copenhagen, Denmark. In 1903 Dane's parents divorced, leaving him in the custody of his mother.

In 1900, Dane and his brother apprenticed as machinists, a job he would perform on and off throughout his life. In 1907, he began compulsory military service in the First Artillery Battalion. With the outbreak of World War I, Dane was called back to duty.

On January 25, 1916, Dane sailed for the United States alone, intending to send for his family later. Speaking no English, he boarded with $25 in his pocket. The ship arrived in February at Ellis Island. Dane passed immigrant inspection and moved to

Brooklyn with a friend named Charles Lindgren. The same day, he found work in a foundry.

In late 1917, Dane appeared in a Vitagraph Studios short filmed New Jersey. He made $3 a day (as a mechanic he had been making $3 a week) for his part. Dane then appeared in Warner Brothers anti-German film My Four Years in Germany

His next film was Wolves of Kultur. He followed that with 'To Hell with the Kaiser'. Before his move to Hollywood, Dane completed three more films; all in the anti-German propaganda style and all released in 1919.

In early 1921, Dane met a Swedish immigrant named Helen Benson. He then quit films, and together the pair moved to Van Nuys, California, where they started a chicken farm. On August 9, 1923, Helen died in childbirth as did the baby. In December 1923, Dane ran into old friend Charles Hutchison who convinced him to appear in a serial he was then producing.

In December 1924, the casting director at MGM recommended Dane for a role in The Big Parade alongside John Gilbert. The movie was a major success, becoming the second highest grossing silent film of all time.

He worked with Rudolph Valentino in Son of the Sheik. After Son of the Sheik, Dane began to appear as a comic relief in several films, including The Scarlet starring Lillian Gish), La Bohème, and Alias Jimmy Valentine.

In 1930 Dane lost his contract with MGM. December 1932, Dane's last film, The Whispering Shadow starring Bela Lugosi, was released.

By the summer of 1933, Dane had given up on films and turned desperately to mining. He spent three months driving up and down the West Coast trying to find a good mining deal. However, he ended up losing $1,100 in September 1933 and the venture never took off. Deeply depressed, Dane took on several jobs, including mechanic, waiter, and carpenter.

By the end of 1933, Dane had purchased a stake in a hot dog stand outside MGM Studios. The business failed. Dane then tried to find work with his former studio as an extra or carpenter but was turned away.

On April 14, Dane was to meet with a woman named Frances Leake, however, he never showed and Leake became worried. She went to his apartment and with the assistance of the landlady, was able to open the door. There they found Dane slumped in his chair with a revolver at his feet. Leake found Dane's final note on a nearby table. The short note read, "To Frances and all my friends-goodbye." Dane had committed suicide by shooting himself in the head. He was 47 years old.

No one came forward to claim his body. Police tagged his body with the note, "May have relatives in Denmark. Hold for awhile". For the next few days, authorities attempted to find his family, even placing ads in major Copenhagen newspapers. However, the Gottliebs did not find out about Dane's death until weeks later. Fellow Danish actor Jean Hersholt stepped forward and insisted MGM pay for a funeral and burial.

Lillian Hall-Davis (23 June 1898 — 25 October 1933) was a British actress during the silent era.

The daughter of a London taxi driver, her films included a part-color version of I Pagliacci (1923), The Passionate Adventure (1924), Quo Vadis (1925), Blighty (1927), The Ring (1927) and The Farmer's Wife (1928), the latter two both directed by Alfred Hitchcock. She also appeared in a comedy short film made in DeForest Phonofilm, As We Lie (1927), co-starring and directed by Miles Mander.

She failed to make the transition to talkies and killed herself at home in Golders Green by turning on the gas supply and cutting her own throat.

*

Bella Darvi

(October 23, 1928 – September 11, 1971) was a Polish-born French actress.

Darvi was born Bayla Wegier. She had three brothers, Robert, Jacques Wegier, Jean-Isidore, and a sister, Sura. Robert died in a concentration camp.Jailed by the Nazis during World War II, she was released in 1943. She was discovered in Paris by the wife of mogul Darryl Zanuck. In 1952, she moved into the Zanuck home. In August 1953, she signed a contract with Zanuck, who changed her name to Bella Darvi, Eventually, she became Zanuck's mistress.She was Richard Widmark's love interest in Sam Fuller's 1954 film Hell and High Water, but is probably best known for the role of Nefer, in The Egyptian.Zanuck left his wife for Darvi, but then left Darvi when he discovered that she was either a lesbian or bisexual. She later publicly dated women, as well as men. Darvi committed suicide, after several failed attempts, in Monte Carlo by gas. Her body remained undiscovered for more than a week.

* **Albert Dekker**

(December 20, 1905 – May 5, 1968) American character actor.

Born Albert Van Ecke in Brooklyn, New York, he adopted his mother's maiden name of Dekker as his stage name. Dekker attended Bowdoin College and made his professional acting debut with a Cincinnati stock company in 1927. Within a few months, Dekker was featured in the Broadway production of Eugene O'Neill's play Marco Millions.

After a decade of theatrical appearances, Dekker transferred to Hollywood in 1937, and made his first film, 1937's The Great Garrick.

He replaced Lee J. Cobb as Willy Loman in the original production of Arthur Miller's Death of a Salesman, and during a five-year stint back on Broadway in the early 1960s he played the Duke of Norfolk in Robert Bolt's A Man for All Seasons.

Dekker appeared in some seventy films from the 1930s to 1960s, but his four most famous screen roles were Dr. Cyclops, The Killers, Kiss Me Deadly, and Sam Peckinpah's western The Wild Bunch. Dekker's role in The Wild Bunch would be his last screen appearance.

On May 5, 1968, Dekker was found dead in his Hollywood home after failing to answer phone calls for two days. Although money and camera equipment were missing, there were no signs of forced entry. He was found naked, kneeling in his bathtub with a noose wrapped around his neck that was looped around the shower's curtain rod. He was also handcuffed, blindfolded, gagged and had sexually explicit words scrawled on his body in red lipstick. The coroner's ruling was accidental death by autoerotic asphyxiation. Dekker was 62 years old.

***Jon Dough** stage name of Chester Anuszak (November 12, 1962 – August 27, 2006) American pornographic actor.

Jon Dough grew up in a steel mill town in western Pennsylvania. Dough attended Albright College in Reading, Pennsylvania, graduating in 1985 with a degree in Biology.

After graduating from college, Jon Dough entered porn through his brother who posed for gay magazines. His first film was a short loop he made for Lance Kinkaid in 1985.

Dough's first marriage was to Deidre Holland, a pornographic actress, whom he later divorced. He remarried, to pornographic actress Monique DeMoan, to whom he remained married until he committed suicide and with whom he had a daughter, who was four years old at the time of his death.

As Dough or one of his other performing aliases, the Pennsylvania native was a veteran of nearly 1,100 adult videos and had directed 71 titles, according to the IAFD. One of his most noteworthy achievements is participating in a gangbang with 101 women, becoming as well the first DVD published by the adult-magazine publisher Hustler.

Dough died on August 27, 2006, in Chatsworth, California of suicide by hanging. He was 43 years old.

 **Dominique Ellen**

Dunne (November 23, 1959 – November 4, 1982) was an American actress.

Dunne was born in Santa Monica, California, the daughter of Ellen Griffin, a ranching heiress, and producer/journalist/novelist Dominick Dunne.

Dunne's first role was in the 1979 made-for-TV movie Diary of a Teenage Hitchhiker. She then got small roles in episodes of popular 1980s television series such as Family, Hart to Hart and Fame. She also appeared in four episodes of the short lived TV series Breaking Away and several more made for TV movies. She was then cast in a major role in producer Steven Spielberg's Poltergeist (1982), directed by Tobe Hooper. After Poltergeist, she appeared in the final season premiere of CHiPs and the 1982 TV movie The Shadow Riders with Tom Selleck and Sam Elliott.

In 1982, after completing work on Poltergeist, Dunne met and later moved in with a Los Angeles chef, (John Thomas Sweeney born and raised in Hazleton, PA), who was sous-chef at the restaurant Ma Maison. The relationship was abusive, and after a short while Dunne ended it. A few weeks later, on October 30, Sweeney strangled Dunne in the driveway of her home after she refused to reconcile with him. She fell into a deep coma for five days. She died on November 4, at Cedars-Sinai Medical Center in Los Angeles, California, less than 20 days before her 23rd birthday.

Michael Dunn

(October 20, 1934 – August 30, 1973) was an American actor and singer

Dunn suffered from dwarfism. As an adult, he stood 3' 10" and weighed about 78 pounds. He was born Gary Neil Miller in Shattuck, Oklahoma, during the time of the Dust Bowl. He was an only child. When he was four, his family moved to Dearborn, Michigan.

Dunn was gifted intellectually and musically. He started reading at age three, was champion of the 1947 Detroit News Spelling Bee and showed early skill at the piano.

He attended Redford High School in Detroit (1947–1951), and then entered University of Michigan in Ann Arbor in September, 1951, just before his 17th birthday.

In 1953, he transferred to the University of Miami, which offered a better climate and more accessible campus. His classmate John Softness recalled, "He could sing like an angel, and he could act and he could write and he was a brilliant raconteur."

At various points, he held different odd jobs— singing in a nightclub, answering telephones for the

Miami Daily News, and working as a hotel detective. He left college in 1956 after completing only his sophomore year, returned to Michigan, and attended summer classes at the University of Detroit, in 1957.

In New York, Dunn re-encountered Softness, who volunteered to be his manager. He also befriended actress Phoebe Dorin in an off Broadway show, "Two by Saroyan," in which both had small parts in the early 1960s. They began singing together casually after their nighttime performances, sitting on the wall of the fountain opposite the Plaza Hotel, and drew a following. Eventually, on the advice of fellow actor Roddy McDowall, the pair started a nightclub act of songs mixed with conversational patter, titled "Michael Dunn and Phoebe." The act received favorable reviews in Time magazine and The New York Times and ultimately led directly to the pair being cast on The Wild Wild West television series, a Western spy spoof with elements of historical fiction and science fiction, which debuted in 1965.

In the pilot episode of Get Smart, Dunn showed his skill with comic farce as the gangster Mr. Big. He also gained wide exposure in his role as Alexander, in the Star Trek episode "Plato's Stepchildren" (1968). He also appeared in an episode of Bonanza, "It's A Small World" (1970.

On the live stage, in 1963, he received the New York critics' Circle Award for best supporting actor for his role as Cousin Lymon in Edward Albee's stage adaptation of The Ballad of the Sad Café. He also received an Oscar nomination for his role as Karl Glocken in Ship of Fools (1965).

His mobility and physical stamina deteriorated throughout his brief life. He suffered especially from deformed hip joints.

He died in his sleep in his room at the Cadogan Hotel in London, on August 30, 1973, at age 38, while on location for The Abdication.

The New York Times reported his cause of death as undisclosed, leading to decades of repeated public speculation about possible suicide

A London physician reportedly prescribed and administered two narcotics and a barbiturate for severe arthritic pain, despite the extreme risk of inducing respiratory depression, apnea, and death in a patient with decreased respiratory reserve. Dunn may have needed the drugs in order to tolerate the physical demands of shooting a movie.

Jeanne Eagels

(June 26, 1890 – October 3, 1929) American actress on Broadway and in several motion pictures.

Jeanne Eagels was born in Kansas City, Missouri. Her father died in 1910 in Kansas City, leaving his 44-year-old widow with six children. Eagels attended St. Joseph's parochial school and Morris Public School. She quit school shortly after her first communion to work as a cash girl in a department store.

It was in Kansas City that she began her acting career. She left Kansas City around the age of 15 and toured the Midwest with the Dubinsky Brothers' traveling theater show. At first, she was a dancer, but in time she went on to play the leading lady in several comedies and dramas put on by the Dubinskys.

Around 1911, she moved to New York City, where she worked in chorus lines, eventually becoming a Ziegfeld Girl. Her hair was brown, but she bleached it when she went to New York. Eagels was in the supporting cast of Mind The Paint Girl at the Lyceum Theatre in 1912. Eagels played opposite George Arliss in three successive plays in 1916 and 1917.

In 1915, she appeared in her first motion picture. In 1918, she appeared in Daddies.

In 1922, she made her first appearance as a star in the play Rain, based on a short story by W. Somerset Maugham. Eagels played her favorite role, that of Sadie Thompson. She went on tour with Rain for two more seasons, and returned to Broadway to give a farewell performance in 1926.

In 1925, Eagels married Edward Harris "Ted" Coy, a former Yale University football star turned stockbroker. They had no children and divorced in 1928.

She next appeared in the comedy Her Cardboard Lover (1927), in which she appeared on stage with Leslie Howard. After a season on Broadway, she took a break to make a movie. She appeared opposite John Gilbert in the MGM film Man, Woman and Sin (1927).

In 1928, she made two "talkies" for Paramount Pictures, including The Letter and Jealousy (both released in 1929).

Just before she was to return to the Broadway stage in a new play, Eagels died suddenly at a private hospital in New York City on October 3, 1929 at the age of 39. Medical examiners disagreed on the exact cause of death, but the available evidence pointed to the effects of alcohol or heroin.

Peg Entwhistle (5 February 1908 – body found 18 September 1932) Welsh-born, English stage and screen actress

Born Millicent Lilian Entwistle in Port Talbot, Wales to English parents, she spent her early life in West Kensington, London. Her mother Emily died when she was very young and her father remarried. In 1916, at age eight, the family immigrated to America and settled in New York City. Her father's second wife also died and in 1922 he was killed by a hit-and-run driver. She and her two younger half-brothers were taken in by their uncle, who had come with them to New York and was the manager of Broadway actor Walter Hampden.

In 1925 Entwistle was living in Boston and was one of the Henry Jewett Players, who were gaining national attention.

Entwistle later had a part in The Wild Duck.

By 1926 Entwistle had been recruited by the New York Theatre Guild and her first credited Broadway performance was in The Man from Toronto.

Entwistle performed in ten Broadway plays as a member of the Theatre Guild between 1926 and 1932, working with noted actors such as George M. Cohan, William Gillette, Bob Cummings, Dorothy Gish, Henry Travers and Laurette Taylor. Her longest-running play was the 1927 hit Tommy in which she starred with Sidney Toler.

In 1927 Entwistle married actor Robert Keith. She was granted a divorce in 1929. Along with charges of cruelty, she claimed her husband did not tell her he had been married before and was the father of six-year-old Brian Keith (who later became an actor.

Aside from a part in the suspense drama Sherlock Holmes and The Strange Case of Miss Faulkner Entwistle was often cast as a comedienne:

In early 1932 Entwistle made her last Broadway appearance in J.M. Barrie's Alice Sit-by-the-Fire. By May 1932, at the height of the Great Depression, Entwistle was in Los Angeles with a role in the Romney Brent play The Mad Hopes starring Billie Burke:

After The Mad Hopes closed Entwistle found her first and only credited film role, for Radio Pictures'. Thirteen Women starred Myrna Loy and Irene Dunne. It premiered on October 14, 1932, a month after her death, at the Roxy Theater in New York City.

On Sunday, September 18, 1932, an anonymous woman telephoned the police and said that while hiking she had found a body below the Hollywood sign.

A detective and two radio car officers found the body of a moderately well-dressed, blonde-haired, blue-eyed woman in the 100-foot ravine below the sign. Entwistle remained unidentified until her uncle connected her two-day absence with the description and initials P.E. on a suicide note which had been found in the purse and published by the newspapers. He said that on Friday the 16th she had told him she was going for a walk to a drugstore and to see some friends. The police surmised that instead, she made her way from his Beachwood Drive home up the nearby southern slope of Mount Lee to the foot of the

Hollywoodland sign, climbed a workman's ladder to the top of the "H" and jumped.

Chris Farley

(February 15, 1964 – December 18, 1997) was an American comedian and actor.

Farley was born in Madison, Wisconsin. Farley graduated from Marquette University in 1986, with a concentration in communications and theater. He got his start in professional comedy at the Ark Improv Theatre in Madison, and at the Improv Olympic theater in Chicago. He then performed at Chicago's Second City Theatre. He was eventually promoted to their main stage.

Farley was one of two new SNL cast members announced in the spring of 1990. During his tenure on SNL, Farley made cameo appearances in the comedy films Wayne's World, Coneheads, Airheads, and Billy Madison.

After Farley completed his contract at Saturday Night Live following the 1994–1995 season, he began focusing on his film career. His first two films were

Tommy Boy and Black Sheep. They established Farley as a star and he was given the title role of Beverly Hills Ninja.

Drug and alcohol problems interfered throughout Farley's film work, and production of his final film, Almost Heroes, was held up several times so Farley could attend rehab. After his sudden death on December 18, 1997, his completed films, Almost Heroes and Dirty Work, were released posthumously.

In the final years of his life, Farley had sought treatment for obesity and drug abuse on seventeen separate occasions. On December 18, Farley was found dead by his younger brother John in his apartment in the John Hancock Center in Chicago. An autopsy later revealed that Farley had died of an overdose of a speedball combination of cocaine and morphine early that morning.

Richard W. Farnsworth (September 1, 1920 – October 6, 2000) was an American actor and stuntman.

Farnsworth was born in Los Angeles, California. He grew up during the Great Depression, living with his aunt, mother, and two sisters in downtown Los Angeles after his father died when he was seven years old.

In 1937, when he was sixteen, he started in films by riding horses in The Adventures of Marco Polo. He performed several horse-riding stunts in the Marx Brothers' A Day at the Races (1937) and Gunga Din (1939). He made uncredited appearances in many films, including Gone with the Wind (1939), Red River (1948), The Wild One (1953), and The Ten Commandments (1956). He was on the set of Spartacus (1960) for eleven months. He laughed when he said he did not look like a gladiator.

Farnsworth's appeared in the 1977 television miniseries Roots.

His breakthrough came when he played stagecoach robber Bill Miner in the 1982 Canadian film The Grey Fox, for which he won a Genie Award. In 1985, he appeared in the Canadian miniseries Anne of Green Gables, winning a Gemini Award for his performance as Matthew Cuthbert. Another of his prominent roles was as a suspicious sheriff in the film version of Stephen King's Misery (1990).

In 1999, he was nominated for an Academy Award for Best Actor for The Straight Story. When David Lynch asked to see if he wanted to be in the simple but emotional movie The Straight Story, Farnsworth had no idea who he was. Farnsworth did not like violence or swearing, and so his agent was very careful to tell him that Lynch was the director who had made The Elephant Man. Fortunately, he liked this movie. When Farnsworth and Lynch met, he reiterated his dislikes.

Farnsworth was diagnosed and treated for prostate cancer in the early 1990s. By 1999, he had been diagnosed as having terminal bone cancer. He made the movie The Straight Story while in considerable pain. Not wanting to live his life in pain, Farnsworth shot himself at his ranch in Lincoln, New Mexico.

Edward Paul Flanders (December 29, 1934 - February 22, 1995)

American actor

Flanders was born in Minneapolis, Minnesota. Flanders began his acting career on Broadway before moving on to guest parts in television series. From 1967 through 1975, Flanders appeared in more than a dozen TV shows, including six appearances on Hawaii Five-O.

In 1982, he began his role in St. Elsewhere. During a scene in which Westphall addressed the staff, Flanders began speaking extemporaneously about the quality of art and had to be edited for broadcast. His exit on St. Elsewhere as a regular cast member was titled Moon for the Misbegotten. The episode gained much publicity as Westphall left the hospital after "mooning" his new boss.

In feature films, Flanders performed in two movies based on novels by William Peter Blatty. In the first, The Ninth Configuration (1980), he plays a self-effacing medic at a secret U.S. army psychiatric facility. The film was based on Blatty's novel Twinkle, Twinkle, "Killer" Kane. Then in 1990, Flanders played Father Dyer alongside star George C. Scott in Blatty's The Exorcist III based on the novel Legion.

One of Flanders' best-remembered TV guest roles was in the first season M*A*S*H episode "Yankee Doodle Doctor", playing film director Duane William Bricker. Bricker, commissioned as a Lieutenant in the Special Services, is making a documentary about M*A*S*H units and comes to the 4077th on the recommendation of General Clayton. When Hawkeye and Trapper react to Bricker's filmmaking by destroying the negatives, Bricker abandons the project and leaves. Hawkeye takes over the making of the film which, instead of a serious documentary, becomes a farce in the style of the Marx Brothers.

Flanders also appeared in the 1979 made-for-TV-horror-mini-series Salem's Lot as Dr. Bill Norton. Flanders continued working in telemovies in the early 1990s, but was suffering from depression, particularly after his 1992 divorce from his second wife and financial problems with his ranch in northern California.

He took his own life by a self-inflicted gunshot wound on February 22, 1995 in Denny, California.

Anita Freel (June 14, 1907 – December 7, 1935) American actress.

Born in Jersey City, New Jersey, the daughter of a physician, Freel was educated at the Bergen School for Girls in Jersey City. She graduated from Smith College. Freel played several eastern stock companies. Among her stage performances was a role in the play

Double Door, which was performed at the Ritz Theater in New York City in the fall of 1933. She was married to Hollywood actor Ross Alexander following a backstage romance.

Having became despondent regarding her career Freel shot herself through the temple on December 6, 1935, and died early the following morning at Emergency Hospital in Los Angeles, California. She was 28 years of age. She was disappointed about some screen tests on which she had high hopes, but which were unsuccessful.

On December 14, 1935, in Sacramento, California, the state of California opened an investigation into the "strange death" of Aleta Freel. The inquiry was requested by Governor of New Jersey Harold G. Hoffman. Friends and relatives of the actress asked Hoffman and Governor Merriam of California for a more exhaustive probe. Freel's father, William, was quoted as saying at the time of his daughter's death, that he was not altogether sure she took her life.

Her husband Ross remarried, but 13 months after Freel's suicide he also shot and killed himself, reportedly with the same gun.

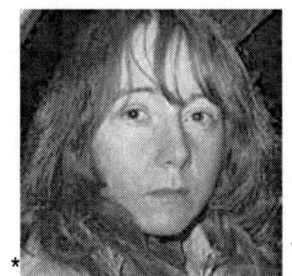*Lynette "Squeaky" Fromme (born October 22, 1948)

Fromme, born in Santa Monica, California, was the daughter of William Fromme, an aeronautical engineer, and Helen Benzinger, a homemaker. While still a child, Fromme performed with a popular local dance group called the Westchester Lariats, which in the late 1950s began touring the U.S. and Europe, appearing on The Lawrence Welk Show and at the White House.

In 1963, the Fromme family moved to Redondo Beach, and Lynette began drinking and using drugs. In 1967, Fromme went to Venice Beach where she met Charles Manson, who had been recently released from federal prison at Terminal Island. The two became friends, traveling together and with other young people such as Mary Brunner and Susan Atkins. She lived in Southern California at Spahn Ranch, and in the desert near Death Valley. When Manson and some of his followers were arrested for the Tate/La Bianca murders in 1969, Fromme and the remaining "Manson family" camped outside of the trial. Fromme copied Manson and his fellow defendants, Patricia Krenwinkel, Leslie Van Houten and Atkins when they carved Xs into their foreheads. Fromme was never charged with involvement in the murders, but was convicted of attempting to prevent Manson's imprisoned followers from testifying, as well as contempt of court when she herself refused to testify. She received short jail sentences for both offenses. On the morning of September 5, 1975, Fromme went to Sacramento's Capitol Park dressed in a nun-like red robe and armed with a .45 pistol that she pointed at Ford. The pistol's magazine was loaded with four rounds, but none was in the firing chamber. She was immediately restrained by a Secret Service agent. After a lengthy trial in which she refused to cooperate with her own defense, she was convicted of the attempted assassination of the president and received a life sentence. On December 23, 1987, Fromme escaped from the Federal Prison Camp, Alderson, in West Virginia, making an attemp to meet Manson, having heard that he had testicular cancer. She was captured two days later and sent to the Federal Medical Center, Carswell in Fort Worth, Texas.

Fromme first became eligible for parole in 1985. She was granted parole in July 2008, but was not released due to the extra time added to her sentence for the 1987 prison escape.

Fromme was released on parole from Federal Medical Center, Carswell on August 14, 2009. She then reportedly moved to Marcy, New York.

David C. Garroway (July 13, 1913 – July 21, 1982) American TV and radio personality.

Born in Schenectady, New York, Garroway was 14 when his family moved to St. Louis, Missouri, where he attended University City High School and Washington University. Before going into broadcasting, Garroway worked as a Harvard University lab assistant, selling books, and as a piston ring salesman. After not being able to successfully sell either, Garroway decided to try his hand in radio.

He began his broadcasting career modestly, starting as an NBC page in 1938, and then graduated from NBC's school for announcers. He landed a job at Pittsburgh radio station KDKA in 1939. He roamed the region, filing a number of memorable reports from a hot-air balloon, from a U.S. Navy submarine in the Ohio River, and from deep inside a coal mine. After two years with KDKA, Garroway left for Chicago.

When the United States entered World War II in 1941, Garroway enlisted in the U.S. Navy, but one trip out to Honolulu convinced the young man that perhaps he was a little better suited for radio instead. The Navy agreed to let him run a yeoman's school instead, and on his off-hours he hosted a radio show, on which he played jazz records and reminisced about the old days back in Chicago.

Later he went back to working in radio, doing "split shift" shows called Garroway AM (mid mornings) and Garroway PM (mid afternoons) for WCBS (AM), New York. Garroway began reading various law books in an effort to try to understand what his lawyer was saying. His attorney told him that he had done enough legal reading to pass the New York State bar exam. On a bet, Garroway Garroway was the first "communicator" on NBC Radio's Monitor when the program began on June 12, 1955. He continued as the Sunday evening host of the news/music program from 1955 to 1961. Garroway worked on the air at WCBS radio in 1964 and briefly hosted the afternoon drive shift at KFI in Los Angeles in late 1970 and early 1971.

Garroway was introduced to the national television audience when he hosted the experimental musical variety show Garroway at Large, telecast live from Chicago. It was carried by NBC from June 18, 1949, to June 24, 1951.

NBC president Sylvester "Pat" Weaver picked Garroway to host his new morning news-and-entertainment experiment, the Today show, in 1951. His familiar "cohost," a chimpanzee with the puckish name of J. Fred Muggs, didn't hurt his genial manner, but his seriousness in dealing with news stories earned him the nickname "The Communicator" and eventually won praise from critics and viewers alike.

At the same time he did Today, Garroway also hosted a Friday night variety series, The Dave Garroway Show, from October 2, 1953, to June 25, 1954, and on October 16, 1955, he began hosting NBC's Sunday afternoon live documentary Wide Wide World, continuing with that series until June 8, 1958.

Garroway's easygoing camera presence masked a man fighting inner demons. Disagreements with staff members became frequent. Some days Garroway would disappear in the middle of the show. Far worse, however, was the 1961 drug-related death of his second wife, Pamela.

In May 1961, Garroway announced his intention to leave Today.

After leaving Today, Garroway returned to television on National Educational Television (the forerunner of PBS) with a science series called Exploring sat for and passed the written exam.

In July 1969, Garroway launched a daytime talk show on WNAC-TV, Tempo Boston, which he hoped would be picked up for national syndication. The program lasted into early 1970 and never aired outside Boston. The show had promise but was canceled when management decided to show old movies instead of local live shows. After leaving the Boston airwaves, Garroway traveled to southern California, hosting a music-and-talk show on KFI radio in Los Angeles. He planned to reenter the television world with a CBS summer replacement show, Newcomers, but the show never made it past the summer of 1971.[1] While in Los Angeles, Garroway began to take acting workshops; he had a role in an episode of the western series Alias Smith and Jones as a judge in 1972.

Garroway appeared sporadically on other television programs without achieving anywhere near the success and recognition levels he enjoyed on Today. The most viewers saw of him for the rest of the 1960s and 1970s was whenever he reemerged for Today anniversaries. His final such appearance was on the 30th anniversary show, on January 14, 1982.

After having undergone heart surgery, Garroway was found dead of a self-inflicted gunshot wound at his Swarthmore, Pennsylvania, home on July 21, 1982.

 **Judy Garland** (June 10, 1922 – June 22, 1969) American actress and singer

After appearing in vaudeville with her sisters, Garland was signed to Metro-Goldwyn-Mayer as a teenager. There she made more than two dozen films, including nine with Mickey Rooney and the 1939 film with which she would be most identified, *The Wizard of Oz*. After 15 years, Garland was released from the studio but gained renewed success through record-breaking concert appearances, and a return to acting.

Despite her professional achievements, Garland battled personal problems throughout her life. She was unhappy about her appearance.

Garland was plagued by financial instability, often owing hundreds of thousands of dollars in back taxes. She married five times, with her first four marriages ending in divorce. Garland died of an accidental drug overdose at the age of 47.

Judy Garland's father and other significant people in her life were homosexuals. Frank Gumm would apparently seduce or at least keep company with very young men or older teens, then move on when told to leave or before his activities could be discovered. Garland's husband Vincente Minnelli was generally known to be a closeted bisexual. From the beginning of her Hollywood career, Garland liked to visit gay bars with openly homosexual friends Roger Edens and George Cukor, to the chagrin of her handlers at MGM.

Trevor Goddard (14 October 1962 – 7 June 2003) English actor.

Goddard was born in Croydon, Surrey, England, in 1962. For much of his career he claimed to be of Australian descent and often played Australian characters.

He appeared in cameo roles in many television shows prior to 1995. That same year, Goddard played Kano in the film adaptation of Mortal Kombat. His performance as Kano became the source of the character's evolution in the video games.

He would go on to act in other movies such as Gone in Sixty Seconds, Men Of War (with Dolph Lundgren and future JAG co-star Catherine Bell) and Hollywood Vampyr. Goddard also played in the television drama series JAG as Lieutenant Commander Mic Brumby and was also featured in TV commercials for the Hoover FloorMate.

He made his last on-screen appearance in the 2003 movie Pirates of the Caribbean: The Curse of the Black Pearl.

On 7 June 2003 Goddard was found dead in his home in North Hollywood (a suburb of Los Angeles), California. Initial reports indicated that Goddard was in the process of getting a divorce and that suicide was suspected. An autopsy later showed that Goddard died from a drug overdose of heroin, cocaine, temazepam and vicodin.

Paula Goodspeed

(1978 - November 11, 2008)   reality TV show contestant and singer.

Best known for her appearances on American Idol, she was considered a huge fan of singer and American Idol judge Paula Abdul, so much so she changed her first name to Paula and modeled her singing career and wardrobe after her.

In 2008, she committed suicide with a drug overdose in her car outside of Paula Abdul's home in Sherman Oaks, California. She reportedly sent Abdul flowers prior to her suicide. Goodspeed had been accused in the press of being nothing more than another celebrity stalker but her relatives disputed that claim.

*

Spalding

Rockwell Gray (June 5, 1941 – January 10, 2004)

American actor, playwright, screenwriter, and performance artist. Gray achieved celebrity status for his monologue Swimming to Cambodia, which was adapted into a film in 1987 by Jonathan Demme.

Gray was born in Providence, Rhode Island, to Rockwell Gray, Sr., the treasurer of Brown & Sharpe, and Margaret Elizabeth "Betty" Horton, a homemaker. He was the middle-born of three sons: Rockwell, Jr.,

Spalding and Channing. He was raised in the Christian Scientist faith and grew up in Barrington, Rhode Island, spending summers at his grandmother's house in Newport.

After graduating from Fryeburg Academy in Fryeburg, Maine, he enrolled at Emerson College as poetry major, where he earned his B.A. in 1963.

In 1965, Gray moved to San Francisco where he became a speaker and teacher of poetry at the Esalen Institute. In 1967, while Gray was vacationing in Mexico City, his mother committed suicide at the age of 52. After his mother's death, Gray moved away from the west coast and permanently settled in New York City.

Theatre historian Don Wilmeth noted Gray's contribution to a unique style of writing and acting: "The 1980s saw the rise of the autobiographical monologue, its leading practitioner Spalding Gray, the WASP from Rhode Island who portrays himself as an innocent abroad in a crazy contemporary world. . . others, like Mike Feder, who grew up in Queens and began telling his life on New York radio, pride themselves on their theatrical minimalism, and simply sit and talk. Audiences come to autobiography for direct connection and great stories, both sometimes hard to find in today's theatre."

After starring in some supporting actor movie roles, such as in The Killing Fields, and television parts, including Saturday Night Live, Gray achieved national prominence with his play 'Swimming to Cambodia', which he wrote in 1985. It was a monologue based entirely on his experiences in Southeast Asia where he played a small role in the 1984 movie The Killing Fields. He was awarded a Guggenheim Fellowship and the National Book Award in 1985.

Aside from his more well-known monologues, Gray was a founding member of the experimental theater company The Wooster Group, and appeared in a large number of plays, including a high-profile revival of Thornton Wilder's Our Town.

In 1992, Gray published his first and only novel, Impossible Vacation. The novel is based upon Gray's own life experiences, including his Christian Scientist upbringing, his WASP background, and his mother's suicide.

In June 2001, he suffered severe injuries in a car crash while on vacation in Ireland. "In the crash, Gray, who had always battled his hereditary depression and bipolar tendencies, suffered a badly broken hip, leaving his right leg almost immobilized, and a fracture in his skull that left a jagged scar on his forehead. He now suffered not only from depression but also from a brain injury. During surgery in which a titanium plate was placed over the break in his skull, surgeons removed dozens of bone fragments from his frontal cortex. Shattered both physically and emotionally, he spent the ensuing months experimenting with every therapy imaginable."

On January 10, 2004, Gray, suffering from increasingly deep episodes of clinical depression in part as a result of his injuries, was declared missing. The night before his disappearance, he had seen Tim Burton's film Big Fish, which ends with the line, "A man tells a story over and over so many times he becomes the story. In that way, he is immortal." Gray's widow, Kathie Russo, has said, "You know, Spalding cried after he saw that movie. I just think it gave him permission. I think it gave him permission to die."

On March 7, 2004, the Office of Chief Medical Examiner of the City of New York reported that Gray's body was pulled from the East River. It is believed that Gray jumped off the side of the Staten Island Ferry. In light of a suicide attempt in 2002, and the fact that his mother had killed herself in 1967, suicide was the suspected cause of death.

Stephen Hubert Avenel Haggard (1911–1943) British actor, writer and poet.

Haggard was born on March 21, 1911, in Guatemala City, Guatemala and was the son of Sir Godfrey Haggard. He was the grandnephew of H. Rider Haggard.

Haggard made his first appearance in New York in 1934 as the poet Thomas Chatterton in her play Come of Age. Returning to Britain, he had successful roles in a number of plays, including Flowers of the Forest, a production of Mazo de la Roche's Whiteoaks, and appeared as Konstantin in Chekhov's The Seagull, and was hailed as one of the most promising and handsome classical actors of the era.

In 1938 Haggard returned to New York to reprise his role as Finch in "Whiteoaks His novel Nya was published in the same year. He appeared as Mozart in the 1936 film Whom the Gods Love. He also appeared in Alfred Hitchcock's 1939 film Jamaica Inn.

He subsequently appeared as Lord Nelson in the 1942 Carol Reed film The Young Mr Pitt.

At the outbreak of the Second World War Haggard joined the British Army, serving as a captain in the Intelligence Corps. Haggard was posted to the Middle East and worked for the Department of Political Warfare. While in the Middle East, Haggard fell in love with a beautiful Egyptian married woman whose husband worked in Palestine. Haggard was overworked and felt that the war had destroyed his acting career. He was on the edge of nervous breakdown when after some months the woman decided to end the relationship. Haggard shot himself on a train between Cairo and Palestine on February 25, 1943 at the age of 31.

Jonathan Hale (March 21, 1891 – February 28, 1966) Canadian-born film and television actor.

Born Jonathan Hatley in Ontario, Canada, Hale was well known as Dagwood Bumstead's boss, Julius

Caesar Dithers, in the Blondie film series in the 1940s. He is also notable for playing Inspector Farnack in various The Saint films by RKO Pictures. He appeared in two different episodes of Adventures of Superman "The Evil Three", in which a he played a murderous "Southern Colonel"-type character, and "Panic in the Sky", one of the most famous episodes, in which he played the lead astronomer at the Metropolis Observatory (actually one of the California observatories).

Hale committed suicide on February 28, 1966.

Jon Hall (February 23, 1915 – December 13, 1979) American actor.

Born Charles Felix Locher in Fresno, California, and raised in Tahiti by his father, the Swiss-born actor Felix Locher. He was a nephew of James Norman Hall, one of the authors of Mutiny on the Bounty. Hall began acting in films in 1935 in minor roles, one of which was Charlie Chan in Shanghai. He achieved success in 1937 when cast opposite another relative newcomer, Dorothy Lamour, in The Hurricane, which was written by James Norman Hall.

He maintained his popularity until the end of the 1940s, usually playing leads in adventure films. In 1940, he portrayed Kit Carson in a biographical film of the frontiersman's life. He is notable for having made six popular Technicolor adventure films with Maria Montez: Arabian Nights (1942), White Savage (1943), Ali Baba and the Forty Thieves (1944), Cobra Woman (1944), Gypsy Wildcat (1944), and Sudan (1945). They typify the type of escapist entertainment which was extremely popular during World War II.

Jon Hall is perhaps best remembered by later audiences as the star of the television series Ramar of the Jungle, which ran from 1952 to 1954. Hall directed and starred the 1965 cult horror film The Beach Girls and the Monster.

When he was stricken with bladder cancer, Hall's health declined to a point that he found unbearable, and after telling friends that the pain of his illness was overwhelming, he committed suicide in North Hollywood, California.

Rusty Hamer

(February 15, 1947 – January 18, 1990)   American
television actor

Born in New Jersey, he grew up on TV as
Rusty Williams, Danny Thomas's freckle-faced son on
Make Room for Daddy. As a five-year-old actor, his
wisecracking behavior made him a popular character
during the airing of the 351 episodes of the program.
Thomas, who occasionally could be spotted trying not
to crack up in Hamer's scenes, would later publicly
praise the child's extraordinary comic timing.

Hamer attempted a brief return to show
business in 1970 as a married medical student in the
show Make Room for Grandaddy, a sequel of Make
Room for Daddy, but the show was canceled after one
season. He appeared occasionally in bit parts on
television shows such as CBS's Green Acres, starring
Eddie Albert and Eva Gabor, but roles became
increasingly sporadic. Hamer eventually moved to
Louisiana where he worked as a short order cook.

On January 18, 1990, Hamer died at the age of
forty-two of a self-inflicted gunshot wound to the head.

Lois   Hamilton

(October 14, 1943 – December 23, 1999)   American
model, author, actress, artist and aviatrix

Hamilton was born Lois Aurino in Philadelphia,
Pennsylvania. Her looks brought an opportunity with
the Ford Modeling Agency where she became one of its
top models during the 1970s.

Moving to Hollywood, she made a successful
transition from model to actress. Within a year, she
landed more TV stints than any other actress at her
agency.

Under the name Lois Hamilton or Lois Areno,
she appeared in several Hollywood films as well as on
television shows including many popular series such as
The Dukes of Hazzard and Three's Company.

When she wasn't involved in a feature film or
television project she was a licensed private pilot.
Hamilton was also an accomplished sculptress, painter
and writer. She exhibited her bronze sculptures and oil

paintings in many one-woman shows in Los Angeles. An author as well, she penned her first novel, Move Over Tarzan, a woman's guide on how to be as assertive as the most aggressive, successful man using a woman's femininity.

On December 23, 1999, Hamilton locked herself in her hotel room at the Sheraton Hotel in Rio de Janeiro, Brazil. Apparently depressed over her lingering injuries from an auto accident earlier in the year, she took a fatal overdose of sleeping pills. She was 56 years old. The official police report states that there are many suspicions around her death, including that the door could have been locked by someone who had a key to the room. The bag placed around her head was also not sealed tight enough to cause death by asphyxiation. Finally, the toxicology report states that the level of sleeping pills in her system was only very minor, and also not enough to cause her death.

Roland Edward Harrah (January 20, 1973 - January 3, 1995) American film and television child actor, actor, songwriter, musician, singer, and artist.

Born in Denver, Colorado, Harrah moved to Riverside, California where he lived for 15 years and acted for 12 years.

Harrah co-starred in adventure dramas, particularly related to Vietnam, which included Braddock: Missing in Action III (1988) with Chuck Norris and in two episodes of the television series Airwolf (1984–1987) with Jan-Michael Vincent.

He died at home in Riverside, allegedly by suicide.

Mary Elizabeth

Hartman (December 23, 1943 – June 10, 1987)
American actress,

Hartman was born in Youngstown, Ohio. After gaining valuable experience in community theater, she relocated to New York City. In 1964, Hartman was signed to play the ingénue lead in the Broadway comedy Everybody Out, the Castle is Sinking.

In 1964, Hartman was screen-tested by MGM and Warner Brothers. In the early autumn of 1964, she was offered a leading role in A Patch of Blue, opposite Sidney Poitier and Shelley Winters.

She went on to star in three well-received films, The Group, You're a Big Boy Now, and The Beguiled. A role as wife of Sheriff Buford Pusser in Walking Tall (1973) was followed ten years later by voice work in 1982's The Secret of NIMH. This proved to be her last Hollywood film role.

Throughout much of her life, Hartman suffered from depression. In her later years, her mental health continued to decline and she moved to Pittsburgh, Pennsylvania to be closer to her family. In the last few years of her life, she gave up acting altogether and worked at a museum. On June 10, 1987, Hartman fell to her death from the fifth floor window of her apartment, in what was believed to be a suicide. Earlier that morning, she had reportedly called her psychiatrist to say that she was feeling low.

Phil Hartman

(September 24, 1948 – May 28, 1998) American actor, comedian, screenwriter, and graphic artist

Born in Brantford, Ontario, Hartman and his family immigrated to the United States when he was ten. After graduating from California State University, with a degree in graphic arts, he designed album covers for bands like Poco and America. Feeling the need for a more creative outlet, Hartman joined the comedy group The Groundlings in 1975 and there helped comedian Paul Reubens develop his character Pee-wee Herman. Hartman co-wrote the screenplay for the film Pee-wee's Big Adventure and made recurring appearances on Reubens' show Pee-wee's Playhouse.

Hartman became well-known in the late 1980s when he joined the sketch comedy show Saturday Night Live. He won fame for his impressions, particularly of President Bill Clinton, and stayed on the show for eight seasons. He also had frequent roles on The Simpsons as Lionel Hutz, Troy McClure and others, and appeared in the films Houseguest, Sgt. Bilko, Jingle All the Way, and Small Soldiers.

Hartman had been divorced twice before he married Brynn (née Omdahl) in 1987; the couple had two children together. However, their marriage was fractured, due in part to Brynn's drug use

On May 28, 1998, Brynn shot and killed her husband while he slept in their Encino home.

Rodney Harvey (July 31, 1967 – April 11, 1998) American actor and model.

Born in Philadelphia, Pennsylvania, Harvey was discovered by director Paul Morrissey in 1984. Morrissey cast Harvey in two of his films Mixed Blood (1985) and Spike of Bensonhurst (1988). After signing with an agent, Harvey moved to Los Angeles where he continued acting and also began modeling In 1990, he landed the role of Sodapop Curtis in the Fox series The Outsiders. After the series ended after one season, Harvey guest starred on Twin Peaks, followed by a role in the Gus Van Sant film My Own Private Idaho. He made his last onscreen appearance in 1996 with a role in the drama God's Lonely Man.

During the making of My Own Private Idaho, Harvey began using heroin. After several stints in jail and attempts to get clean, he died of a heroin and cocaine overdose on April 10, 1998 at the Hotel Barbizon in Los Angeles.

Phyllis Haver

(January 6, 1899 – November 19, 1960) American film actress

She was born Phyllis Haver in Douglass, Kansas. When she was young, her family moved to Los Angeles, California. Haver attended Los Angeles

Polytechnic High. After graduating, she played piano to accompany the new silent films in local theaters.

Haver auditioned for comedy producer Mack Sennett on a whim. Sennett hired her as one of his original Bathing Beauties. Within a few years, she was appearing as a leading lady in two-reelers.

At the Sennett Studios, Haver played the part of Roxie Hart in the first film adaptation of 'Chicago' in 1927. She performed in the 1928 comedy film 'The Battle of the Sexes', directed by D. W. Griffith. The next year, she appeared with Lon Chaney, Sr. in his last silent film.

Haver retired in Sharon, Connecticut. She died at age 61 from an overdose of barbiturates in 1960, a suspected suicide.

James Hayden (November 25, 1953 – November 8, 1983) American actor.

Apart from starring on Broadway, he is perhaps best known for playing Patrick 'Patsy' Goldberg in the film Once Upon a Time in America.

Hayden trained and served as a medic in the United States Army during the Vietnam War. Upon his discharge he returned to New York and attended the American Academy of Dramatic Arts and began working as an actor.

In 1983, the year of his death, he portrayed a heroin addict in the critically acclaimed play American Buffalo, co-starring with his friend Al Pacino.

Ironically, Hayden died of a heroin overdose.

*Christa Helm: Who killed her?

Christa Helm (November 11th, 1949 - February 12, 1977)

American actress.

Born Sandra Clements in Milwaukee, Christina left home at age 17 hoping to become a go-go dancer. She married at 18, gave birth to a daughter and allowed the child to be adopted. It is said that her husband was killed in a motorcycle accident. Moving to New York, she found work as a fashion model. There she met Lea and Perrin heir Stuart Duncan. Duncan produced the film 'Lets Go For Broke', and made Helm, his new love interest, the star.

Later, Helm moved to Hollywood where she used her sexual attractions as a vehicle into films. She had little success, landing only a small part in a Starsky and Hutch episode and one commercial.

Helm became involved with narcotics, eventually ran upon hard times, and took employment as a waitress.

On February 2nd, 1977, while attending a party, she was stabbed to death. The murder was never solved.

*

Ernest   Miller

Hemingway (July 21, 1899 – July 2, 1961)

American author and journalist.

Hemingway was raised in Oak Park, Illinois. His father, Clarence Edmonds Hemingway was a physician, and his mother, Grace Hall-Hemingway, was a musician. I high school, he took part in a number of sports, boxing, track and field, water polo, and football, and he had good grades in English classes. With his sister Marcelline h performed in the school orchestra for two years. After finishing high school he worked as a reporter for a few months for The Kansas City Star, before leaving for the Italian front to enlist with the World War I ambulance drivers. In 1918, he was seriously wounded and returned home. His wartime experiences formed the basis for his novel A Farewell to Arms. In 1922, he married Hadley Richardson, the first of his four wives. The couple moved to Paris, where he worked as a foreign correspondent, and fell under the influence of the modernist writers and artists of the 1920s "Lost Generation" expatriate community.

The Sun Also Rises, Hemingway's first novel, was published in 1926.

After his 1927 divorce from Hadley Richardson, Hemingway married Pauline Pfeiffer. They divorced after he returned from Spanish Civil War where he had acted as a journalist, and after which he wrote For Whom the Bell Tolls. Martha Gellhorn became his third wife in 1940. They separated when he met Mary Welsh in London during World War II; during which he was present at the Normandy Landings and liberation of Paris.

Shortly after the publication of The Old Man and the Sea, Hemingway went on safari to Africa in 1952, where he was almost killed in a plane crash that left him in pain or ill-health for much of the rest of his life. Hemingway had permanent residences in Key West, Florida, and Cuba during the 1930s and 1940s, but in 1959 he moved from Cuba to Ketchum, Idaho, where in the early morning hours of July 2, 1961, Hemingway "quite deliberately" shot himself with his favorite shotgun. He unlocked the basement storeroom where his guns were kept, went upstairs to the front entrance foyer of their Ketchum home, and "pushed two shells into the twelve-gauge Boss shotgun ...put the end of the barrel into his mouth, pulled the trigger and blew out his brains."

Margaux

Hemingway(February 16, 1954[1] – July 1, 1996)

American fashion model and actress.

Margot Louise Hemingway was born in Portland, Oregon, and was the older sister of actress Mariel Hemingway and the granddaughter of writer Ernest Hemingway. When she learned that she was named for the wine, Château Margaux, which her parents, Puck and Jack Hemingway (eldest son of Ernest), were drinking the night she was conceived, she changed the original spelling from 'Margot' to 'Margaux' to match.

At six feet tall, Hemingway experienced success as a model, including a million-dollar contract for Fabergé as the spokesmodel for Babe perfume in the 1970s. Her lucrative contract with Fabergé was the first million dollar contract ever awarded to a fashion model.

During the height of her modeling career in the mid-to late 1970s, Hemingway was a regular attendee of New York City's exclusive discothèque Studio 54 - often in the company of such celebrities as Liza Minnelli, Halston, Bianca Jagger, Andy Warhol and Grace Jones. It was at such social mixers that Hemingway began to experiment with alcohol and drugs.

She made her film debut in the 1976 Lamont Johnson-directed drama Lipstick alongside her then fourteen year-old sister Mariel.

She supported herself later in life by appearing in a few direct-to-video films, autographing her nude photos from Playboy magazine, and endorsing a psychic telephone hotline owned by her cousin Adiel Hemingway

On July 1, 1996, one day before the anniversary of her grandfather's own suicide, Hemingway was found dead in her studio apartment in Santa Monica, California, at age 42. She had taken an overdose of phenobarbital, according to the Los Angeles County coroner's findings one month later.

Benjamin

Hendrickson (August 26, 1950 – July 3, 2006)

American actor

Hendrickson was born in Huntington, New York. He studied at the Juilliard School as part of the institution's first drama division class.

Prior to his television appearances, Hendrickson acted in theatre. From 1973-1984, he appeared in a host of productions that included The Elephant Man, Awake and Sing, and Strider. He also had roles in Dreams Don't Die (1982), Manhunter (1986), Russkies (1987), Regarding Henry (1991), Consenting Adults (1992) and Spanking the Monkey (1994).

Hendrickson made appearances on daytime television in the early 1980s; his credits included Another World, Texas, and a notable role on Guiding Light. Years later, he also appeared as a judge on Boston Legal.

Hendrickson was probably best known for playing Harold "Hal" Munson Jr., the Chief of Detectives for the mythical town of Oakdale on the long-running daytime soap opera As the World Turns.

He played Hal for over 20 years, from October 1985 to September 2004 and from June 2005 to July 2006.

Hendrickson's body was discovered on July 3, 2006 at his Huntington, New York home. The Suffolk County Police labeled his death a suicide; his body had been found with a gunshot wound to the head.

Evelyn Hoey

(December 15, 1910 – September 11, 1935) Broadway theatre torch singer and actress.

Hoey began performing at the age of 10 in Minneapolis. As an adult she appeared in London, England and Paris, France. She had one movie credit: a role in the 1930 comedy Leave It To Lester.

Hoey was found shot to death in an upstairs bedroom of oil heir Henry H. Rogers III.

A bullet was discharged in her brain on the night of September 11. She had been a guest at the home for a week. Rogers was the son of a deceased millionaire, Colonel Henry Huddleston Rogers, a former Standard Oil executive. Henry H. Rogers III was excluded from the provisions of his father's will through the careful wording of lawyers. He lived on $500,000 annually from a trust fund.

At a coroner's inquest the jury returned an open verdict that Hoey killed herself in the second floor bedroom.

* **William Holden**

(April 17, 1918 – November 12, 1981) was an American actor

Holden, was born William Franklin Beedle, Jr. in O'Fallon, Illinois.

The family moved to South Pasadena, California when he was three. After graduating from South Pasadena High School, Holden attended Pasadena Junior College, where he became involved in local radio plays. He was spotted by a talent scout from Paramount Pictures in 1937 while playing the part of an 80-year-old man. His first film role was in Prison Farm the following year.

Holden's first starring role was in Golden Boy (1939), in which he played a violinist turned boxer. That was followed by the role of George Gibbs in the film adaptation of Our Town.

After Columbia Pictures picked up half of his contract, he alternated between starring in several minor pictures for Paramount and Columbia before serving as a 2nd lieutenant in the United States Army Air Forces during World War II, where he acted in training films. Beginning in 1950, his career took off when Billy Wilder tapped him to star as the down-at-the-heels screenwriter Joe Gillis, who is taken in by faded silent-screen star Norma.

Following this breakthrough film, he played a series of roles that combined good looks with cynical detachment, including a prisoner-of-war entrepreneur in Stalag 17 (1953, a young engineer/family man in Executive Suite (1954), stage director in The Country Girl (1954), a jet pilot in The Bridges at Toko-Ri (1954), Picnic (1955), correspondent in Love Is a Many-Splendored Thing (1955), POW in The Bridge on the River Kwai (1957) and World War II tug boat captain in The Key (1958).

He also played in The Moon is Blue (1953), in Born Yesterday (1950), Forever Female (1953), and as Humphrey Bogart's younger brother, a playboy, in Sabrina (1954.

In 1969, Holden starred in director Sam Peckinpah's Western The Wild Bunch.

Holden was married to actress Ardis Ankerson (stage name Brenda Marshall) from 1941 until their divorce (after many long separations) in 1971.

In 1954, during the filming of Sabrina, Holden and Audrey Hepburn became romantically involved, and she hoped to marry him and have children. She broke off the relationship when Holden revealed that he had undergone a vasectomy.

He maintained a home in Switzerland and also spent much of his time working for wildlife conservation as a managing partner in an animal preserve in Africa.

In 1966, in Italy, he killed another driver in a drunk driving accident, and received an eight-month suspended sentence for vehicular manslaughter.

According to the Los Angeles County Coroner's autopsy report, on November 12, 1981, Holden was alone and intoxicated in his apartment in Santa Monica, California, when he slipped on a throw rug, severely lacerated his forehead on a teak bedside table, and bled to death. Evidence suggests he was conscious for at least half an hour after the fall. It is probable that he may not have realized the severity of the injury and did not summon aid, or was unable to call for help. His body was found four days later.

Judd Holdren (October 16, 1915 - March 11, 1974) American film actor

He was born near Villisca, Iowa. He dropped out of high school to travel to Omaha, Nebraska, where he studied at the Omaha Playhouse. During World War II he served in the United States Coast Guard, and then moved to Hollywood. Two of his early film roles were in 'All the King's Men' (1949) and Francis the Talking Mule (1950), Purple Heart Diary (1951), and Captain Video: Master of the Stratosphere (1951). After The Lost Planet (1953), He appeared in a number of TV series, such as Dragnet, and The Lone Ranger. His last film appearances were minor roles in Jeanne Eagels (1957), Ice Palace (1960), and The Rise and Fall of Legs Diamond (1960).

After 1960, Holdren became a full-time insurance salesman. During his Hollywood years, he was seen in public as the escort of many different Hollywood beauties, but never married.

Holdren committed suicide on March 11, 1974, by shooting himself in the head.

Russell Hopton (February 18, 1900 – April 7, 1945) American film actor.

Harry Russell Hopton was born in New York City. Apart from an appearance, in "Ella Cinders" (1926), he worked on the stage until 1930, when he settled in Hollywood. Hopton appeared in 105 films. His most memorable role was in director King Vidor's "Street Scene" (1931. Among his other credits are "Min and Bill" (1930), "Arrowsmith" (1931), "Law and Order" (1932), "I'm No Angel" (1933), "Men in White" (1934), "'G' Men" (1935), "Made For Each Other" (1939), and "Tall in the Saddle" (1944).

Finding himself reduced to an occasional unaccredited bit in B films, he committed suicide with an overdose of sleeping pills.

Leslie Howard (3 April 1893 – 1 June 1943) English stage and film actor, director, and producer.

Howard was born Leslie Howard in Forest Hill, London, UK. He was educated at Alleyn's School, London. He worked as a bank clerk before enlisting at the outbreak of the First World War. He served in the British Army as a subaltern in the Northamptonshire Yeomanry, but suffered shell shock, which led to his relinquishing his commission in May 1916.

Howard began acting on the London stage in 1917 but had his greatest theatrical success in the United States on Broadway, in plays such as Aren't We All? (1923), Outward Bound (1924), and The Green Hat (1925). He became an undisputed Broadway star in Her Cardboard Lover (1927). After his success as time traveler Peter Standish in Berkeley Square (1929), he by repeated the Standish role in the 1933 film version of the play.

Following his move to Hollywood, he appeared in the film version of Outward Bound (1930), and in Berkeley Square (1933). He played the title character in

The Scarlet Pimpernel (1934) and later Professor Henry Higgins Pygmalion (1938).

Howard co-starred with Bette Davis in The Petrified Forest (1936). Howard had earlier co-starred with Davis in the film adaptation of W. Somerset Maugham's book Of Human Bondage (1934) and later in the romantic comedy It's Love I'm After (1937). Howard starred with Ingrid Bergman in Intermezzo (1939) and Norma Shearer in a film version of Shakespeare's Romeo and Juliet (1936).

Howard is best remembered for his role as Ashley Wilkes in Gone With the Wind (1939). He returned to England to help with the Second World War effort. He starred in a number of Second World War films including 49th Parallel (1941), Pimpernel Smith (1941), and The First of the Few (1942).

Howard died in 1943 when flying to Bristol, UK, from Lisbon, Portugal. The aircraft he was aboard, a Douglas DC-3, was shot down by Luftwaffe fighter aircraft over the Bay of Biscay.

The news of Howard's death was published in the same issue of The Times that reported the "death" of Major William Martin, the red herring used for the ruse involved in Operation Mincemeat.

A long-standing hypothesis states that the Germans believed that UK Prime Minister Winston Churchill, who had been in Algiers, was on board the flight. Churchill himself can be blamed for the spread of the theory; in his autobiography, he expresses sorrow that a mistake about his activities might have cost Howard his life.

Paul Hurst

(October 15, 1888 – February 27, 1953) American film actor and director.

Hurst was born in Traver, California, and raised on a ranch. He appeared in hundreds of films during the '20s, '30s and '40s.

Hurst is best remembered for his roles as the Yankee deserter who is shot by Scarlett in Gone with the Wind (1939), of the drunken and sadistic vigilante Smith in The Ox Bow Incident (1943), and the rancher who refuses water to a Quaker family in the movie Angel and the Badman. It was after this role that Republic Pictures signed him as the comic sidekick in Monte Hale's Western series.

His last film was John Ford's The Sun Shines Bright.

Hurst was diagnosed with terminal cancer in late 1952, and committed suicide in February 1953.

Leona Hutton

(ca. 1892 – April 1, 1949) was an American actress.

Hutton's motion picture debut was in The Crimson Stain (1913), a three-reel drama short. Among her co-stars were William S. Hart, William Russell, Charles Ray, and Sessue Hayakawa.

Her final role was in The Man Who Would Not Die (1916).

During World War I, Hutton served overseas with the American and French Red Cross.

Hutton, also known as Mrs. Mary Epstein, committed suicide in 1949, by an overdose of codeine. She died in an iron lung in Maumee Hospital in Toledo, Ohio, eighteen hours after she was discovered by her husband. She had been confined to her home for ten weeks because of a leg fracture.

Phyllis   Linda

Hyman (July 6, 1949 – June 30, 1995) American

soul singer and actress.

Phyllis Hyman was born in Philadelphia. She appeared in the film Lenny (1974). She also did a two-year stint leading a band called Phyllis Hyman and the P/H Factor. Hyman was discovered in 1975 by internationally known pop artist and music industry veteran Sid Maurer, and former Epic Records promoter Fred Frank, and signed to their Roadshow Records/Desert Moon imprint.

Hyman sang with Pharoah Sanders and the Fatback Band while working on her first solo album, Phyllis Hyman, released in 1977 on the Buddah Records label. When Arista Records bought Buddha, she was transferred to that label. Her first album for Arista, Somewhere in My Lifetime, was released in 1978; the title track was produced by then labelmate Barry Manilow. Her follow-up album, You Know How to Love Me, made the R&B Top 20 and also performed well on the club–dance charts. In the late 1970s, Hyman married her manager Larry Alexander (who is the brother of Jamaican pianist and melodica player Monty Alexander), but both the personal and professional associations ended in divorce. Alexander introduced Hyman to cocaine, which led to a life-long dependency and spent a lot of her money during the years.

In 1983, Hyman recorded the song "Never Say Never Again" as the title song for the James Bond movie of the same name, written by Stephen Forsyth and Jim Ryan. However, Warner Brothers informed Forsyth that Michel Legrand, who wrote the score for the film, had threatened to sue them, claiming he contractually had the rights to the title song. An alternate title song composed by Legrand was eventually used for the film and performed by singer Lani Hall.

Hyman's last album, I Refuse to Be Lonely, was a journey into her personal life. Both the title track and the single "I'm Truly Yours" became minor R&B hits.

On the afternoon of June 30, 1995, Hyman committed suicide by overdosing on pentobarbital and secobarbital in her New York City apartment.

Thomas Ince (1882–1924), American silent film actor , director, screenwriter and producer.

Ince was born in Newport, Rhode Island, into a family of stage actors, and first appeared on the stage at age six. He made his Broadway debut in 1898 when he was 15, in Shore Acres. Ince was hired by Biograph in New York. Working exclusively in films, and making $5 per day, he was regularly under employed.

In 1910, a chance encounter with an employee from his acting troupe led Ince to get work at the Independent Motion Pictures Co. That same year he was given an opportunity to direct.

He advanced the idea of working full time in that capacity to IMP's owner Carl Laemmle. Laemmle hired him, and sent him to Cuba to make films. Ince's output, however, was small. He was drawn to westerns and American civil war dramas., and he wanted to achieve the effects accomplished by D.W. Griffith. This, he believed, could only be accomplished in Hollywood.

In September 1911, in an attempt to convey the appearance of a successful director by wearing a borrowed suit and a diamond, Ince walked into the offices of Charles O. Baumann at the New York Motion Picture Company which had decided to establish a West Coast studio to make westerns. Ince was offered $100 a week to go to California.

In November 1911, he arrived at NYMP's studios. It was during this period that Ince began to revolutionize the filmmaking process. He hit upon the method of pre-planning his films on paper introducing the use of a detailed "shooting script.

Ince's aspirations led him to leave Edendale and find a location that would give him more room. He settled upon a 460-acre tract of land located at Sunset Blvd. and Pacific Coast Highway in the Santa Monica hills.

By 1912 he had earned enough money to purchase the ranch and was granted permission by NYMP to lease another 18,000 acres in the Palisades Highlands. It was here that Ince built a studio that was the first of its kind, offering, offices, labs, dressing rooms, props houses, elaborate sets, and other necessities all in one location. While the site was still under construction Ince hired the Miller Brothers 101 Ranch Wildwest Show, including many cowboys, horses, cattle and a Sioux Indian tribe, who set up their teepees on the property. When construction was completed the streets were lined with a variety of structures, from humble cottages to mansions, designed in the style and architecture of different countries. Extensive outdoor western sets were also built.

Most of the cowboys, American Indians and assorted workmen lived on the site, while the actors came from Los Angeles.

Two of his most successful films were among his first, War on the Plains (1912) and Custer's Last Fight (1912), which featured many Indians who had actually been in the battle.

Even though he directed most of his early productions, by 1913 Ince eventually ceased full-time directing to concentrate on producing, giving up this responsibility to such proteges as Francis Ford, and his brother John.

In his last years Ince began to make social dramas. One was a version of Anna Christie (1923). He also produced Human Wreckage (1923) which was an early anti-drug movie.

In 1925, Cecil B. Demille acquired Ince Studios, renaming it the DeMille Studios. Besides DeMille, among those who filmed on the lot include Pathé, and RKO, producer Howard Hughes, and Desilu Productions. In 1991, Sony Pictures Entertainment purchased the property as the home for its television shows, renaming it Culver Studios.

On Saturday, November 15, 1924, William Randolph Hearst's lavish 280-foot yacht, the Oneida, set sail from San Pedro. Among his guests that weekend were his mistress Marion Davies, silent film star Charlie Chaplin, and newspaper columnist Louella Parsons. Ince, the guest of honor as it was his 42nd birthday, was late and the yacht left without him.

Ince took a train to San Diego where he joined the guests the next morning. At dinner that Sunday night, the group celebrated his birthday. Sometime later, Ince suffered an acute bout of indigestion. Ince was brought back ashore in San Diego, accompanied by Dr. Goodman and then put on a train bound for Los Angeles. While en route Ince's condition worsened. At Del Mar, he was removed from the train, and then taken to a hotel where he was promptly given medical treatment. Later, he was taken to his home in Hollywood where he died the next day, November 19.

Less than forty-eight hours after leaving the Oneida, Ince had died, officially of a heart attack. Dr. Ida Cowan Glasgow, his personal physician, signed the death. The front page of the Wednesday morning Los Angeles Times, however, told another story; "'Movie Producer Shot on Hearst Yacht!" headlines that mysteriously vanished in the evening edition. Ince's body was cremated.

The first stories in Hearst's newspapers about Ince's death said the producer had fallen ill while visiting the Hearst ranch in San Simeon and had been rushed home by ambulance. The rumor mill in Los Angeles began circulating stories about the incident, often revolving around a claim that Hearst shot Ince in the head by mistake.

The story goes that Hearst suspected that Davies and Chaplin were secretly lovers. In order to keep tabs on the two, he invited them both on board the yacht. Supposedly, he found the couple in a compromising clinch and went for his gun. Davies' screams awakened Ince who rushed to the scene. A scuffle ensued, followed by a gunshot and Ince took the bullet for Chaplin. A second version of the story had Davies and Ince alone in the galley late Sunday night. Ince, who suffered from ulcers, was supposedly looking for something to ease his upset stomach when Hearst walked in. Mistaking Ince for Chaplin, Hearst shot him. A third version tells of a struggle over a gun below decks between unidentified passengers. The gun fired accidentally and the bullet ripped through a plywood partition straight into Ince's room where it struck him.

Chaplin's secretary, Toraichi Kono, told his wife that Ince's head was "bleeding from a bullet wound" when he saw Ince ashore. The story quickly spread among the Japanese domestic workers throughout Beverly Hills. Whether Ince was killed in a fit of jealousy or by accident, the story stuck, with many believing Hearst was using his power to cover up the incident. One month after Ince's death, the rumors ran so rampant that the San Diego District Attorney's Office was forced to take action.

The D.A. only interviewed Dr. Goodman. According to Goodman, Ince got sick on the train so they disembarked in Del Mar and checked into a hotel. Goodman then called a doctor, as well as Nell Ince. Concerned for her husband, Nell agreed to come to Del Mar immediately. Goodman, unclear whether Ince was suffering from a heart attack or indigestion, claimed he left Del Mar before Nell arrived. The D.A. quickly closed the investigation.

Nonetheless, the rumors and suspicions continued to be fueled by the very people who celebrated with Ince that ill-fated weekend. Chaplin denied even being there, insisting that he, Hearst and Davies visited the ailing Ince later that week. He also stated that Ince died two weeks after their visit. In reality, Ince was dead within forty-eight hours after leaving the Oneida with Chaplin attending the memorial services that Friday.

Davies also added to the mystery in her attempts to deny the incident. She never acknowledged that Chaplin, Parsons or Goodman were aboard the yacht that weekend. She insisted that Nell Ince called her late Monday afternoon at United Studios to inform her of Ince's death.

When the Oneida sailed, Parsons was a New York movie columnist for one of Hearst's papers. After the Ince affair, Hearst gave her a lifetime contract and expanded her syndication. Hearst also provided Nell Ince with a trust fund just before she left for Europe. She refused an autopsy and ordered her husband's immediate cremation. Rumor also has it that Hearst paid off Ince's mortgage on his Château Élysée apartment building in Hollywood. D.W. Griffith said of the incident:

"All you have to do to make Hearst turn white as a ghost is mention Ince's name. There's plenty wrong there, but Hearst is too big."

 **Rick Jason** (May 21, 1923 – October 16, 2000) American actor.

He served in the U.S. Army Air Corps during World War II from 1943 to 1945.

After the War, he attended the American Academy of Dramatic Arts on the GI Bill, and held a seat on the New York Stock Exchange. While in attendance at a New York play, he was spotted by Hume Cronyn, who cast him in Now I Lay me Down to Sleep. The role earned Jason a Hollywood contract with Columbia Pictures.

M-G-M, searching for an actor to replace Fernando Lamas in the movie Sombrero, gave the role to Jason. It was a success and it led to The Saracen Blade and This Is My Love.

Fox signed him for the male lead role in The Lieutenant Wore Skirts and later signed for a multi-picture contract. His first project was The Wayward Bus. In 1958, Jason played the lead in The Fountain of Youth, a pilot written and directed by Orson Welles.

In 1954, he played Joaquin Murietta in an episode of Stories of the Century. Jason starred in 1960 as insurance investigator Robin Scott in The Case of the Dangerous Robin. Jason also appeared on the NBC interview program Here's Hollywood and co-starred in 1969 in the ABC movie The Monk.

In 1962, he starred as Platoon Leader 2nd Lt. Gil Hanley on the series Combat. The show lasted for five seasons and 152 episodes.

After Combat!, Rick returned to theater. His TV career went well in the '70s and '80s, when he appeared in shows like Matt Houston, Police Woman, Murder, She Wrote, Moonlighting, Wonder Woman, Fantasy Island, and Dallas. In 1973, he was a frequent character on The Young and the Restless.

In 2000, Jason attended a Combat! reunion in Las Vegas with fellow cast members. He died from a self-inflicted gunshot wound one week later on October 16, 2000 in Moorpark, California.

Ryan   Jenkins

(February 8, 1977 – August 23, 2009) Reality show star.

Ryan Alexander Jenkins was a reality show contestant. He appeared on the popular VH1 show "Megan Wants a Millionaire" and went on later to star on "I Love Money". Jenkins married Jasmine Fiore, a former model, after meeting her in a Las Vegas casino. On August 15, 2009, just a few days later, his wife's body was discovered. She had been strangled and stuffed into a suitcase, her remains mutilated to prevent recognition. She was eventually identified by the serial numbers of her breast implants. Jenkins was the only suspect in the murder. Fiore was 28 years old at the time of her death. On August 23, 2009, Jenkins was found dead in a hotel room in Hope, British Columbia, Canada. He was 32 years old. Jenkins committed suicide by hanging himself on a coat rack.

 **Richard Jeni**

(April 14, 1957 – March 10, 2007), American stand-up comedian and actor.

Raised in an Italian-American family in Bensonhurst, Brooklyn, he graduated with honors from Hunter College, earning a bachelor's degree in Comparative Politics.

Jeni first received recognition through a series of Showtime specials and appearances on The Tonight Show. Jeni also starred on the short-lived UPN sitcom Platypus Man and appeared in the Jim Carrey film The Mask. Jeni composed the theme song ("I'm A Platypus Man") for his TV series. He appeared in The Aristocrats, Dad's Week Off, Burn, Hollywood, Burn, and Chasing Robert

After making his "Tonight Show" debut in 1988 with Johnny Carson, Jeni appeared on The Tonight Show with Jay Leno more than any other stand-up comedian

On March 10, 2007, Jeni was found by his girlfriend with an apparent self-inflicted handgun wound to the face, in West Hollywood, California. Police found him alive, but gravely injured when they arrived. He was transported to Cedars-Sinai Medical Center in Los Angeles, where he died.

Anissa Jones

(March 11, 1958 – August 28, 1976) American child actress

Jones was born in West Lafayette, Indiana. Her parents were students at Purdue University at the time of her birth and they soon moved to Playa Del Rey, California. When she was two years old her mother enrolled Jones in dance classes. In 1964 when she was six, Jones' mother took her to an open audition for a breakfast cereal commercial, which became her first television appearance

Jones was eight when her acting skills drew the attention of television producers and she was cast as Elizabeth "Buffy" Patterson-Davis on the CBS sitcom Family Affair (1966). That year she also had a small role in the Elvis Presley comedy film The Trouble with Girls.

Family Affair was cancelled in 1971 after five seasons and 138 episodes. By then Jones was 13 years old and said she was happy at the thought of no longer needing to be seen with the doll. She wanted to act in films but, as can happen with any successful actor, child or adult, Jones couldn't find the kind of work she wanted. She auditioned unsuccessfully for the part of Regan MacNeil in the film The Exorcist. Meanwhile Brian Keith kept in touch with her through letters and offered Jones a young-adult role on The Brian Keith Show (1972–1974). Keith told her she would not need to audition for the part, but by then Jones did not want to work in television.

On her 18th birthday in March 1976, Jones gained control of saved earnings from her work in Family Affair, about $180,000 (roughly equal to $700,000 in 2009) which was being held in a trust fund and U.S. Savings Bonds. Jones and her brother Paul then rented an apartment together not far from their mother.

Five and a half months later, in the early morning hours of August 28, 1976 after partying all night in the beach town of Oceanside, California with her new boyfriend and others, Jones was found dead . The coroner's report listed her death as an accidental drug overdose. Cocaine, PCP, Quaaludes and Seconal were found in her body during an autopsy. The coroner who examined Jones reported she had died from one of the most severe drug overdoses he had ever seen.

In 1984 her brother John Paul Jones, Jr. also died of a drug overdose.

 # Janis Joplin

(January 19, 1943 – October 4, 1970) American singer, songwriter and music arranger.

Janis Joplin was born in Port Arthur, Texas, on January 19, 1943.

As a teenager, she befriended a group of outcasts, one of whom had albums by African-American blues artists Bessie Smith and Leadbelly, whom Joplin later credited with influencing her decision to become a singer.

She first began singing blues and folk music with friends. While at Thomas Jefferson High School, she stated that she was mostly shunned. Joplin was quoted as saying, "I was a misfit. I read, I painted, I didn't hate niggers."

As a teen, she became overweight and her skin broke out so badly she was left with deep scars which required dermabrasion.

Joplin graduated from high school in 1960 and attended Lamar State College of Technology in Beaumont, Texas, during the summer and later the

University of Texas at Austin. The campus newspaper ran a profile of her in 1962 headlined "She Dares To Be Different."

Her first song recorded on tape, at the home of a fellow student in December 1962, was "What Good Can Drinkin' Do". She left Texas for San Francisco in January 1963, where she lived in North Beach and later Haight-Ashbury. In 1964, Joplin and future Jefferson Airplane guitarist Jorma Kaukonen recorded a number of blues standards. Around this time her drug use increased, and she acquired a reputation as a "speed freak" and occasional heroin user. She also used other psychoactive drugs and was a heavy drinker.

In the spring of 1965, Joplin's friends, noticing the physical effects of her amphetamine habit persuaded her to return to Port Arthur, Texas. In May 1965, Joplin's friends threw her a bus-fare party so she could return home. In Port Arthur, she changed her lifestyle, avoiding drugs and alcohol. During a year at Lamar University, she commuted to Austin to perform solo, accompanying herself on guitar.

In 1966, Joplin's bluesy vocal style attracted the attention of the rock band Big Brother and the Holding Company. Her first public performance with them was at the Avalon Ballroom in San Francisco.

On August 23, 1966, during a four week engagement in Chicago, the group signed a deal with independent label Mainstream Records. Shortly after the five band members drove from Chicago to Northern California , they moved with the Grateful Dead to a house in Lagunitas, California. It was there that Joplin relapsed into hard drugs.

During the spring of 1968, Joplin and Big Brother made their nationwide television debut on The Dick Cavett Show.

TIME magazine called Joplin "probably the most powerful singer to emerge from the white rock movement," and Richard Goldstein, in Vogue magazine, wrote that Joplin was "the most staggering leading woman in rock... she slinks like tar, scowls like war... clutching the knees of a final stanza, begging it not to leave... Janis Joplin can sing the chic off any

By early 1969, Joplin was addicted to heroin, allegedly shooting at least $200 worth of heroin per day.

Joplin and the Kozmic Blues Band toured North America and Europe throughout 1969, appearing at Woodstock in August. By most accounts, Woodstock was not a happy affair for Joplin. Faced with a ten hour wait after arriving at the festival, she shot heroin and was drinking alcohol. At the end of the year, the group broke up. Their final gig with Joplin was at Madison Square Garden in New York City on the night of December 19–20, 1969.]

On Saturday, October 3, Joplin visited the Sunset Sound Recorders in Los Angeles to listen to the instrumental track for Nick Gravenites' song "Buried Alive in the Blues" prior to recording the vocal track, scheduled for the next day. When she failed to show up at the studio for the recording session by Sunday afternoon, producer Paul A. Rothchild became concerned. Full Tilt Boogie's road manager, John Cooke, drove to the Landmark Motor Hotel in Hollywood Heights where Joplin had been a guest since August 24. He saw Joplin's Porsche in the parking lot. Upon entering her room, he found her dead on the floor. The official cause of death was an overdose of heroin, possibly combined with the effects of alcohol.] Cooke believes that Joplin had accidentally been given heroin which was much more potent than normal, as several of her dealer's other customers also overdosed that week. She was 27.

Stephen Keats

(February 6, 1945 – May 8, 1994) American actor

Keats grew up in Brooklyn, New York, and graduated from the New York School for the

Performing Arts . After serving a tour of duty in Vietnam with the Air Force from 1965–1966, Keats attended the Yale School of Drama in 1969 and 1970.

Keats debuted on Broadway in Oh! Calcutta!, and appeared in over 80 films and TV shows. He was nominated for an Emmy in 1977 for his role in Seventh Avenue. He also portrayed Thomas Edison in the science fiction TV series, Voyagers!.

Keats' performance in the Hester Street was acclaimed.

At the end of his career, Keats was playing the part of Ed McClain on the soap opera Another World.

On May 8, 1994, he was found dead in his apartment in Manhattan; his death was ruled a suicide

Brian   Keith

(November 14, 1921 – June 24, 1997) American film, television , and stage actor

Keith was born Robert Alba Keith in Bayonne, New Jersey, to actor Robert Keith and stage actress Helena Shipman. His parents divorced. His mother continued to perform on stage and radio, while Robert's grandmother helped to raise him in Long Island, New

York. He spent a lot of hours back stage while his parents performed. Helena fondly recalled keeping little Brian in the dressing room in one of her dressing room drawers. From 1927 through 1929, Keith's stepmother was Peg Entwistle, a well-known Broadway actress who committed suicide by jumping from the "H" of the famous Hollywood Sign in 1932.

After graduation from East Rockaway High School in 1939, in East Rockaway, New York, he joined the United States Marine Corps (1942–1945). He served as a Radio-Gunner in the rear cockpit of a two-man Douglas SBD Dauntless dive.

After the war, Keith became a stage actor, later branching out into films and then into television. In 1952, he played in three episodes of Tales of Tomorrow. This led him to roles in shows such as Police Story, Eye Witness, The United States Steel Hour, Robert Montgomery Presents, The Motorola Television Hour, The Pepsi-Cola Playhouse, The Adventures of Ellery Queen, and Jane Wyman Presents: The Fireside Theatre. In 1955, Keith starred in his own series, Crusader.

In 1960, he stared in Sam Peckinpah's short-lived series The Westerner (1960). The following year, Keith appeared as the father of twins in the 1961 film The Parent Trap, co-starring Hayley Mills and Maureen O'Hara.

In 1966, Keith landed the role of Uncle Bill Davis in Family Affair. By the end of its fifth season in 1971, Family Affair had high ratings, but was canceled after 138 episodes.

Keith went on to star as the pediatrician Dr. Sean Jamison in the NBC sitcom The Brian Keith Show. The series was canceled after two seasons in 1974.

Keith returned to series television in 1983 in, Hardcastle and McCormick.

In his last film, Keith played President William McKinley in Rough Riders (1997).

During the later part of his life, Keith suffered from emphysema and lung cancer. On June 24, 1997, he was found dead of a self-inflicted gunshot wound in Malibu, California, two months after his daughter Daisy committed suicide.

* **Paul Michael**

Kelly (August 9, 1899 – November 6, 1956) was an American child actor who later as an adult became a stage, film, and television actor.

Born in Brooklyn, New York, the ninth of ten children, Kelly began his career as a child actor at age 7.

In 1911 Kelly began making silent films at age 12 with the Vitagraph Studios, which was based in Brooklyn, and where he was billed as Master Paul Kelly. Kelly was possibly the first male child actor to be given any starring roles in American films predating better known child stars such as Bobby Connelly and Jackie Coogan.

Kelly made his talking film debut in 1933's 'Broadway Through a Keyhole'.

In the course of his long career, and relatively short life, it's estimated that Kelly worked on stage, screen, and television in over four hundred roles. Later in his film career, as an adult, Kelly appeared in films mostly as a tough guy character actor in the 1930s, 1940s and 1950s. In 1948, Kelly won a Best Actor Tony Award his role in Command Decision. The award was shared with Henry Fonda for Mister Roberts and Basil Rathbone for The Heiress.

His career momentum was briefly halted with a two-year (1927–1929) forced hiatus when he served 25 months for manslaughter in California's San Quentin prison for the death of actor Ray Raymond. Kelly later played the part of San Quentin Warden Clinton Duffy in the film Duffy of San Quentin. Raymond's widow, Dorothy MacKaye, later married Kelly. She was briefly imprisoned for being an accomplice in the killing; and, wrote about her experiences, titled, "Women in Prison," that became a 1933 film, Ladies They Talk About, with Barbara Stanwyck.

He married a bit player, he met on the set of Flight Command (1940), Claire Owen (née Zona Mardelle Zwicker), on January of 1941. She retired from acting, and went on to survive him.

He died of a heart attack in 1956, aged 57.

 **Victor Kilian** (March
6, 1891 – March 11, 1979) was an American actor Born
in Jersey City, New Jersey, Victor Kilian began his
career at the age of eighteen by joining a vaudeville
company. In the mid 1920s he was performing in
Broadway plays and 1930 had made his debut in motion
pictures. For the next twenty years he worked as a
character actor films such as The Adventures of Tom
Sawyer (1938). Frequently cast as a villain, while staging
a fight scene with John Wayne for a 1942 film, Kilian
suffered a serious injury that resulted in the loss of one
eye.

In the 1950s, Victor Kilian was blacklisted for
his political beliefs but because the Actors' Equity
Association refused to go along with the ban, Kilian
was able to earn a living by performing on stage. After
Hollywood's blacklisting ended, he began doing guest
roles during the 1970s. He is best known for his role as
Grandpa Larkin in the television soap opera spoof
Mary Hartman, Mary Hartman (1976).

Kilian's wife, Daisy Johnson, to whom he had
been married for 46 years, died in 1961. Living alone, in
1979 he was beaten to death by robbers burglarizing his
Hollywood apartment. He was 88.

 **Andrew   Koenig**

August 17, 1968 – February 2010

From 1985 to 1989, Koenig played a recurring role in the first four seasons of the ABC sitcom Growing Pains. During the same period, he guest starred on My Sister Sam and My Two Dads as well as 21 Jump Street.

In the early 1990s he provided a voice for the animated series G.I. Joe, and had a minor role in the 1993 Star Trek: Deep Space Nine episode "Sanctuary".

Koenig played the the Joker in the 2003 film Batman: Dead End.

Onstage, he starred as the M.C. in the 2007 interactive theater play The Boomerang Kid and performed with the improv group Charles Whitman Reilly and Friends.

Though he continued his career in the 2006 The Theory of Everything (2006), Koenig spent more time behind the scenes. He wrote, produced and/or directed the shorts Good Boy (2003), Woman in a Green Dress, and Instinct vs. Reason (2004).

In February 2010, Koenig was reported missing. He was last seen in Vancouver, British Columbia, Canada, on February 14, and missed a scheduled flight back to the US on February 16. On February 25, 2010, CNN reported that his body was found in Stanley Park in Vancouver.

Koenig's father told reporters at an evening press conference that his son "took his own life.

* **Ruslana Korshunova** (July 2, 1987 – June 28, 2008) Russian/American model.

She posed in Vogue and represented designers such as Vera Wang and Nina Ricci. Discovered in 2003, she was immediately distinguished by her knee-length, chestnut-colored hair. On June 28, 208, Ruslana fell from of her ninth-floor balcony, shortly after watching the movie "Ghost" with a former boyfriend in Manhattan. Friends have said that she was usually a cheerful person and had never shown any signs of distress or feelings of failure, although there were things written on some social networking sites that seemed to suggest otherwise. She at one time stated "Death is a celebration of life...there is hope" and "I'm so lost. Will I ever find myself?" Ruslana Korshunova's death was ruled as a suicide because the police could find no other witnesses.

Alan Ladd

(September 3, 1913 – January 29, 1964) American actor

Ladd was born in Hot Springs, Arkansas. His father died when he was four, and his mother relocated to Oklahoma City. The family then moved again to North Hollywood, California where Ladd became a high-school swimming and diving champion and participated in high school dramatics. He opened his own hamburger and malt shop, which he called Tiny's Patio. He worked briefly as a studio and for a short time was part of the Universal Pictures studio school for actors. But Universal decided he was too blond and too short and dropped him. Intent on acting, he found work in radio.

Ladd began by appearing in dozens of films in small roles, including Citizen Kane in which he played one of the "faceless". He first gained some recognition with a featured role in the wartime thriller Joan of Paris, 1942. His next role was in This Gun For Hire.

Ladd went on to star in many Paramount Pictures' films with a brief timeout for military service with the United States Army Air Force's First Motion Picture Unit. He appeared in The Glass Key, and Lucky Jordan.

In 1946, he starred in a trio of silver screen classics: Two Years Before the Mast, The Blue Dahlia, and the World War II espionage thriller, O.S.S..

Ladd and Robert Preston starred in the 1948 western film, Whispering Smith. In 1949's version of The Great Gatsby, Ladd had the featured role of Jay Gatsby.

Ladd played the title role in the 1953 western Shane.

In November 1962, Ladd was found lying unconscious in a pool of blood with a bullet wound near his heart, an unsuccessful suicide attempt. In 1963 Ladd filmed a supporting role in The Carpetbaggers. He would not live to see its release. On January 29, 1964 he was found dead in Palm Springs, California, of an acute overdose of alcohol and sedatives at the age of 50, which was ruled accidental.

He had married a high-school acquaintance, Midge Harrold, with whom he had a son, Alan Ladd, Jr. His stepfather died suddenly. Then his mother, who suffered from depression, committed suicide by poison.

Despite Alan Ladd's fathering three children, he regularly socialized with members of Hollywood's gay subculture in the luxurious home of George Cukor. It was the site of weekly Sunday afternoon parties attended by closeted celebrities and the attractive young men they met in bars and gyms and brought with them.

*   **Carole   Landis**

(January 1, 1919 – July 5, 1948)   American film and stage actress

Landis was born Frances Lillian Mary Ridste in Fairchild, Wisconsin. Her early years were filled with poverty and sexual abuse.

In January 1934, 15-year-old Landis married her 19-year-old neighbor, Irving Wheeler, but the marriage was annulled in February 1934. They later remarried on August 25, 1934. Wheeler named Busby Berkeley in an alienation of affections lawsuit in 1938 involving Landis, and they divorced in 1939.

Landis dropped out of high school at age 15. She started out as a hula dancer in a San Francisco nightclub and later sang with a dance band. After saving $100 she moved to Hollywood.

Her 1937 film debut was as an extra in A Star Is Born. She continued appearing in bit parts until 1940 when Hal Roach cast her as a cave girl in One Million B.C.. The movie turned Carole into a star.

Landis appeared in a string of successful films in the early forties. In a time when the singing of many actresses was dubbed in, Landis's own voice was used in her musical roles. Landis landed a contract with 20th Century Fox and began a sexual relationship with Darryl F. Zanuck. She had roles playing opposite fellow pin-up girl Betty Grable in Moon Over Miami and I Wake Up Screaming, both in 1941. When Carole ended her relationship with Zanuck, her career suffered and she was assigned roles in B-movies.

In 1942, she toured with comedienne Martha Raye, and actress Kay Francis with a USO troupe in England and North Africa. Two years later, she entertained soldiers in the South Pacific with Jack Benny. Landis traveled more than 100,000 miles during the war and spent more time visiting troops than any other actress

In 1945 she starred on Broadway in the musical A Lady Says Yes with Jacqueline Susann, with whom she reportedly had an affair. Susann purportedly based the character Jennifer North in her book Valley of the Dolls on Landis.

Landis wrote several newspaper and magazine articles about her experiences during the war, including the 1944 book Four Jills in a Jeep, which was later made into a movie, costarring Kay Francis, Martha Raye, and Mitzi Mayfair.

She nearly died from amoebic dysentery and malaria she contracted while traveling overseas while entertaining American troops.

In 1945, Landis married Broadway producer W. Horace Schmidlapp. By 1948, her career was in decline and her marriage with Schmidlapp was collapsing. She entered into a romance with actor Rex Harrison, who was married to actress Lilli Palmer at the time. Landis was reportedly crushed when Harrison refused to divorce his wife for her. Unable to cope, she committed suicide at her Pacific Palisades home by taking an overdose of Seconal. She had spent her final night alive with Harrison. The next afternoon, he and the maid discovered her on the bathroom floor. According to some sources, Landis left two suicide notes, one for her mother and the second for Harrison who instructed his lawyers to destroy it. During a coroner's inquest, Harrison denied knowing any motive for her suicide and told the coroner he did not know of the existence of a second suicide note.

Florence

Lawrence (January 2, 1886 – December 28, 1938)

Canadian inventor and silent film actress.

Born Florence Annie Bridgwood in Hamilton, Ontario, After her father's death, Florence, her mother and two older brothers moved from Hamilton, Ontario to Buffalo, New York.

After graduating from school, Lawrence joined her mother's dramatic company. The company disbanded after a series of disputes. Lawrence and her mother moved to New York City around 1906.

In 1906, at age 20, she appeared in her first motion picture. The next year, she appeared in 38 movies for the Vitagraph film company.

During the spring and summer of 1906, Lawrence auditioned for a number of Broadway productions, with no success. However, on 27 December 1906, she was hired by the Edison Manufacturing Company to play Daniel Boone's daughter in Daniel Boone.

In 1907 she went to work for the Vitagraph Company in Brooklyn, New York.

She returned briefly to stage acting, playing the leading role in a road show production of Melville B. Raymond's Seminary Girls.

In the spring of 1908 she returned to Vitagraph where she played the lead role in The Dispatch Beare. Largely as a result of her equestrian skills, she received parts in eleven films in the next five months.

Lawrence managed to convince Solter and Griffith that she was the best suited for the starring role in The Girl and the Outlaw.

After her success in this role, she appeared in Betrayed by a Handprint and in The Red Girl. In total, she had parts in most of the 60 films directed by Griffith in 1908.

She continued to work for Biograph in 1909. Her demand to be paid by the week rather than daily was met, and she received double the normal rate

Lawrence joined the Independent Moving Pictures Company of America in 1909. The company, founded by Carl Laemmle, was looking for experienced filmmakers and actors. Needing a star, he lured Lawrence away from Biograph by promising to give her a marquee. First though, Carl Laemmle organized a publicity stunt by starting a rumor that Lawrence had been killed by a street car in New York City.

Then, after gaining media attention, he placed ads in the newspapers that announced, "We nail a lie", and included a photo of Lawrence. The ad declared that she was alive and making The Broken Oath, a new movie for his IMP Film Company.

Laemmle then had Lawrence make an appearance in St. Louis to show her fans that she was alive. Partially as a result of Laemmle's ingenuity, the "star system" was born and before long, Florence Lawrence became a household name. Lawrence worked for IMP for eleven months, making fifty films. After that, she went on vacation in Europe. When she returned to the US, she joined a film company headed by Siegmund Lubin. Lawrence was once again teamed with Arthur Johnson, and the pair made 48 films together under Lubin's direction.

In 1912, Lawrence made a deal with Carl Laemmle and they formed their own company. Laemmle gave them complete artistic freedom in the company, called Victor Film Company, and paid Lawrence five hundred dollars a week as the leading lady. They established a film studio in Fort Lee, New Jersey and made a number of films starring Lawrence and Owen Moore before selling out to the new Universal Pictures in 1913.

Despite her mooted retirement, Lawrence was induced to return to work in 1914 for her company. During one of the films, Pawns of Destiny, a fire got out of control. Lawrence was burned and she suffered a serious fall. She went into shock for months. She returned to work, but collapsed after its completion. She blamed Solter for making her do the stunt in which she was injured and the two divorced. To add to her problems, Universal refused to pay her medical expenses.

In the spring of 1916, she returned to work for Universal and completed another feature film, Elusive Isabel. However, the strain of working took its toll on her and she suffered a serious relapse. She was completely paralyzed for four months. By the time she returned to the screen in 1921, few people remembered her.

Lawrence's mother died in 1929. By then, in her mid-forties, demand for her in films had long since disappeared and the stock market crash and the ensuing Great Depression saw Lawrence's fortune decline.

Alone, discouraged, and suffering with chronic pain, she was found unconscious in her West Hollywood apartment on 27 December 1938 after she had attempted suicide by eating ant paste. She was rushed to a hospital but died a few hours later.

Lawrence invented the first turn signal, a device attached to a motor vehicle's rear fender. Dubbed as the "auto signaling arm", when a driver pressed a button, an arm raised or lowered, with a sign attached indicating the direction of the intended turn. Following this, she developed a brake signal based on the same concept where an arm with a sign reading "STOP" was raised whenever the driver stepped on the brake pedal. However, Lawrence's inventions were not patented, and others in the rapidly expanding auto industry developed their own versions.

Pepi Lederer

(March 18, 1910 – June 11, 1935) American actress and writer

She was nicknamed "Peppy" for her high-spirited personality. Later she formally adopted the name. Her mother was a stage actress and the sister of Marion Davies.

After her Aunt Marion became involved with William Randolph Hearst, Hearst took responsibility for Pepi and her several siblings, who included Charlie Lederer, later a well-known screenwriter. She spent a good deal of her youth at Hearst Castle.

The Hearsts arranged for Pepi to get a few small parts in movies such as Her Cardboard Lover, and gave her a token job on Hearst's magazine, The Connoisseur.

She did some writing for the 'Los Angeles Examiner' newspaper. A known lesbian, she ran around with Tallulah Bankhead and Louise Brooks who became one of her best friends.

Lederer had a voracious appetite for rich food, alcohol, and cocaine.

In 1935, her drug addiction worsening, Davies and Hearst committed her to a mental hospital to receive a drug cure.

Not long afterward, she committed suicide by jumping out of a window. She was 25.

Heath Andrew Ledger (4 April 1979 – 22 January 2008) Australian television and film actor.

Ledger moved to the United States in 1998 to advance his film career. His films included 10 Things I Hate About You (1999), The Patriot (2000), A Knight's Tale (2001), Brokeback Mountain (2005), and The Dark Knight (2008). He produced and directed music videos and aspired to be a film director.

Ledger died on 22 January 2008, from an accidental "toxic combination of prescription drugs". A few months before his death, Ledger had finished filming his penultimate performance, as the Joker in The Dark Knight. His death came during editing of the film and cast a shadow over the subsequent promotion of the $180 million production. At the time of his death, he had completed about half of his work performing the role of Tony in Terry Gilliam's film The Imaginarium of Doctor Parnassus.

Philip Loeb (March 28, 1891 – September 1, 1955), was an American stage, film, and television actor.

Born in Philadelphia, Pennsylvania, Loeb first performed in a high school production of Lady Gregory's The Workhouse Ward. He served in the Army, and then worked as stage manager of The Green Goddess. His stage career gained strength in the early 1920s when he became associated with the newly-formed Theatre Guild in New York City. He worked in a number of plays throughout the decade. His stage work lessened in the 1930s, while he worked with Actors Equity Association. (It is his work with Equity that is thought to have prompted the charges of Communist leanings.)

In 1948, Loeb portrayed the role of Jake Goldberg on Broadway in Gertrude Berg's play Me and Molly which was based on Berg's long running radio show The Goldbergs. After the play, he reprised the role on the television adaptation of The Goldbergs on CBS. Loeb became a viewer favorite as the sometimes exasperated but always loving husband Jake to Berg's sometimes meddlesome but always bighearted Molly Goldberg, and it looked as though he would become a television fixture.

In June 1950, Red Channels: The Report of Communist Influence in Radio and Television, named Loeb as a Communist. Loeb denied being a Communist, but the sponsors of The Goldbergs, General Foods, insisted that he be dropped from the show's cast due to his "controversiality".

Berg (who had created the show and owned it on both radio and television) refused to fire Loeb, but Loeb soon resigned, accepting a settlement which was estimated at $40,000. Loeb's last acting job was in the 1952 Broadway production of Time Out For Ginger and its subsequent Chicago production in 1954.

In his memoirs, Inside Out, blacklisted screenwriter Walter Bernstein describes Loeb as being depressed as a result of the blacklisting. Loeb was the sole support of a mentally disturbed son, and was burdened with money worries

Loeb committed suicide by taking an overdose of sleeping pills in the Taft Hotel in midtown New York City on September 1, 1955.

* **Jeanette Loff**

(October 9, 1906 - August 4, 1942) American motion picture actress and singer

Born Janette Lov in Orofino, Idaho.

The family moved to Canada in 1907 where her father found work as a violinist.

At the age of 11, Loff played the title role in Snow White and the Seven Dwarfs. At 16 she had the leading role in an operetta, Treasure Hunters. When she was seventeen the family moved to Portland, Oregon, where Loff completed her musical education at the Ellison and White Conservatory of Music. She played the organ in theaters in Portland as Jan Lov.

Loff's motion picture career began with an uncredited role in the silent film Uncle Tom's Cabin.

Cecil B. DeMille signed her to a contract and she was soon cast in ingénue roles. She decided to take a break from her movie career and perform on stage. Her last screen role before she briefly retired was in The King of Jazz (1930). She remained under contract to Universal Pictures for some months but made no additional films. She went to New York City and appeared in musical plays and with orchestras.

Loff returned to films with a role in Mating Time. Her final motion picture performances

On August 4, 1942, Jeanette Loff died of ammonia poisoning in Los Angeles, California in 1942. Loff was only thirty five years old.

Charles Manson

(November 12, 1934 -) American killer

Born to an unmarried 16-year-old named Kathleen Maddox, in Cincinnati General Hospital, Ohio, Manson was first named "no name Maddox." This was later changed to Charles Milles Maddox. For a short time his mother was married to a laborer named William Manson, and he became Charles Manson. The boy's biological father appears to have been a "Colonel Scott," against whom Kathleen Maddox filed a bastardy suit that resulted in an agreed judgment in 1937. Several statements in Manson's 1951 case file from the seven months he would later spend at the National Training School for Boys in Washington, D.C., allude to the possibility that "Colonel Scott" was African American. These include the first two sentences of his family background section, which read: "Father: unknown. He is alleged to have been a colored cook by the name of Scott, with whom the boy's mother had been promiscuous at the time of pregnancy." When asked about these official records by attorney Vincent Bugliosi in 1971, Manson denied that his father had been of African American ancestry.

Manson's mother was allegedly a heavy drinker. According to a family member, she once sold her son for a pitcher of beer. His uncle retrieved him some days later. When Manson's mother and her brother were sentenced to five years' imprisonment for robbing a Charleston, West Virginia, service station in 1939, Manson was placed in the home of an aunt and uncle in McMechen, West Virginia. Upon her 1942 parole, Kathleen took her son and lived with him in run-down hotel rooms. In 1947, the court placed Manson in Gibault School for Boys, in Terre Haute, Indiana. After 10 months, he fled from there to his mother, who rejected him.

By committing burglary of a grocery store, Manson obtained cash that enabled him to rent a room. He committed a string of burglaries of other stores, including one from which he stole a bicycle. He was eventually caught and sent to an Indianapolis juvenile center. He escaped after one day, and was recaptured and placed in Boys Town. Four days after his arrival there, he escaped with another boy. Caught at age 13, during a break-in of a grocery store, Manson was sent to the Indiana Boys School, where, he would later claim, he was sexually brutalized . He escaped with two other boys in 1951. In Utah, the three were caught driving to California in cars they had stolen. They had burglarized several gas stations along the way. For the federal crime of taking a stolen car across a state line, Manson was sent to Washington, D.C.'s National Training School for Boys.

In October 1951, on a psychiatrist's recommendation, Manson was transferred to Natural Bridge Honor Camp, a minimum security institution. Less than a month before a scheduled February 1952 parole hearing, he "took a razor blade and held it against another boy's throat while he sodomized him." He was transferred to the Federal Reformatory, Petersburg, Virginia, where he was considered "dangerous." In September 1952, a number of other serious disciplinary offenses resulted in his transfer to the Federal Reformatory at Chillicothe, Ohio. There he became a model resident. Good work habits and a rise in his educational level from the lower fourth to the upper seventh grade won him a May 1954 parole.

After temporarily honoring a parole condition that he live with his aunt and uncle in West Virginia, Manson moved in with his mother in that same state. In January 1955, he married a hospital waitress named Rosalie Jean Willis, with whom, by his own account, he found genuine, if short-lived, marital happiness. He supported their marriage via small-time jobs and auto theft.

In October, about three months after he and his pregnant wife arrived in Los Angeles in a car he had stolen in Ohio, Manson was again charged with a federal crime for taking the vehicle across state lines. After a psychiatric evaluation, he was given five years' probation. His subsequent failure to appear at a Los Angeles hearing on an identical charge filed in Florida resulted in his March 1956 arrest in Indianapolis. His probation was revoked and he was sentenced to three years' at Terminal Island, San Pedro, California.

While Manson was in prison, Rosalie gave birth to their son, Charles Manson, Jr. During his first year at Terminal Island, Manson received visits from Rosalie and his mother, who were now living together in Los Angeles. In March 1957, when the visits from his wife ceased, his mother informed him Rosalie was living with another man. Less than two weeks before a scheduled parole hearing, Manson tried to escape by stealing a car. He was subsequently given five years probation, and his parole was denied.

Manson received five years' parole in September 1958, the same year in which Rosalie was granted a divorce.In September 1959, he pleaded guilty to a charge of attempting to cash a forged U.S. Treasury check. He received a 10-year suspended sentence and probation after a young woman with an arrest record for prostitution made a "tearful plea" before the court that she and Manson were "deeply in love... and would marry if Charlie were freed." Before the year's end, the woman did marry Manson, possibly so testimony against him would not be required of her.

After Manson took two woman from California to New Mexico for purposes of prostitution, he was held and questioned for violation of the Mann Act. When he violated of his probation, a warrant was issued. Arrested in Laredo, Texas, in June, when one of the women was arrested for prostitution, Manson was returned to Los Angeles. For violation of his probation on the check-cashing charge, he was ordered to serve his 10-year sentence.

In July 1961, after a year spent unsuccessfully appealing the revocation of his probation, Manson was transferred from the Los Angeles County Jail to the United States Penitentiary at McNeil Island. Although the Mann Act charge had been dropped, the attempt to cash the Treasury check was still a federal offense. In 1963, Leona was granted a divorce, in the pursuit of which she alleged that she and Manson had had a son, Charles Luther. In June 1966, Manson was again sent to Terminal Island. By March 21, 1967, his release day, he had spent more than half of his 32 years in prisons and other institutions. On his release day, Manson received permission to move to San Francisco, where, with the help of a prison acquaintance, he moved into an apartment in Berkeley. In prison, bank robber Alvin Karpis had taught him to play steel guitar. Now, living mostly by panhandling, he soon got to know Mary Brunner, a 23-year-old graduate of the University of Wisconsin–Madison. Brunner was working as an assistant librarian at University of California, Berkeley, and Manson moved in with her.

Manson established himself as a guru in San Francisco's Haight-Ashbury, which, during 1967's "Summer of Love," was emerging as the signature hippie locale. Expounding a philosophy that included some of the Scientology he had studied in prison, he soon had his first group of young followers, most of them female. Before the summer ended, Manson and eight or nine of his enthusiasts piled into an old school bus they had re-wrought in hippie style, with colored rugs and pillows in place of the many seats they had removed. They roamed as far north as Washington state, then southward through Los Angeles, Mexico, and the southwest. Returning to the Los Angeles area, they lived in Topanga Canyon, Malibu, and Venice—western parts of the city and county.

The events that would culminate in the murders began in late spring 1968, when, by some accounts, Dennis Wilson, of The Beach Boys, picked up two hitchhiking Manson women and brought them to his Pacific Palisades house for a few hours. Returning home in the early hours of the following morning from a night recording session, Wilson was greeted in the driveway of his own residence by Manson, who emerged from the house. Uncomfortable, Wilson asked the stranger whether he intended to hurt him. Assuring him he had no such intent, Manson began kissing Wilson's feet. Inside the house, Wilson discovered 12 strangers, mostly women. Over the next few months, as their number doubled, the Family members who had made themselves part of Wilson's Sunset Boulevard household cost him approximately $100,000. This included a large medical bill for treatment of their gonorrhea and $21,000 for the accidental destruction of his uninsured car, which they borrowed. Wilson would sing and talk with Manson, whose women were treated as servants to them both. Wilson paid for studio time to record songs written and performed by Manson, and he introduced Manson to acquaintances of his with roles in the entertainment business. These included Gregg Jakobson, Terry Melcher, and Rudi Altobelli (the last of whom owned a house he would soon rent to actress Sharon Tate and her husband, director Roman Polanski). Jakobson, who was impressed by "the whole Charlie Manson package" of artist/lifestylist/philosopher, also paid to record Manson material.

Manson established a base for the group at Spahn's Movie Ranch not far from Topanga Canyon in August 1968 after Wilson's manager told the Family to move out of Wilson's home. The entire Family then relocated to the ranch. The ranch had been a television and movie set for Western productions. However, by the late 1960s, the buildings had deteriorated and the ranch was earning money primarily by selling horseback rides.

Family members did helpful work around the grounds. Also, Manson ordered the Family's women, including Lynette "Squeaky" Fromme, to occasionally have sex with the nearly blind, 80-year-old owner, George Spahn. The women also acted as seeing-eye guides for Spahn. In exchange, Spahn allowed Manson and his group to live at the ranch without charge. Charles Watson soon joined the group. Watson, a Texan who had quit college and moved to California, met Manson at Dennis Wilson's house. Watson gave Wilson a ride while Wilson was hitchhiking after his cars had been wrecked.

In the first days of November 1968, Manson established the Family at alternative headquarters in Death Valley's environs, where they occupied two unused or little-used ranches, Myers and Barker. The former, to which the group had initially headed, was owned by the grandmother of a new woman in the Family. The latter was owned by an elderly, local woman to whom Manson presented himself and a male Family member as musicians in need of a place congenial to their work.

For some time, Manson had been saying that racial tension between blacks and whites was growing and that blacks would soon rise up in rebellion in America's cities. He had emphasized Martin Luther King, Jr.'s assassination, which had taken place on April 4, 1968. On a bitterly cold New Year's Eve at Myers Ranch, the Family members, gathered outside around a large fire, listened as Manson explained that the social turmoil he had been predicting had also been predicted by the Beatles. The White Album songs, he declared, told it all, although in code. In fact, he maintained (or would soon maintain), the album was directed at the Family itself, an elect group that was being instructed to preserve the worthy from the impending disaster.

In early January 1969, the Family escaped the desert's cold and positioned itself to monitor L.A.'s supposed tension by moving to a canary-yellow home in Canoga Park, not far from the Spahn Ranch. Because this locale would allow the group to remain "submerged beneath the awareness of the outside world," Manson called it the Yellow Submarine, another Beatles reference. There, Family members prepared for the impending apocalypse, which, around the campfire, Manson had termed "Helter Skelter," after the song of that name.

By February, Manson's vision was complete. The Family would create an album whose songs, as subtle as those of the Beatles, would trigger the predicted chaos. Ghastly murders of whites by blacks would be met with retaliation, and a split between racist and non-racist whites would yield whites' self-annihilation. Blacks' triumph, as it were, would merely precede their being ruled by the Family, which would ride out the conflict in "the bottomless pit"—a secret city beneath Death Valley. At the Canoga Park house, while Family members worked on vehicles and pored over maps to prepare for their desert escape, they also worked on songs for their world-changing album.

On May 18, 1969, Terry Melcher visited Spahn Ranch to hear Manson and the women sing. Melcher arranged a subsequent visit, not long thereafter, on which he brought a friend who possessed a mobile recording unit; but he himself did not record the group.

By June, Manson was telling the Family they might have to show blacks how to start "Helter Skelter". When Manson tasked Watson with obtaining money supposedly intended to help the Family prepare for the conflict, Watson defrauded a black drug dealer named Bernard "Lotsapoppa" Crowe. Crowe responded with a threat to wipe out everyone at Spahn Ranch. Manson countered on July 1, 1969, by shooting Crowe at his Hollywood apartment. Manson's mistaken belief that he had killed Crowe was seemingly confirmed by a news report of the discovery of the dumped body of a Black Panther in Los Angeles. Although Crowe was not a member of the Black Panthers, Manson, concluding he had been, expected retaliation from the group. He turned Spahn Ranch into a defensive camp, with night patrols of armed guards. "If we'd needed any more proof that Helter Skelter was coming down very soon, this was it," Tex Watson would later write, "[B]lackie was trying to get at the chosen ones."

On July 25, 1969, Manson sent sometime Family member Bobby Beausoleil along with Mary Brunner and Susan Atkins to the house of acquaintance Gary Hinman, to persuade him to turn over money Manson thought Hinman had inherited. The three held the uncooperative Hinman hostage for two days, during which Manson showed up with a sword to slash his ear. After that, Beausoleil stabbed Hinman to death, ostensibly on Manson's instruction. Before leaving the Topanga Canyon residence, Beausoleil, or one of the women, used Hinman's blood to write "Political piggy" on the wall and to draw a panther paw, a Black Panther symbol.

In magazine interviews of 1981 and 1998–99, Beausoleil would say he went to Hinman's to recover money paid to Hinman for drugs that had supposedly been bad; he added that Brunner and Atkins, unaware of his intent, went along idly, merely to visit Hinman. On the other hand, Atkins, in her 1977 autobiography, wrote that Manson directly told Beausoleil, Brunner, and her to go to Hinman's and get the supposed inheritance—$21,000. She said Manson had told her privately, two days earlier, that, if she wanted to "do something important," she could kill Hinman and get his money.

Beausoleil was arrested on August 6, 1969, after he had been caught driving Hinman's car. Police found the murder weapon in the tire well. Two days later, Manson told Family members at Spahn Ranch, "Now is the time for Helter Skelter."

On the night of August 8, Manson directed Watson to take Atkins, Linda Kasabian, and Patricia Krenwinkel to "that house where Melcher used to live" and "totally destroy everyone in [it], as gruesome as you can." He told the women to do as Watson would instruct them. Krenwinkel was one of the early Family members, one of the hitchhikers who had allegedly been picked up by Dennis Wilson. The current occupants of the house, all of whom were strangers to the Manson followers, were movie actress Sharon Tate, wife of famed director Roman Polanski and eight and a half months pregnant; her friend and former lover Jay Sebring, a noted hairstylist; Polanski's friend and aspiring screenwriter Wojciech Frykowski, and Frykowski's lover Abigail Folger, heiress to the Folger coffee fortune. Tate's husband, Polanski, was in London working on a film project; Tate had been visiting with him and had returned to the United States only three weeks earlier.

When the murder team arrived at the entrance to the Cielo Drive property, Watson, who had been to the house on at least one other occasion, cut the phone line. It was now around midnight and into August 9, 1969. Backing their car down to the bottom of the hill that led up to the place, the group parked there and walked back up to the house. Thinking the gate might be electrified or rigged with an alarm, they climbed a brushy embankment at its right and dropped onto the grounds. Just then, headlights came their way from farther within the angled property. Watson ordered the women to lie in the bushes. He then stepped out and ordered the approaching driver, 18-year-old student and hi-fi enthusiast Steven Parent, to halt. As Watson leveled a 22-caliber revolver at Parent, the frightened youth begged Watson not to hurt him, claiming that he wouldn't say anything. Watson first slashed at Parent with a knife, giving him a defensive slash wound on the palm of his hand (severing tendons and tearing the boy's watch off his wrist), then shot him four times in the chest and abdomen. Watson then ordered the women to help push the car further up the driveway After traversing the front lawn and having Kasabian search for an open window of the main house, Watson cut the screen of a window. He then removed the screen, entered, and let Atkins and Krenwinkel in through the front door. As Watson whispered to Atkins, Frykowski awoke on the living-room couch; Watson kicked him in the head. When Frykowski asked him who he was and what he was doing there, Watson replied, "I'm the devil, and I'm here to do the devil's business."

On Watson's direction, Atkins found the house's three other occupants and, with Krenwinkel's help, brought them to the living room. Watson began to tie Tate and Sebring together by their necks with rope he'd brought and slung up over a beam. Sebring's protest – his second – of rough treatment of the pregnant Tate prompted Watson to shoot him. Folger was taken momentarily back to her bedroom for her purse, out of which she gave the intruders $70. After that, Watson stabbed the groaning Sebring seven times.

Frykowski's hands had been bound with a towel. Freeing himself, Frykowski began struggling with Atkins, who stabbed at his legs with the knife with which she had been guarding him. As he fought his way toward and out the front door, onto the porch, Watson joined in against him. Watson struck him over the head with the gun multiple times, stabbed him repeatedly, and shot him twice. Watson broke the gun's right grip in the process.

Around this time, Kasabian was drawn up from the driveway by "horrifying sounds." She arrived outside the door. In a vain effort to halt the massacre, she told Atkins falsely that someone was coming. Inside the house, Folger had escaped from Krenwinkel and fled out a bedroom door to the pool area. Folger was pursued to the front lawn by Krenwinkel, who stabbed – and finally, tackled – her. She was dispatched by Watson; her two assailants had stabbed her 28 times. As Frykowski struggled across the lawn, Watson stabbed him to death. Back in the house, Tate pleaded to be allowed to live long enough to have her baby, and even offered herself as a hostage in an attempt to save the life of her unborn child; her killers would have none of it, as either Atkins, Watson, or both killed Tate, who was stabbed 16 times. Watson later wrote that Tate cried, "Mother... mother..." as she was being killed. Earlier, as the four Family members had headed out from Spahn Ranch, Manson had told the women to "leave a sign... something witchy". Using the towel that had bound Frykowski's hands, Atkins wrote "pig" on the house's front door, in Tate's blood. En route home, the killers changed out of bloody clothes, which were ditched in the hills, along with their weapons. In initial confessions to cellmates of hers at Sybil Brand Institute, Atkins would say she killed Tate. In later statements to her attorney, to prosecutor Vincent Bugliosi, and before a grand jury, Atkins indicated Tate had been stabbed by Tex Watson. In his 1978 autobiography, Watson said that he stabbed Tate and that Atkins never touched her.

The next night, six Family members—Leslie Van Houten, Steve "Clem" Grogan, and the four from the previous night—rode out at Manson's instruction. Displeased by the panic of the victims at Cielo Drive, Manson accompanied the six, "to show [them] how to do it." After a few hours' ride, in which he considered a number of murders and even attempted one of them, Manson gave Kasabian directions that brought the group to 3301 Waverly Drive. This was the home of supermarket executive Leno LaBianca and his wife,

Rosemary, a dress shop co-owner. Located in the Los Feliz section of Los Angeles, it was next door to a house at which Manson and Family members had attended a party the previous year.

According to Atkins and Kasabian, Manson disappeared up the driveway and returned to say he had tied up the house's occupants; then he sent Watson up with Krenwinkel and Van Houten. In his autobiography, on the other hand, Watson stated that, having gone up alone, Manson returned to take him up to the house with him. After Manson pointed out a sleeping man through a window, the two of them entered through the unlocked back door. Watson added that, at trial, he "went along with" the women's account, which he figured made him "look that much less responsible." As Watson tells it, Manson roused the sleeping Leno LaBianca from the couch at gunpoint and had Watson bind his hands with a leather thong. After Rosemary LaBianca was brought briefly into the living room from the bedroom, Watson followed Manson's instructions to cover the couple's heads with pillowcases. He bound these in place with lamp cords. Manson left, sending Krenwinkel and Leslie Van Houten into the house with instructions that the couple be killed.

Before leaving Spahn Ranch, Watson had complained to Manson of the inadequacy of the previous night's weapons. Now, sending the women from the kitchen to the bedroom, to which Rosemary LaBianca had been returned, he went to the living room and began stabbing Leno LaBianca with a chrome-plated bayonet. The first thrust went into the man's throat.

Sounds of a scuffle in the bedroom drew Watson there to discover Mrs. LaBianca keeping the women at bay by swinging the lamp tied to her neck. After subduing her with several stabs of the bayonet, he returned to the living room and resumed attacking Leno, whom he stabbed a total of 12 times with the bayonet. When he had finished, Watson carved "WAR" on the man's exposed abdomen. He stated this in his autobiography. In an unclear portion of her eventual grand jury testimony, Atkins, who did not enter the LaBianca house, possibly said she believed Krenwinkel had carved the word. In a ghost-written newspaper account based on a statement she had made earlier to her attorney, she said Watson carved it.

Returning to the bedroom, Watson found Krenwinkel stabbing Rosemary LaBianca with a knife from the LaBianca kitchen. Heeding Manson's instruction to make sure each of the women played a part, Watson told Van Houten to stab Mrs. LaBianca too. She did, stabbing her approximately 16 times in the back and the exposed buttocks. At trial, Van Houten would claim, uncertainly, that Rosemary LaBianca was dead when she stabbed her. Evidence showed that many of Mrs. LaBianca's 41 stab wounds had, in fact, been inflicted post-mortem. While Watson cleaned off the bayonet and showered, Krenwinkel wrote "Rise" and "Death to pigs" on the walls and "Healter [sic] Skelter" on the refrigerator door, all in LaBianca blood. She gave Leno LaBianca 14 puncture wounds with an ivory-handled, two-tined carving fork, which she left jutting out of his stomach. She also planted a steak knife in his throat. Hoping for a double crime, Manson had gone on to direct Kasabian to drive to the Venice home of an actor acquaintance of hers, another "piggy." Depositing the second trio of Family members at the man's apartment building, he drove back to Spahn Ranch, leaving them and the LaBianca killers to hitchhike home. Kasabian thwarted this murder by deliberately knocking on the wrong apartment door and waking a stranger. As the group abandoned the murder plan and left, Susan Atkins defecated in the stairwell.

The Tate murders had become news on August 9, 1969. The Polanski's housekeeper, Winifred Chapman, had arrived for work that morning and discovered the murder scene. On August 10, detectives of the Los Angeles County Sheriff's Department, which had jurisdiction in the Hinman case, informed Los Angeles Police Department (LAPD) detectives assigned to the Tate case of the bloody writing at the Hinman house. Thinking the Tate murders a consequence of a drug transaction, the Tate team ignored this and the crimes' other similarities. The Tate autopsies were under way and the LaBianca bodies were yet to be discovered.

Steven Parent, the shooting victim in the Tate driveway, was determined to have been an acquaintance of William Garretson, who lived in the guest house. Garretson was a young man hired by Rudi Altobelli to take care of the property while Altobelli himself was away. As the killers arrived, Parent had been leaving Cielo Drive, after a visit to Garretson. Held briefly as a Tate suspect, Garretson told police he had neither seen nor heard anything on the murder night. He was released on August 11, 1969, after undergoing a polygraph examination that indicated he had not been involved in the crimes. Interviewed decades later, he stated he had, in fact, witnessed a portion of the murders, as the examination suggested. (See "Later events", below.) The LaBianca crime scene was discovered at about 10:30 pm on August 10, approximately 19 hours after the murders were committed. Fifteen-year-old Frank Struthers— Rosemary's son from a prior marriage and Leno's stepson—returned from a camping trip and was disturbed by seeing all of the window shades of his home drawn, and by the fact that his step-father's speedboat was still attached to the family car, which was parked in the driveway. He called his older sister and her boyfriend. The boyfriend, Joe Dorgan, accompanied the younger Struthers into the home and discovered Leno's body. Rosemary's body was found by investigating police officers. On August 12, 1969, the LAPD told the press it had ruled out any connection between the Tate and LaBianca homicides. On August 16, the sheriff's office raided Spahn Ranch and arrested Manson and 25 others, as "suspects in a major auto theft ring" that had been stealing Volkswagens and converting them into dune buggies. Weapons were seized, but because the warrant had been misdated the group was released a few days later. The LaBianca detectives were generally younger than the Tate team. In a report at the end of August, when virtually all leads had gone nowhere, they noted a possible connection between the bloody writings at the LaBianca house and "the singing group the Beatles' most recent album."

Still working separately from the Tate team, the LaBianca team checked with the sheriff's office in mid-October about possible similar crimes. They learned of the Hinman case. They also learned that the Hinman detectives had spoken with Beausoleil's girlfriend, Kitty Lutesinger. She had been arrested a few days earlier with members of "the Manson Family." The arrests had taken place at the desert ranches, to which the Family had moved and whence, unknown to authorities, its members had been searching Death Valley for a hole in the ground—access to the Bottomless Pit. A joint force of National Park rangers and officers from the California Highway Patrol and the Inyo County Sheriff's Office—federal, state, and county personnel—had raided both the Myers Ranch and Barker Ranch after following clues unwittingly left when Family members burned an earthmover owned by Death Valley National Monument. The raiders had found stolen dune buggies and other vehicles and had arrested two dozen people, including Manson. A Highway Patrol officer found Manson hiding in a cabinet beneath Barker's bathroom sink. A month after they, too, had spoken with Lutesinger, the LaBianca detectives made contact with members of a motorcycle gang she'd told them Manson had tried to enlist as his bodyguards while the Family was at Spahn Ranch. While the gang members were providing information that suggested a link between Manson and the murders, a dormitory mate of Susan Atkins succeeded in informing LAPD of the Family's involvement in the crimes. As one of those arrested at Barker, Atkins had been booked for the Hinman murder after she'd confirmed to the sheriff's detectives that she'd been involved in it, as Lutesinger had said. Transferred to Sybil Brand Institute, a detention center in Los Angeles, she had begun talking to bunkmates Ronnie Howard and Virginia Graham, to whom she gave accounts of the events in which she had been involved.

On December 1, 1969, acting on information from these sources, LAPD announced warrants for the arrest of Watson, Krenwinkel, and Kasabian in the Tate case; the suspects' involvement in the LaBianca murders was noted. Manson and Atkins, already in custody, were not mentioned; the connection between the LaBianca case and Van Houten, who was also among those arrested near Death Valley, had not yet been recognized. Watson and Krenwinkel, too, were already under arrest, authorities in McKinney, Texas, and Mobile, Alabama, having picked them up on notice from LAPD. Informed that there was a warrant out for her arrest, Kasabian voluntarily surrendered to authorities in Concord, New Hampshire, on December 2.

Before long, physical evidence such as Krenwinkel's and Watson's fingerprints, which had been collected by LAPD at Cielo Drive, was augmented by evidence recovered by the public. On September 1, 1969, the distinctive .22-caliber Hi Standard "Buntline Special" revolver Watson used on Parent, Sebring, and Frykowski had been found and given to the police by Steven Weiss, a 10-year-old who lived near the Tate residence. In mid-December, when the Los Angeles Times published a crime account based on information Susan Atkins had given her attorney, Weiss' father made several phone calls which finally prompted LAPD to locate the gun in its evidence file and connect it with the murders via ballistics tests. Acting on that same newspaper account, a local ABC television crew quickly located and recovered the bloody clothing discarded by the Tate killers. The knives discarded en route from the Tate residence were never recovered, despite a search by some of the same crewmen and, months later still, by LAPD. A knife found behind the cushion of a chair in the Tate living room was apparently that of Susan Atkins, who lost her knife in the course of the attack.

The trial began June 15, 1970. On Friday, July 24, the first day of testimony, Manson appeared in court with an X carved into his forehead. He issued a statement that he was "considered inadequate and incompetent to speak or defend [him]self" – and had "X'd [him]self from [the establishment's] world." Over the following weekend, the female defendants duplicated the mark on their own foreheads, as did most Family members within another day or so

During the trial, Family members loitered near the entrances and corridors of the courthouse. To keep them out of the courtroom itself, the prosecution subpoenaed them as prospective witnesses, who would not be able to enter while others were testifying. When the group established itself in vigil on the sidewalk, some members wore a sheathed hunting knife that, although in plain view, was carried legally. Each of them was also identifiable by the X on his or her forehead.

Some Family members attempted to dissuade witnesses from testifying. Prosecution witnesses Paul Watkins and Juan Flynn were both threatened; Watkins was badly burned in a suspicious fire in his van. Former Family member Barbara Hoyt, who had overheard Susan Atkins describing the Tate murders to Family member Ruth Ann Moorehouse, agreed to accompany the latter to Hawaii. There, Moorehouse allegedly gave her a hamburger spiked with several doses of LSD. Found sprawled on a Honolulu curb in a drugged semi-stupor, Hoyt was taken to the hospital, where she did her best to identify herself as a witness in the Tate-LaBianca murder trial. Before the incident, Hoyt had been a reluctant witness; after the attempt to silence her, her reticence disappeared. On August 4, despite precautions taken by the court, Manson flashed the jury a Los Angeles Times front page whose headline was "Manson Guilty, Nixon Declares." This was a reference to a statement made the previous day when U.S. President Richard Nixon had decried what he saw as the media's glamorization of Manson. Voir dired by Judge Older, the jurors contended that the headline had not influenced them. The next day, the female defendants stood up and said in unison that, in light of Nixon's remark, there was no point in going on with the trial. On October 5, Manson was denied the court's permission to question a prosecution witness whom the defense attorneys had declined to cross-examine. Leaping over the defense table, Manson attempted to attack the judge. Wrestled to the ground by bailiffs, he was removed from the courtroom with the female defendants, who had subsequently risen and begun chanting in Latin. Thereafter, Older allegedly began wearing a revolver under his robes.

On November 16, the prosecution rested its case. Three days later, after arguing standard dismissal motions, the defense stunned the court by resting as well, without calling a single witness. Shouting their disapproval, Atkins, Krenwinkel, and Van Houten demanded their right to testify. In chambers, the women's lawyers told the judge their clients wanted to testify that they had planned and committed the crimes and that Manson had not been involved. By resting their case, the defense lawyers had tried to stop this; Van Houten's attorney, Ronald Hughes, vehemently stated that he would not "push a client out the window." In the prosecutor's view, it was Manson who was advising the women to testify in this way as a means of saving himself. Speaking about the trial in a 1987 documentary, Krenwinkel said, "The entire proceedings were scripted – by Charlie."

The next day, Manson testified. Lest Manson's address violate the California Supreme Court's decision in People v. Aranda by making statements implicating his co-defendants, the jury was removed from the courtroom. Speaking for more than an hour, Manson said, among other things, that "the music is telling the youth to rise up against the establishment." He said, "Why blame it on me? I didn't write the music." "To be honest with you," Manson also stated, "I don't recall ever saying 'Get a knife and a change of clothes and go do what Tex says.' "

As the body of the trial concluded and with the closing arguments impending, attorney Ronald Hughes disappeared during a weekend trip. When Maxwell Keith was appointed to represent Van Houten in Hughes' absence, a delay of more than two weeks was required to permit Keith to familiarize himself with the voluminous trial transcripts. No sooner had the trial resumed, just before Christmas, than disruptions of the prosecution's closing argument by the defendants led Older to ban the four defendants from the courtroom for the remainder of the guilt phase. Older said it had become obvious the defendants were acting in collusion with each other and were simply putting on a performance.

On January 25, 1971, guilty verdicts were returned against the four defendants on each of the 27 separate counts against them. Not far into the trial's penalty phase, the jurors saw, at last, the defense that Manson—in the prosecution's view—had planned to present. Atkins, Krenwinkel, and Van Houten testified the murders had been conceived as "copycat" versions of the Hinman murder, for which Atkins now took credit. The killings, they said, were intended to draw suspicion away from Bobby Beausoleil, by resembling the crime for which he had been jailed. This plan had supposedly been the work of, and carried out under the guidance of, not Manson, but someone allegedly in love with Beausoleil—Linda Kasabian. Among the narrative's weak points was the inability of Atkins to explain why, as she was maintaining, she had written "political piggy" at the Hinman house in the first place. Midway through the penalty phase, Manson shaved his head and trimmed his beard to a fork; he told the press, "I am the Devil, and the Devil always has a bald head." In what the prosecution regarded as belated recognition on their part that imitation of Manson only proved his domination, the female defendants refrained from shaving their heads until the jurors retired to weigh the state's request for the death penalty. The effort to exonerate Manson via the "copycat" scenario failed. On March 29, 1971, the jury returned verdicts of death against all four defendants on all counts. On April 19, 1971, Judge Older sentenced the four to death. On the day the verdicts recommending the death penalty were returned, news came that the badly decomposed body of Ronald Hughes had been found wedged between two boulders in Ventura County. It was rumored, although never proven, that Hughes was murdered by the Family, possibly because he had stood up to Manson and refused to allow Van Houten to take the stand and absolve Manson of the crimes.Though he might have perished in flooding, Family member

Sandra Good stated that Hughes was "the first of the retaliation murders."

Protracted proceedings to extradite Watson from his native Texas, where he had resettled a month before his arrest, resulted in his being tried separately. The trial commenced in August 1971; by October, he, too, had been found guilty on seven counts of murder and one of conspiracy. Unlike the others, Watson had presented a psychiatric defense; prosecutor Vincent Bugliosi made short work of Watson's insanity claims. Like his co-conspirators, Watson was sentenced to death.

In February 1972, the death sentences of all five parties were reduced to life in prison

In a 1971 trial that took place after his Tate/LaBianca convictions, Manson was found guilty of the murders of Gary Hinman and Donald "Shorty" Shea and was given a life sentence. Shea was a Spahn Ranch stuntman and horse wrangler who had been killed approximately 10 days after the August 16, 1969, sheriff's raid on the ranch. Manson, who suspected that Shea helped set up the raid, had apparently believed Shea was trying to get Spahn to run the Family off the ranch. Manson may have considered it a "sin" that the white Shea had married a black woman; and there was the possibility that Shea knew about the Tate/LaBianca killings. In separate trials, Family members Bruce Davis and Steve "Clem" Grogan were also found guilty of Shea's murder. Before the conclusion of Manson's Tate/LaBianca trial, a reporter for the Los Angeles Times tracked down Manson's mother, remarried and living in the Pacific Northwest. The former Kathleen Maddox claimed that, in childhood, her son had suffered no neglect; he had even been "pampered by all the women who surrounded him."

On September 5, 1975, the Family rocketed back to national attention when Squeaky Fromme attempted to assassinate US President Gerald Ford. The attempt took place in Sacramento, to which she and Manson follower Sandra Good had moved to be near Manson while he was incarcerated at Folsom State Prison. A subsequent search of the apartment shared by Fromme, Good, and a Family recruit turned up evidence that, coupled with later actions on the part of Good, resulted in Good's conviction for conspiring to send threatening communications through the United States mail and transmitting death threats by way of interstate commerce. Fromme was sentenced to 15 years to life, becoming the first person sentenced under United States Code Title 18, chapter 84 (1965), which made it a Federal crime to attempt to assassinate the President of the United States.

Manson will be eligible to re-apply for parole in 2012.

* **Marie**

McDonald (July 6, 1923 – October 21, 1965)

American singer and actress

Born Cora Marie Frye in Burgin, Kentucky, she was the daughter of a Ziegfeld Follies girl. After her parents divorced, she moved with her mother and stepfather to Yonkers, New York. At the age of 15, McDonald began modeling and competed in numerous beauty pageants and was crowned Miss New York in 1939. At 17, she landed a showgirl role in a 1940 Broadway production at the Earl Carroll Theatre called Earl Carroll's Vanities. Shortly thereafter, she moved to Hollywood.

Marie McDonald's singing voice brought work with Tommy Dorsey & His Orchestra on his radio show and she later performed with other Big bands. In 1942, she was put under contract by Universal Studios. That year, she appeared in three motion pictures, most notably, Pardon My Sarong. The following year she co-starred in A Scream in the Dark. In 1945 she worked for a small independent production company in another "B" film called Getting Gertie's Garter. She then costarred with Gene Kelly in MGM's Living in a Big Way (1947).

Between 1945 and 1950 she appeared in two films and not again until 1958 when she was cast in The Geisha Boy. In 1957, she toured the world in a very successful nightclub act. In 1963, she made her last appearance in the film, Promises! Promises.

McDonald was one of Bugsy Siegel's mistresses at one time. In all, she married seven times, including twice to millionaire Harry Karl, who later married Debbie Reynolds. There were also romances with Eddie Fisher and Michael Wilding. She suffered multiple miscarriages before adopting two children and giving birth to a daughter, Tina Marie, in 1956. McDonald's personal life overshadowed her career. The media often reported on her romances, auto accidents, and an escape from an Australian psychiatric clinic. She made headlines in 1957, when she claimed to have been kidnapped by two men.

In 1965, McDonald was found dead of a drug overdose in her Calabasas, California home.

Three months after McDonald's death, in January 1966, her sixth husband, Donald F. Taylor, who was a producer who had occasionally acted under the name Don Taylor, committed suicide.

Margurite

McNamara (June 18, 1928 – February 18, 1978)

American stage, film, and television actress.

Born in New York City, McNamara was one of four children. She attended Textile High School in New York and worked as a teen model while studying drama and dance. McNamara became one of the most successful models of John Robert Powers' modeling agency.

In 1951, she began her acting career when she took over Barbara Bel Geddes' role as Patty O'Neill in the stage production of The Moon Is Blue. Later that year, she made her Broadway debut in The King of Friday's Men.

In 1953, she went to Hollywood to reprise her role in Otto Preminger's film version of The Moon Is Blue. McNamara's second film role was in Three Coins in the Fountain (1954). Although her career started off well, she made only two more films after Three Coins. In the early 1960s, she appeared in several television shows including an episode of The Twilight Zone entitled "Ring-a-Ding Girl." McNamara's last onscreen role was in a 1964 episode of The Alfred Hitchcock Hour entitled "The Body in the Barn."

[McNamara was married to actor/director David Swift. The marriage ended in divorce and McNamara never remarried. After her last onscreen role in 1964, McNamara fell out of public view and spent her later years working as a typist in New York City. In February 1978, she was found dead after a deliberate overdose of sleeping pills.

Kendall McComas

(October 29, 1916 – October 15, 1981) American child actor.

McComas was born in Holton, Kansas. He first appeared in the Mickey McGuire short subjects series as a member of Mickey McGuire's.

In 1931, he joined the Our Gang series. Even though he was well into his teens during his Our Gang tenure, McComas, very short for his age, capably portrayed his grade-school-age character Breezy.

After growing up, he gave up show business to be an electrical engineer at the U.S. Naval Weapons Center in China Lake, California.

He committed suicide on October 15, 1981.

* **Mayo Methot** (March 3, 1904–June 9, 1951), also known as Mayo Methot Bogart, American film and theater actress

Methot was born in Portland, Oregon. A petite brunette, she became a popular actress on Broadway during the 1920s. While on Broadway she originated a role in the musical Great Day (1929), introducing the song "More Than You Know" and several others.

She moved to Hollywood in the early 1930s and began work for Warner Brothers Studios. She found herself usually cast as unsympathetic second leads in Warner's crime melodramas such as Jimmy the Gent and Marked Woman, where she met Humphrey Bogart. They married in 1938. It was her third marriage, having first wed at age 19 to Cosmopolitan Productions cameraman Jack La Mond, whom she divorced in 1927.

Methot and Bogart became a couple of high-profile Hollywood celebrities, but it was not a smooth marriage. Both drank heavily, and Methot gained a reputation for her violent actions when drunk.

During World War II, the Bogarts traveled Europe, entertaining the troops. During their travels, they often stayed in officers' quarters. They had no trouble borrowing guns, and enjoyed "shooting up the place" in the middle of the night. Afterwards, the army banned married couples from entertaining the troops for the remainder of the war.

At one point, in their travels during the war, they linked up with director John Huston in Italy. During a night of heavy drinking, Methot insisted that everyone listen to her perform a song. Though they told her no, she sang anyway. The performance was so bad and embarrassing, Huston and Bogart remembered it and based a scene in Key Largo on the incident. It was the scene in which the alcoholic girlfriend (Claire Trevor) of the mobster (played by Edward G. Robinson) sang a number of key and while intoxicated. The performance won Trevor an Oscar.

Numerous battles took place at the Hollywood residence of the famous couple including one in which Methot stabbed Bogart in the shoulder. Actress Gloria Stuart told of a dinner party at which Methot produced a pistol and threatened to shoot Bogart. At one point, when Methot was depressed, she slashed her wrists. Methot's career went into a rapid decline as a result of her drinking, and her marriage to Bogart ended in 1945, when he left her to marry Lauren Bacall.

Methot was unable to renew her career and settled into a pattern of alcoholism and depression. Following her divorce from Bogart in May, she moved back to Oregon where her mother helped take care of her. By the early 1950s, struggling to support herself and ill from years of alcoholism, she died in a motel room in Multnomah, Oregon, on June 9, 1951. Her body lay undiscovered for several days. When Bogart heard the news (while shooting The African Queen) his comment was "Such a waste".

Milos   Milos

(Serbian) (July 1, 1941 – January 30, 1966) was a Hollywood actor, a stunt double and bodyguard.

In the 1950s Milos Milosevic and his friend Stevan Markovic were involved in a street fight in Belgrade. They met Alain Delon, who was filming a movie in Belgrade. Delon hired Milos Milos and Stevan Markovic as bodyguards, and Milos later moved to Hollywood, California. There he met gangster Nikola Milinkovich. Milinkovich gave Milos $200,000 to fight for him in street fights, from which Nikola benefited $2,000,000.

As a young Hollywood actor Milos is best known for his performance as a Soviet naval officer in the 1966 comedy The Russians Are Coming, the

Russians Are Coming and for his titular role in the 1965 Esperanto horror movie, Incubus.

In 1965, Barbara Ann Thomason (stage name Carolyn Mitchell) began an affair with Milos. The two were found dead in her husband Mickey Rooney's Los Angeles house in 1966. The American official inquiry stated that Milos had shot Thomason with Rooney's chrome-plated .38 caliber revolver and then committed suicide. The official inquiry provoked rumors and doubts that they were actually both murdered in revenge for having an affair.

Sal Mineo (January 10, 1939 – February 12, 1976), American film and theatre actor

Mineo was born in The Bronx, the son of Sicilian coffin makers. His mother enrolled him in dancing and acting school at an early age. He had his first stage appearance in The Rose Tattoo (1951. He also played the young prince opposite Yul Brynner in the stage musical The King and I.

Mineo had also auditioned for a part in The Private War of Major Benson as a cadet colonel opposite Charlton Heston. His breakthrough then came in Rebel Without A Cause, in which he played John "Plato" Crawford, the sensitive teenager smitten with Jim Stark (played by James Dean).

Mineo played a Mexican boy in Giant (1956), but many of his subsequent roles were variations of his role in Rebel Without a Cause. In the Disney adventure Tonka, for instance, Mineo starred as a young Sioux named White Bull who traps and domesticates a clear-eyed, spirited wild horse named "Tonka" who becomes the famous Comanche.

By the early 1960s, he was becoming too old to play the type of role that had made him famous and was not considered appropriate for leading roles. He auditioned for David Lean's film Lawrence of Arabia but was not hired. Mineo was baffled by his sudden loss of popularity, later saying "One minute it seemed I had more movie offers than I could handle, the next, no one wanted me." He did appear on The Patty Duke Show in its second season (1964). The episode was called "Patty Meets a Celebrity". There are stories he attempted to revive his career by camping out on the front lawn of Francis Ford Coppola's home for a chance to win the role of Fredo in The Godfather, but the role went to John Cazale.

A small role in Escape from the Planet of the Apes (1971) as the chimpanzee Dr. Milo was Mineo's last appearance in a motion picture. In 1973, Mineo appeared as Rachman Habib, assistant to the president of a Middle Eastern country, in the episode "A Case of Immunity" on the NBC crime drama Columbo. He also appeared in two episodes of Hawaii Five-O, in 1968 and 1975.

By 1976, Mineo's career had begun to turn around. Playing the role of a bisexual burglar in a series of stage performances of the comedy P.S. Your Cat Is Dead in San Francisco, Mineo received substantial publicity from many positive reviews, and he moved to Los Angeles along with the play. Arriving home after a rehearsal on February 12, 1976, Mineo was stabbed to death in the alley behind his apartment building in West Hollywood, California. He was 37 years old. Mineo was stabbed just once, not repeatedly as first reported, but the knife blade struck his heart.

* **Miroslava Stern**

(February 26, 1926 – March 9, 1955) Czechoslovakian-born Mexican film actress.

Born Miroslava Šternová in Czechoslovakia (now the Czech Republic), Stern moved to Mexico as a child with her adoptive parents in the late 1930s, seeking to escape war in their native country.

After winning a national beauty contest, Miroslava began to study acting. She participated in various Mexican films and also spent some time in Hollywood.

She was offered a role in Ensayo de un crimen (Rehearsal for a Crime) in 1955, directed by Luis Buñuel. Soon after the final wrap of the film, Miroslava committed suicide by overdosing on sleeping pills. Her body was found lying outstretched over her bed, she had a portrait of bullfighter Luis Miguel Dominguín in one hand. Her friends stated her suicide was due to unrequited love for Dominguín, who had recently married Italian actress Lucia Bosé. Bosè would go on to star in Buñuel's next movie, Cela s'appelle l'aurore (1956).

In his 1983 autobiography, Mon dernier soupir ("My Last Breath"), Buñuel recalls the irony of Miroslava's cremation following her suicide, when compared to a scene in Ensayo de un crimen, her last film, in which the protagonist cremates a wax reproduction of her character. Her life is the subject of a short story by Guadalupe Loaeza which was adapted by Alejandro Pelayo for his 1992 Mexican film called Miroslava, starring Arielle Dombasle.

American films included Adventures of Casanova" (1947) as Casania's sister, The Brave Bulls (1951) as Linda de Calderón, and Stranger on Horseback (1955) as Amy Lee Bannerman.

Marilyn Monroe

(June 1, 1926 – August 5, 1962) born Norma Jeane Mortenson, but baptized Norma Jeane Baker. American actress, singer and model.

After spending much of her childhood in foster homes, Monroe began a career as a model, which led to a film contract in 1946. Her early film appearances were minor, but her performances in The Asphalt Jungle and All About Eve (both 1950) were well received. By 1953, Monroe had progressed to leading roles. Her "dumb blonde" persona was used to comedic effect in such films as Gentlemen Prefer Blondes (1953), How to Marry a Millionaire (1953) and The Seven Year Itch (1955).

The final years of Monroe's life were marked by illness, personal problems, and a reputation for being unreliable and difficult to work with.

On August 5, 1962, LAPD police sergeant Jack Clemmons received a call at 4:25 a.m. from Dr. Ralph Greenson, Monroe's psychiatrist, proclaiming that Monroe was found dead at her home in Brentwood, Los Angeles, California. She was 36 years old. At the subsequent autopsy, eight milligram percent of Chloral hydrate and 4.5 milligram percent of Nembutal were found in her system, and Dr. Thomas Noguchi of the Los Angeles County Coroner's office recorded cause of death as "acute barbiturate poisoning", resulting from a "probable suicide". Many theories, including murder, circulated about the circumstances of her death and the timeline after the body was found. Some conspiracy theories involved John and Robert Kennedy, while other theories suggested CIA or Mafia complicity.

Chester

Morris (February 16, 1901 – September 11, 1970) was an American actor

He was born John Chester Brooks Morris in New York City, the son of Broadway stage actor William Morris and the performer Etta Hawkins. He made his Broadway debut at 17 in Lionel Barrymore's The Copperhead. At 17, he billed himself as "the youngest leading man in the country". His film career began in 1917 in An Amateur Orphan. He was nominated for the Academy Award for Best Actor for Alibi (1929) directed by Roland West. He also starred in The Bat Whispers (1930) and Corsair (1931), both directed by West.

He starred in the early prison film The Big House (1930). His career gradually declined in the late 1930s, with roles in B-movies such as Smashing the Rackets with Edward J. Pawley (1938) and Five Came Back (1939). His career revived when from 1941 to 1949 he played the character Boston Blackie in 14 low-budget movies produced by Columbia Pictures, starting with Meet Boston Blackie, and one season of radio shows.

During World War II he performed hundreds of free magic shows for the U.S.O. at army and navy camps, war bond drives and hospitals. In 1944, a B-17 "Flying Fortress" airplane was christened "The Chester and Lili Morris" in honor of him and his wife, and their contributions to the United States war effort. Morris also contributed original tricks to magician's journals and often incorporated magic into his film performances, including "Boston Blackie and The Law" (1946).

Through the 1950s and 1960s, Morris worked mainly in television, with a recurring role as detective Lieutenant Max Ritter in the CBS summer replacement series, Diagnosis: Unknown, which aired from July to September 1960. He also made occasional forays into regional theatre, and a few films, notably a role in the science-fiction film The She Creature, where he played Dr. Carlo Lombardi. After his last Boston Blackie movie, he only performed in three more films, including his final role in The Great White Hope (1970) which was released after his death.

Morris was dying of cancer when he committed suicide in room 202 at the former Holiday Inn of New Hope by taking an overdose of barbiturates in 1970. At the time of his death, he was appearing in a stage production of The Caine Mutiny Court Martial at the Bucks County Playhouse in New Hope, Pennsylvania.

*

Jim Morrison

(December 8, 1943 – July 3, 1971) American singer and poet.

James Douglas Morrison was born in Melbourne, Florida, teson of a future Admiral.

With his father in the United States Navy, Morrison's family moved often. He spent part of his childhood in San Diego, California.

In January 1964, Morrison moved to Los Angeles, California, to attend the University of California, Los Angeles (UCLA). Morrison completed his undergraduate degree at UCLA's film school and the Theater Arts department of the College of Fine Arts in 1965. He made two films while attending UCLA. First Love, the first of these films, made with Morrison's classmate and roommate Max Schwartz, was released to the public when it appeared in a documentary about the film Obscura. During these years, while living in Venice Beach, he became friends with writers at the Los Angeles Free Press. Morrison was an advocate of the underground newspaper until his death in 1971.

Morrison died on July 3, 1971. In the official account of his death, he was found in a Paris apartment bathtub by Courson. Pursuant to French law, no autopsy was performed because the medical examiner claimed to have found no evidence of foul play. The absence of an official autopsy has left many questions regarding Morrison's cause of death.

In Wonderland Avenue, Danny Sugerman discussed his encounter with Courson after she returned to the U.S. According to Sugerman's account, Courson stated that Morrison had died of a heroin overdose, having insufflated what he believed to be cocaine. Sugerman added that Courson had given numerous contradictory versions of Morrison's death, at times saying that she had killed Morrison, or that his death was her fault. Courson's story of Morrison's unintentional ingestion of heroin, followed by accidental overdose, is supported by the confession of Alain Ronay, who has written that Morrison died of a hemorrhage after snorting Courson's heroin, and that Courson nodded off instead of phoning for medical help, leaving Morrison bleeding to death

Courson died of a heroin overdose three years later. Like Morrison, she was 27 years old at the time of her death.

Al Mulock (June 30, 1925 - May 1968) was a character actor

He is best known for his roles in the Spaghetti Western movies, most notably in his two collaborations with Sergio Leone.

Mulock, for reasons which are still not clear, committed suicide in May 1968, in Guadix, Spain during the shooting of Once Upon a Time in the West, by jumping from a hotel window. He was wearing his movie costume as he jumped.

Ona Munson (June 16, 1903 – February 11, 1955) was an American actress

She first came to fame on Broadway as the singing and dancing ingenue in the original production of No, No, Nanette. From this, Munson had a very successful stage and radio career in 1930s in New York. She introduced the song "You're the Cream in My Coffee" in the 1927 Broadway musical Hold Everything.

Her first starring role was in a Warner Brothers talkie called Going Wild (1930). Originally this film was intended as musical but all the numbers were removed prior to release due to the public's distaste for musicals which had virtually saturated the cinema in 1929-1930. Munson appeared the next year in a musical comedy called Hot Heiress in which she sings several songs along with her co-star Ben Lyon. She also starred in Broadminded (1931) and Five Star Final (1931). She briefly retired from the screen, only to return in 1938. Another roll was as "Mother Gin Sling" in the (1941) "The Shanghai Gesture"

When David O. Selznick was casting his production Gone with the Wind, he first announced that Mae West was to play Belle, but this was a publicity stunt. Tallulah Bankhead refused the role as too small. Munson herself was the antithesis of the voluptuous Belle: freckled and of slight build. But her skills as an actress electrified her screen test: it was all in the voice. She spoke deep and throaty in her test, and her voice conveyed sexiness and worldliness. The rest could be remedied by the wardrobe and makeup departments.

In 1955, plagued by ill health, she committed suicide at the age of 51 with an overdose of barbiturates in her apartment in New York. A note found next to her deathbed read, "This is the only way I know to be free again...Please don't follow me."

* **Brittany Murphy**

(November 10, 1977 – December 20, 2009) American actress and singer.

Brittany Anne Murphy was born in Atlanta, Georgia. Her parents divorced when she was two years old, and Murphy was raised by her mother in Edison, New Jersey, where she attended Edison High School.Murphy attended Verne Fowler School of Dance and Theatre Arts in Colonia, New Jersey, in 1982. At the age of four, she continued to train in singing, dancing, and acting until her move to California at 13. Murphy made her Broadway debut in A View From The Bridge.Murphy landed her first job in Hollywood when she was 13, starring as Brenda Drexell in the series Drexell's Class. She then went on to play Molly Morgan in Almost Home. Murphy also guest-starred on several television series, including Parker Lewis Can't Lose, Blossom, seaQuest 2032, Murder One, and Frasier. She also had recurring roles on Sister, Sister; Party of Five and Boy Meets World.Murphy starred in several films, including Clueless (1995); Girl, Interrupted (1999); Drop Dead Gorgeous (1999); Don't Say a Word (2001); the TV adaptation of the novel The Devil's Arithmetic (2001); 8 Mile (2002) and Uptown Girls (2003). In 2003, she starred in the romantic comedies Just Married and Little Black Book (2004), and Sin City (2005). She also starred in two Edward Burns films: Sidewalks of New York (2001) and The Groomsmen (2006).Murphy was also a voice actor. She voiced the character Luanne Platter on the FOX animated sitcom King of the Hill for the entirety of the show's run from 1997 to 2009. She also provided the voice for Gloria the penguin in the 2006 feature Happy

Feet. Murphy completed her last film, Abandoned, in June 2009.In May 2007, Murphy married British screenwriter Simon Monjack in a private ceremony in Los Angeles.In the early 2000s, Murphy lost a large amount of weight, which led to rumors of cocaine addiction. In 2005, Murphy disputed such claims to Jane magazine, saying, "No, just for the record I have never tried it in my entire life, I've never even seen it, and I don't leave the house too much, except to go to work."At 08:00 on December 20, 2009, the Los Angeles Fire Department responded to "a medical request" at the Los Angeles home Murphy and Monjack shared. She had collapsed in a bathroom. She was transported to Cedars-Sinai Medical Center, where she was pronounced dead.On February 4, 2010, the Los Angeles County coroner stated that the primary cause of Murphy's death was pneumonia, with secondary factors of iron-deficiency anemia and multiple drug intoxication.

On May 23, 2010, her widower Simon Monjack was found dead at the same Hollywood Hills residence. In July 2010, Los Angeles Assistant Chief Coroner Ed Winter stated that the cause of his death was acute pneumonia and severe anemia.

*

Jack Nance

(December 21, 1943 – December 30, 1996   American actor.

Nance was born in Boston, Massachusetts and was raised in Dallas, Texas, where he graduated from South Oak Cliff High School. He worked for some time with the American Conservatory Theater in San Francisco. In the 1970s, Nance met David Lynch, who cast him as the lead in Eraserhead. At the time, Nance was married to the actress Catherine E. Coulson (the future Log Lady in Twin Peaks). They divorced in 1976.

Nance was married to Kelly Jean Van Dyke (who worked in the adult film industry under the name Nancee Kelly), in May 1991. Kelly was the daughter of Coach star Jerry Van Dyke. Kelly Van Dyke committed suicide by hanging on November 17, 1991. According to his younger brother Richard Nance, Jack, who was in Oregon filming Meatballs 4 at the time, attempted to console her on the phone as she threatened suicide. A lightning storm knocked out the phones in Oregon, subsequently taking over 45 minutes for Nance and the director, Bobby Logan, to find a deputy sheriff who contacted LA police and the apartment manager. They broke in and found that she had hanged herself.

In his later years, Nance grew a small white moustache and was a distinctive presence in many films with his peculiar twisted smile and bug eyes. After Eraserhead, Nance remained on good terms with Lynch, who cast him in Dune (1984): a small role as the Harkonnen Captain Iakin Nefud, Blue Velvet (1986): a supporting role as Paul, a friend of Dennis Hopper's villain character, The Cowboy and the Frenchman (1988): plays Pete, one of the cowboys, Wild at Heart (1990): a small role as '00 Spool', Twin Peaks (1990–1991): co-starring role as Pete Martell, the henpecked sawmill gaffer, Twin Peaks: Fire Walk with Me (1992): reprised his role as Peter Martell, but his scenes were deleted, Lost Highway (1997): a small role as a garage mechanic named Phil (his final acting role).

Nance died in South Pasadena, California on December 30, 1996 under mysterious circumstances. Nance claimed to have been involved in a brawl outside a Winchell's Donuts on the morning of December 29. It is unclear if he was still drunk from the previous night, or if he had already begun drinking that morning, but it is certain that he was intoxicated at the time; he would later tell friends that he had "'popped-off' to "a couple of beaners" in the parking lot at 5am that day. He told them to get a haircut and a job. One of them socked him in the eye, his glasses flew off and he went down."

Later that day, he lunched with friends Leo Bulgarini and Catherine Case. Nance had a visible "crescent shaped bruise" under his eye and when asked about it, related to them the story about the fight. He soon went home, complaining of a headache. The injuries he received caused a subdural hematoma, resulting in his death the following morning. Nance died alone in his apartment. His body was discovered on the bathroom floor by Bulgarini. An autopsy revealed that the actor's blood alcohol level was .24 percent at the time of his death.

* **Alan** **Scott**

Newman (September 23, 1950 – November 20, 1978) was an American film and television actor and stuntman.

Born in Cleveland, Ohio to Paul Newman and his first wife Jackie Witte, Scott Newman was only a year old when the family moved to New York City.

When Scott was still a young boy with two younger sisters, Susan and Stephanie, his father moved to California to further his career, leaving his family in New York. By 1958, his parents had divorced and his father had married Joanne Woodward. In a later interview, Paul Newman said of his children, "When they were growing up I wasn't there much, and when I was there I was very inconsistent with them. It was hard for them to get a balance." Scott attended expensive private schools but was dismissed from some of them for bad behavior. He came to resent the absence of his father, blaming Woodward and refusing to speak to her.By the late 1960s, Newman had dropped out of college and started to take jobs as a stuntman in his father's films, making over 500 parachute jumps to become a certified instructor. He also took on menial jobs and refused to ask his father for financial help. In the early 1970s, his father decided to use his influence to try to initiate an acting career for his son, and arranged a part for him in The Great Waldo Pepper, starring Robert Redford. At the time, Scott stated, "I'm not taking any acting help from my father. I want my work to stand on its own merit." He had started to drink heavily, and was arrested for minor drink-related offences. He also assaulted a police officer, kicking him in the head in a squad car after being arrested for vandalizing a school bus while drunk. Newman's father paid the resulting $1000 fine.

He later played an acrophobic fireman in The Towering Inferno, in which his father also starred. He also played small parts in various TV series during 1975, such as Marcus Welby, M.D., Harry O and S.W.A.T.; and in the Charles Bronson film, Breakheart Pass.

Newman subsequently appeared in the 1977 film, Fraternity Row, but this was to be his last appearance. His alcoholism became more severe, and by 1978 he was sleeping on friends' floors and working as a laborer. He also tried his hand at cabaret singing in small clubs, billing himself as William Scott. Around this time, he confided to family friend A. E. Hotchner, "It's hell being his son, you know... I don't have his blue eyes. I don't have his talent. I don't have his luck. I don't have anything... that's me."

He suffered a motorcycle accident in the fall of 1978, and was taking painkillers to ease the discomfort of his injuries. He also accepted an offer of psychiatric help, paid for by his father. However, in Los Angeles on the night of November 19, he took a fatal dose of valium with alcohol and other drugs. Scott Steinberg, one of the minders appointed by his father, called an ambulance, but Newman was pronounced dead on arrival, the official verdict being an accident. His father later said, "It was the saddest day of my life. The memory of it can never be erased." He told Hotchner: "There's nothing you can say that will repair my guilt about Scott. It will be with me as long as I live."

*

Ramon

Novarro (February 6, 1899 – October 30, 1968)

Mexican actor.

> Born José Ramón Gil Samaniego in
> Durango, Mexico, he moved with his
> family to Los Angeles, California, to escape
> the Mexican Revolution in 1913.
>
> He was a second cousin of the Mexican
> actresses Dolores del Río and Andrea
> Palma.
>
> He entered films in 1917 in bit parts; and
> he supplemented his income by working as
> a singing waiter. From 1923, he began to
> play more prominent roles. His role in
> Scaramouche (1923) brought him his first
> major success.

In 1925, he achieved his greatest success in Ben-Hur. Novarro appeared with Norma Shearer in The Student Prince in Old Heidelberg (1927) and with Joan Crawford in Across to Singapore (1928). He made his first talking film, starring as a French soldier, in Devil-May-Care (1929). Novarro starred with Greta Garbo in Mata Hari (1932.

In the 1940s, he had several small roles in American films, including John Huston's We Were Strangers (1949. A Broadway tryout was aborted in the 1960s; but Novarro kept busy on television, appearing in NBC's The High Chaparral as late as 1968.

At the peak of his success in the late 1920s and early 1930s, he was earning more than US$100,000 per film. He invested some of his income in real estate, and his Hollywood Hills residence is one of the more renowned designs (1927) by architect Lloyd Wright. After his career ended, he was still able to maintain a comfortable lifestyle.

Novarro had been troubled all his life as a result of his conflicting views over his Roman Catholic religion and his homosexuality, and his life-long struggle with alcoholism is often traced to these issues. He was a friend of adventurer and author Richard Halliburton, also a celebrity in the closet, and was romantically involved with journalist Herbert Howe, who was also his publicist during the late 1920s.

Novarro was murdered by two brothers, Paul and Tom Ferguson (aged 22 and 17, respectively), whom he had hired from an agency to come to his Laurel Canyon home for sex. According to the prosecution in the murder case, the two young men believed that a large sum of money was hidden in Novarro's house. The prosecution accused them of torturing Novarro for several hours to force him to reveal where the nonexistent money was hidden. They left with a mere twenty dollars they took from his bathrobe pocket before fleeing the scene. Novarro allegedly died as a result of asphyxiation, choking to death on his own blood after being brutally beaten.

 **Haing S. Ngor**

(March 22, 1940 – February 25, 1996)

Cambodian American physician, actor and author

Ngor is best known for winning the 1985 Academy Award for Best Supporting Actor for his debut performance in the movie The Killing Fields, in which he portrayed Cambodian journalist and refugee Dith Pran. As of 2010, Ngor remains the only Asian to win an Oscar for Best Supporting Actor

Born in Samrong Young, Cambodia, Ngor trained as a surgeon and gynecologist. He was practicing in the capital, Phnom Penh, in 1975 when Pol Pot's Khmer Rouge seized control of the country and proclaimed it Democratic Kampuchea. He was compelled to conceal his education, medical skills, and even the fact that he wore glasses to avoid the new regime's intense hostility to intellectuals and professionals. He was expelled from Phnom Penh along with the bulk of its two million inhabitants as part of the Khmer Rouge's "Year Zero" social experiment and imprisoned in a concentration camp along with his wife, My-Huoy, who subsequently died giving birth. Although a gynecologist, he was unable to treat his wife who required a Cesarean section as he would have been exposed and both he and his wife (as well as the child) would very probably have been killed. After the fall of the Khmer Rouge in 1979, Ngor worked as a doctor in a refugee camp in Thailand and left with his niece for the United States on August 30, 1980. Ngor was not able to resume medical practice in the U.S. He never remarried.

Ngor appeared in other movies and TV shows, most memorably in Oliver Stone's Heaven & Earth and the Vanishing Son miniseries. He also appeared in a supporting role in the 1989 Vietnam War drama, The Iron Triangle. He guest-starred in a two-episode storyline on the acclaimed series China Beach (episodes "How to Stay Alive in Vietnam 1 & 2 as a wounded Cambodian POW who befriends Colleen McMurphy while under her care.

On February 25, 1996, Ngor was shot dead outside his home in Chinatown, in downtown Los Angeles, California.

* **Hugh Edward Ralph O'Connor** (April 7, 1962 – March 28, 1995) American actor

Hugh O'Connor was born in Rome, Italy. When he was six days old, he was adopted by Carroll O'Connor and his wife Nancy. Carroll was in Rome filming Cleopatra. He was named after Carroll O'Connor's brother, who died in a motorcycle accident in 1961. When he was 16, Hugh was diagnosed with Hodgkins Lymphoma. He survived the cancer with chemotherapy and two surgeries, but became addicted to drugs. He had been taking prescription drugs for the pain and marijuana for nausea. He quickly became addicted to harder drugs. Despite numerous stays at rehabilitation clinics, he never conquered his addiction.

O'Connor had a role in [Brass (1985) as James Flynn, and in In the Heat of the Night (1988-1995) as Det./ Lt. Lonnie Jamison,

He married Angela Clayton, on March 28, 1992, and their son Sean Carroll O'Connor was born in 1993.

On March 28, 1995, the third anniversary of his marriage, O'Connor called his father to tell him he was going to end his life. He said he could not beat the drugs and could not face another drug rehabilitation program.

He shot himself in the head. The police later determined he had cocaine in his blood.

Lani O'Grady

(October 2, 1954 – September 25, 2001)

Born Lanita Rose Agrati in Walnut Creek, California to Mary Grady, a children's talent agent, O'Grady began acting at the age of 13 with a role in the television series High Chaparral.

In the early 1970s, she appeared on Harry O and had a role in the 1975 television movie Cage Without a Key, starring Susan Dey. In 1976, she co-starred in Massacre at Central High. The following year, she landed the role of Mary Bradford in the ABC series Eight Is Enough. After the series ended in 1981, O'Grady had a role in the 1982 television movie The Kid with the Broken Halo starring Gary Coleman. She also reprised the role of Mary Bradford in two Eight Is Enough reunion television movies in 1987 and 1989. O'Grady's last acting role was as Mrs. Kramer in the soap opera Days of our Lives in 1990.

After suffering from agoraphobia and memory blackouts in the early 1990s, O'Grady retired from acting and became a talent agent. She also began taking medication for a diagnosed brain chemical imbalance. In a 1994 interview with the Los Angeles Times, O'Grady said she had suffered from severe panic attacks since the age of 18 but was not diagnosed with panic disorder until she was 21. She also admitted that she abused prescription drugs and alcohol, including Valium.

In December 1998, she checked into the Thalians Mental Health Department at Cedars-Sinai Medical Center for detox.

O'Grady died in her home in Valencia, Santa Clarita, California at age 46 on September 25, 2001. An autopsy revealed toxic levels of the painkiller Vicodin and antidepressant Prozac in her bloodstream, and the Los Angeles County Coroner's office said she died of "multiple drug intoxication."

Robert Pastorelli

(June 21, 1954 – March 8, 2004) American actor

Pastorelli was born in New Brunswick', New Jersey.

Robert Pastorelli was a former boxer and an admitted drug addict before he cleaned up his act and pursued theater work in New York in such 1970s productions as Rebel Without a Cause, The Rainmaker, and Death of a Salesman.

He turned to film and TV in 1982. He worked with Bette Midler and Shelley Long in Outrageous Fortune (1987), and Eddie Murphy in Beverly Hills Cop II (1987). His first big film role came with Kevin Costner's Dances with Wolves (1990).

It was his TV role as Candice Bergen's house painter in "Murphy Brown" (1988) that made him a star. He stayed with the show for seven seasons. After that came Sister Act 2: Back in the Habit (1993), Michael (1996), and Modern Vampires (1998). He played the role of Luther Billis in the remake of South Pacific (2001) with Glenn Close.

Pastorelli was found dead in his home at Hollywood Hills in 2004; a syringe, a spoon and a plastic bag with white powder were discovered near his body. The Coroner's Office later reported that Pastorelli died of "acute cocaine-morphine (heroin) toxicity.

Pastorelli's death occurred at the time the authorities were reopening the investigation into the March 1999 shooting death of his then-girlfriend, 25-year-old Charemon Jonovich, at their home. Pastorelli, who knew of the investigation, had been considered a person of interest. During the initial investigation, Jonovich's death had been ruled an accident or undetermined. However, police investigating the incident, acting on new evidence that implicated Pastorelli, changed the cause of death to murder in 2004. Pastorelli was never formally charged with the crime, and the Jonovich case file was closed four months after Pastorelli's death.

Chris Penn

(October 10, 1965 – January 24, 2006) American film and television actor

Penn was born in Los Angeles, California, the youngest son of Leo Penn, an actor and director, and

Eileen Ryan, an actress. . His brothers are actor Sean Penn and musician Michael Penn.

Penn never married. From 1993 to 1999 he dated and lived with Filipino-American model Steffiana de la Cruz. Penn started acting at the age of 12 at the Loft Studio and made his film debut in 1979's Charlie and the Talking Buzzard . In 1983, he was featured in Francis Ford Coppola's youth drama Rumble Fish and appeared in the high school football drama All the Right . He also appeared in the hit dance movie Footloose in 1984; Pale Rider (1985); and At Close Range (1986).

Two of his more popular performances were in Reservoir Dogs and True Romance.

In Robert Altman's ensemble film Short Cuts, Penn played a troubled swimming pool cleaner. He also appeared as the couch-potato, drug-dealing, high school janitor in Murder by Numbers .

Penn was found dead in his Santa Monica condominium on January 24, 2006, at the age of 40. Although Penn had used multiple drugs in the past, an autopsy performed by a Los Angeles County medical examiner revealed the primary cause of death was "nonspecific heart disease, with the prescription drug promethazine with codeine and an enlarged heart being possible contributing circumstances.

George Periolat

(February 5, 1874 – February 20, 1940)   American actor.

Born in Chicago, Illinois, George Periolat began his career as a Broadway actor. Making his film debut with the Essanay Studios in Chicago, he moved to Hollywood in 1911 and starred in over 170 films throughout his career. He was a very versatile actor, often playing multiple roles in a single production, as when he played two leading characters, the count and the crook, in the 1916 production of The Counterfeit Earl. The story of Norma Desmond, though fictitious, is not far removed from the plight of many silent film stars, and the advent of the sound film brought about a swift end to Periolat's career. He made his last appearance in 1932's What Price Hollywood? On February 20, 1940, he committed suicide by ingesting arsenic in his Hollywood mansion.

Christopher

Pettiet (February 12, 1976 – April 12, 2000)

Pettiet began his career as a child actor making appearances in television series such as SeaQuest DSV, Star Trek: The Next Generation, Chicago Hope, Judging Amy, Picket Fences and Undressed. He also appeared in several films such as Point Break (1991). In 1991, he won the role of a young Jesse James on The Young Riders.

After the cancellation of The Young Riders in 1992, Pettiet's career went downhill. According to his manager, Bob Villard, Pettiet was just about broke. Villard's open letter also notes that Pettiet's problem with drugs had been a long standing one and that he had tried "for over two years" to get Pettiet into treatment. Despite attending "a couple" of AA meetings, he refused to admit that he had a substance abuse problem.

Pettiet died on April 12, 2000, of a drug overdose in Los Angeles at the age of 24.

* River Phoenix

(August 23, 1970 – October 31, 1993)

Phoenix began acting at age 10 in television commercials. He appeared in diverse roles, making his first notable appearance in the 1986 film Stand by Me, a well-received coming-of-age film based on a novella by Stephen King. Phoenix made a transition into more adult-oriented roles with Running on Empty (1988), playing the son of fugitive parents in a well-received performance that earned him an Academy Award for Best Supporting Actor nomination, and My Own Private Idaho (1991), playing a gay hustler in search for his estranged mother.

On October 31, 1993, Phoenix died of a drug overdose on the sidewalk outside the West Hollywood nightclub the Viper Room.

At some point in the evening, Phoenix went to the bathroom to take drugs with various friends and dealers.[22] It is frequently reported that an acquaintance or dealer offered him Persian Brown (a powerful form of heroin mixed with methamphetamine, which is commonly snorted); his autopsy report revealed lethal doses of cocaine and morphine. His blood also contained diazepam, ephedrine and marijuana.

Rosamond

Pinchot (October 26, 1904 – January 24, 1938)

American stage and film actress

Pinchot was born in New York City, the daughter of a wealthy attorney. At the age of nineteen, Pinchot was discovered by Max Reinhardt while traveling on an ocean liner with her mother. Reinhardt cast her The Miracle. Pinchot's appearance in the play led to considerable attention from the press. She made her only film appearance in the 1935 adaptation of The Three Musketeers, as Queen Anne.

Pinchot married William "Big Bill" Gaston (previously married to Kay Francis), who was said to be abusive. The couple had two children. On January 24, 1938, Pinchot committed suicide by carbon monoxide poisoning in the garage of her family's home.

Luigi Pistilli (July 19, 1929 – April 21, 1996) actor of stage, screen, and television.

Pistilli made his feature film debut with an uncredited role in Dark Passage (1947).

He appeared in many spaghetti Westerns such as The Good, the Bad and the Ugly (1966) (as the priest brother of Eli Wallach's character Tuco) and in For a Few Dollars More (1965) as the cunning second-in-command.

Pistilli committed suicide in his Milan home on April 21, 1996. A show had been harshly panned by critics and audiences and this apparently threw Pistilli into a deep depression.

Edward Platt (Feb. 14, 1916 – March 19, 1974) American actor

Platt was born in Staten Island, New York. He studied at Princeton University, majoring in Romance languages, and switched to music at the Juilliard School, intending to be an opera singer. He sang with Paul Whiteman's Orchestra, performing in such musicals as The Pirates of Penzance and The Mikado. During WW2 He served as a radio operator in the US Army.

A powerful bass-baritone, he debuted on Broadway in the Rodgers and Hammerstein musical Allegro. He landed his first film role in The Shrike. In 1955, he appeared in Rebel Without a Cause.

In 1959, he played Cary Grant's attorney in North by Northwest.

His most famous role was the role of "Chief" in the television series Get Smart (1965–1970).

Edward Platt committed suicide on March 19, 1974, aged 58. He left four children from two marriages.

Dana Plato

(November 7, 1964 – May 8, 1999) American actress television.

Plato was born to Linda Strain, an unwed 16-year-old, who was already caring for an 18-month-old. Strain put her infant daughter Dana up for adoption.

By the age of seven, Plato began doing television commercials, reportedly appearing in over 100 spots for companies as diverse as Kentucky Fried Chicken, Dole, and Atlantic Richfield. Plato made her film debut in 1977, at the age of thirteen in Return to Boggy Creek. Other credits include California Suite, High School U.S.A. and Exorcist II: The Heretic.

In 1978, 'Diff'rent Strokes' debuted on NBC. Plato appeared on the show until 1984. During that year, she became pregnant by her boyfriend, a musician named Lanny Lambert. The producers of 'Diff'rent Strokes' did not feel that a pregnancy would fit the show's wholesome image, so Plato was let go. Although rumors of drug use and other "problems on the set" swirled around her dismissal, the producers were

Edward Platt (Feb. 14, 1916 – March 19, 1974) American actor

Platt was born in Staten Island, New York. He studied at Princeton University, majoring in Romance languages, and switched to music at the Juilliard School, intending to be an opera singer. He sang with Paul Whiteman's Orchestra, performing in such musicals as The Pirates of Penzance and The Mikado. During WW2 He served as a radio operator in the US Army.

A powerful bass-baritone, he debuted on Broadway in the Rodgers and Hammerstein musical Allegro. He landed his first film role in The Shrike. In 1955, he appeared in Rebel Without a Cause.

In 1959, he played Cary Grant's attorney in North by Northwest.

His most famous role was the role of "Chief" in the television series Get Smart (1965–1970).

Edward Platt committed suicide on March 19, 1974, aged 58. He left four children from two marriages.

Dana Plato

(November 7, 1964 – May 8, 1999) American actress television.

Plato was born to Linda Strain, an unwed 16-year-old, who was already caring for an 18-month-old. Strain put her infant daughter Dana up for adoption.

By the age of seven, Plato began doing television commercials, reportedly appearing in over 100 spots for companies as diverse as Kentucky Fried Chicken, Dole, and Atlantic Richfield. Plato made her film debut in 1977, at the age of thirteen in Return to Boggy Creek. Other credits include California Suite, High School U.S.A. and Exorcist II: The Heretic.

In 1978, 'Diff'rent Strokes' debuted on NBC. Plato appeared on the show until 1984. During that year, she became pregnant by her boyfriend, a musician named Lanny Lambert. The producers of 'Diff'rent Strokes' did not feel that a pregnancy would fit the show's wholesome image, so Plato was let go. Although rumors of drug use and other "problems on the set" swirled around her dismissal, the producers were adamant that the pregnancy was the only reason her character was written out

After leaving Diff'rent Strokes in 1984, Plato had breast implants and appeared in a June 1989 Playboy pictorial. She started taking roles in such B-movies as Bikini Beach Race and Lethal Cowboy.

In 1991, Plato ended up in Las Vegas out of work. She took a job at a dry-cleaning store to support herself. On Feb. 28, she entered a video store, produced a gun, and demanded the money from the register. Plato was given five years' probation. She made headlines and became part of the national debate over troubled child stars, particularly given the difficulties of her Diff'rent Strokes co-stars, Gary Coleman and Todd Bridges. In January 1992, she was again arrested, this time for forging a prescription for Valium. She served 30 days in jail for violation of the terms of her probation and entered a drug program.

Just before her death, she and her fiancé, Robert Menchaca, were living in a recreation vehicle in Navarre, Florida. Returning from a trip the couple stopped at Menchaca's mother's home in Moore, Oklahoma, for a Mother's Day visit. Plato went to lie down inside her recreational vehicle parked outside the house and subsequently died of an overdose from Vanadom (Soma) and Lortab. Her death at the age of 34 was eventually ruled a suicide.

Almost 11 years to the day of Dana Plato's death, on May 6, 2010, Plato's son Tyler Lambert died of a self-inflicted gunshot wound to the head in Tulsa, Oklahoma, at age 25. His grandmother, Joni Richardson, stated that Lambert was experimenting with both drugs and alcohol, which may have contributed to his suicide.

* **Freddy Prinze** (June 22, 1954 – January 29, 1977)

Prinze was born Frederick Karl Pruetzel in New York City.

Prinze worked at several comedy clubs in New York City, including The Improv and Catch a Rising Star where he introduced himself to audiences as a "Hungarican" (part Hungarian, part Puerto Rican).

Elvis Presley (January 8, 1935 – August 16, 1977)

Elvis Presley was born on January 8, 1935, in Tupelo, Mississippi, to 18-year-old Vernon Elvis and 22-year-old Gladys Love Presley. Jesse Garon Presley, his identical twin brother, was delivered 35 minutes before him, stillborn. Presley moved to Memphis, Tennessee, with his family at the age of 13. He began his career there in 1954 when Sun Records owner Sam Phillips, eager to bring the sound of African American music to a wider audience, saw in Presley the means to realize his ambition. Accompanied by guitarist Scotty Moore and bassist Bill Black, Presley was one of the originators of rockabilly, an uptempo, backbeat-driven fusion of country and rhythm and blues. RCA Victor acquired his contract in a deal arranged by Colonel Tom Parker, who would manage the singer for over two decades. Presley's first RCA single, "Heartbreak Hotel", released in January 1956, was a number one hit. He became the leading figure of the newly popular sound of rock and roll with a series of network

During 1973, he made his first television appearance on one of the last episodes of The Jack Paar Show. In December 1973, his biggest break came with an appearance on The Tonight Show Starring Johnny Carson. Prinze was the first young comedian to be asked to have a sit-down chat with Carson on his first appearance. From 1974 to 1977, Prinze starred as Francisco "Chico" Rodriguez in the NBC TV series Chico and the Man with Jack Albertson. The show was an instant hit.

About four months prior to his death, Prinze had signed a multi-year deal with NBC worth US$6 million over five years. In the months before he died, he had a strong fixation on how John F. Kennedy was assassinated. He also developed an obsession with the film Taxi Driver, viewing it repeatedly.

Prinze married Katherine Cochran in October 1975, with whom he had one son, future actor Freddie Prinze, Jr. In 1976, after his arrest for driving under the influence of quaaludes, his wife filed for divorce on the grounds that his escalating drug dependence was endangering their son.

Prinze suffered from depression, and on January 28, 1977, shot himself with a small semi-automatic pistol after talking on the telephone with his estranged wife.

television appearances and chart-topping records. His energized interpretations of songs, many from African American sources, and his uninhibited performance style made him enormously popular—and controversial. In November 1956, he made his film debut in Love Me Tender.

Journalist Tony Scherman writes that by early 1977, "Elvis Presley had become a grotesque caricature of his sleek, energetic former self. Hugely overweight, his mind dulled by the pharmacopoeia he daily ingested, he was barely able to pull himself through his abbreviated concerts." In Alexandria, Louisiana, the singer was on stage for less than an hour and "was impossible to understand". Presley failed to appear in Baton Rouge: he was unable to get out of his hotel bed, and the rest of the tour was By this point, he suffered from multiple ailments—glaucoma, high blood pressure, liver damage, and an enlarged colon, each aggravated, and possibly caused, by drug abuse.

Presley was scheduled to fly out of Memphis on the evening of August 16, 1977, to begin another tour. That afternoon, he was discovered unresponsive on his bathroom floor. Attempts to revive him failed, and death was officially pronounced at 3:30 pm at Baptist Memorial Hospital. Drug use was believed to be heavily implicated in Presley's death.

Marie Prevost

(November 8, 1898 – January 21, 1937)

Born Mary Bickford Dunn in Sarnia, Ontario, she was still a child when her family moved first to Denver, Colorado and then later to Los Angeles. While working as a secretary, she applied for and obtained an acting job at the Hollywood studio owned by Mack Sennett. Sennett, who was from a small town outside of Montreal, dubbed her as the exotic "French girl", adding Dunn to his collection of bathing beauties under the stage name of Marie Prevost.

In 1919, Prevost secretly married socialite Sonny Gerke who left her after six months of marriage. Gerke's mother had forbidden him to associate with Prevost because she was an actress, so he was scared to tell his mother of the marriage—and he couldn't get a divorce without revealing that he was married. Prevost, fearful of the bad publicity a divorce would cause, would stay secretly married to Gerke until 1923.

One of her first publicly successful film roles came in the 1920 romantic film Love, Honor, and Behave, opposite George O'Hara.

She worked in several films for Sennett's studio until 1921 when she signed with Universal.

Just as her career was blossoming, Prevost's mother was killed in an automobile accident while traveling in Florida with actress Vera Steadman, another Canadian friend, and Hollywood studio owner, Al Christie in 1926.

Devastated by the loss of her only remaining parent, Prevost began drinking heavily and developed an addiction to alcohol. After seeing Prevost in The Beautiful and Damned, Howard Hughes cast her as the lead in The Racket (1928). During filming, Hughes and Prevost had a brief affair. Hughes quickly broke off the affair leaving Prevost heartbroken and furthering her depression. After playing the lead in The Racket, Prevost's days as a leading lady were over.

Prevost's depression caused her to binge on food resulting in significant weight gain. By the 1930s, she was working less and being offered only secondary parts. A notable exception was Paid (1930), a role which, while secondary to star Joan Crawford, still garnered her good reviews. As a result of all this, her financial income declined and her growing dependency on alcohol added to her weight problems. By 1934, she had no work at all and her financial situation deteriorated dramatically. The downward spiral became greatly aggravated when her weight problems forced her into repeated crash dieting in order to keep whatever bit part a movie studio offered.

On January 21, 1937, at the age of 38, Prevost died from heart failure brought on by acute alcoholism and malnutrition. Her body was not discovered until January 23, after neighbors complained about her dog's incessant barking. A bellboy, who ignored the note Prevost posted on the door asking that no one knock on the door more than once, finally forced the door open. Prevost was found lying face down on her bed, her legs marked with tiny bites. Prevost's pet dachshund, Maxie, had nipped at her legs in an attempt to wake her up.

*
Glenn Quinn (28 May 1970 – 3 December 2002) Irish actor in television and film

Quinn was born in Dublin, Ireland, and raised in both America and then again as a teenager in Cabinteely, County Dublin Ireland. As a teenager, he played drums in a rock band called Revival (who peaked at supporting Irish AOR Band Winter's Reign and also had a demo played on the radio 'How could I know'-Rock with BOC - BLB Radio). He also acted in productions at small local theaters. Quinn attended Clonkeen College and moved to the Long Beach area of California in 1988 with his mother, Bernadette, and two sisters, Sonya and Louisa. His older brother, Ciaran, who lives in Dublin, Ireland, was recently reunited with his mother and two sisters. Glenn worked odd jobs at power plants, restaurants, and more before deciding to pursue an acting career.

Quinn did commercials for Pepsi and Ray-Ban, appeared in the music video for the Richard Marx song "Satisfied," and had his first speaking line in the pilot of Beverly Hills, 90210 after having endured eight separate auditions for the roles of both "Brandon Walsh" and then "Steve Sanders." Having lost out to Jason Priestley and Ian Ziering, respectively, casting director Johanna Ray gave him a small role with two lines in the pilot, but Glenn was barely visible in the final broadcast version. His first substantial speaking part was as a guest-star in an episode of the short-lived The Outsiders.

In 1991, Quinn had his first major role in a movie, Shout, which starred John Travolta and in which he shared an on-screen kiss with Gwyneth Paltrow. Later, one of Quinn's more visible roles was that of Mark Healy, Becky Conner's boyfriend, and later husband, in Roseanne. Quinn took on the role as youngest son Cedric on the US and UK TV series Covington Cross. While shooting the series in England, he suffered a serious injury to his back falling from his horse while shooting a scene In 1992 he starred alongside Holly Marie Combs in Dr. Giggles. Also in 1992, Glenn's management was approached by Robert Redford who was then casting A River Runs through It and expressed interest in Glenn reading for the role opposite Brad Pitt. At the time Glenn was tired from working non-stop for over a year and had planned to go on a fishing trip with his uncle, and as nothing could dissuade his intention to take that short break, the role went to Craig Sheffer.

Although he spent years doing an American accent on Roseanne, Quinn was pleased producers made Doyle on Angel Irish because it would allow him to use his native accent. In an interview with The Irish Times, Quinn said of his accent, "I've been hiding it for so long that it's amazing to have some freedom. It was like putting on an old pair of shoes. It's bringing my soul back to life." His last film work was in 2002's R.S.V.P..

In addition to acting, he also co-owned a nightclub called "Goldfingers" in Los Angeles, California.

Quinn was found dead on 3 December 2002 of a drug overdose. He was 32 years old. Police and autopsy reports revealed the cause of death to be an accidental heroin overdose. His body was found on the couch of a friend he was visiting in North Hollywood, California.

Richard Quine

(November 12, 1920 – June 10, 1989)

American stage, film, and radio actor and director.

Quine made his Broadway debut in the Jerome Kern/Oscar Hammerstein II musical Very Warm for May in 1939 and appeared in My Sister Eileen the following year. His screen acting credits include The World Moves On (1934), Jane Eyre (1934), Babes on Broadway (1941), My Sister Eileen (1942), and Words and Music (1948), among others.

During World War II, Quine served in the United States Coast Guard. He married actress Susan Peters in November 1943. His directing credits include Pushover (1954), My Sister Eileen (1955), Operation Mad Ball (1957), Bell, Book and Candle (1958), Strangers When We Meet (1960), and The World of Suzie Wong (1960).

He also produced such films as the comedy Paris, When It Sizzles (1964) with Audrey Hepburn and William Holden, How to Murder Your Wife (1965) with Jack Lemmon, Synanon (1966), and Hotel (1967).

In the 1970s, Quine made only a few films, none of which did well. Moving to television, he co-created with Blake Edwards the first Mickey Rooney series. Quine later directed three episodes of Peter Falk's Columbo. His final work was on The Prisoner of Zenda (1979) with Peter Sellers.

His first wife, Susan Peters, was crippled from the waist down on a hunting trip with Quine in 1945. They divorced in 1948, and she died of the effects of anorexia nervosa in 1952, at age 31.

Quine was later engaged to Kim Novak, but the two did not marry. He also married Barbara Bushman, Fran Jeffries, and Diana Balfour.After an extended period of depression and poor health, Quine committed suicide by shooting himself in Los Angeles on June 10, 1989.

David Stephen

Rappaport (November 23, 1951 – May 2, 1990)
English Dwarf actor, television and film

Rappaport was born in London, England. He played the drums professionally. Rappaport studied psychology at the University of Bristol, graduating with a degree.

He married his college girlfriend, and they had a son. Rappaport settled down as a teacher, but as his marriage broke down, he decided to follow a career as an actor.

One of his most popular roles was as Randall, the leader of the gang of dwarves in the Terry Gilliam film Time Bandits. During the mid80s he played in the BBC production of Robin of Sherwood.

On May 2, 1990, he committed suicide by shooting himself in the chest in Laurel Canyon Park in the San Fernando Valley, California. Just before his death, he had been cast and began filming for the role of Kivas Fajo in the Star Trek: The Next Generation episode "The Most Toys". Rappaport's death was one of the main reasons why Terry Gilliam decided to shelve the intended sequel to Time Bandits.

Virgina Rappe

(July 7, 1891 – September 9, 1921) American actress.

Rappe was born to unwed mother Mabel Rapp in New York City. Mabel died when Virginia was 11, and Virginia was then raised by her grandmother in Chicago. At age 14 she began working as a commercial and art model in Chicago. Rappe had at least two abortions by the time she was 15.

In 1916 she relocated to San Francisco to pursue her career as an artist's model, where she met dress designer Robert Moscovitz and they became engaged. Shortly after the engagement her fiancé was killed in a streetcar accident and she moved to Los Angeles. In early 1917 she was hired by director Fred Balshofer and given a prominent role in his Paradise Garden. In 1918 she gave birth to a child, which was put into foster care. Balshofer then hired her again to costar with early drag performer Julian Eltinge and newcomer Rudolph Valentino in Over the Rhine, for which she was awarded the title of "Best Dressed Girl in Pictures".

While working at Mack Sennett Comedies Corporation, Rappe had numerous sexual relationships with cast and crew members. An epidemic of pubic lice--for which she was blamed—caused Mack Sennett to have the studio closed and fumigated

The circumstances of Rappe's death in 1921 became a Hollywood. During a party held on Labor Day, September 5, 1921 in Roscoe "Fatty" Arbuckle's suite at the St. Francis Hotel in San Francisco, California, Rappe allegedly suffered a trauma. She died on September 9, 1921, from a ruptured bladder and secondary peritonitis.

The exact events of that party are unknown, with witnesses relating various versions of what happened. It was alleged that she died as a result of a violent sexual assault by Roscoe Arbuckle.

Marvel   Rea

(November 9, 1901 – June 17, 1937)

American silent film actress.

Rea's family moved from Nebraska to California in 1910. She entered silent films in 1918 joining the Keystone Film Company and becoming one of Mack Sennett's Bathing Beauties.

Rea was in movies from 1917 through 1921. Among more than twenty-five screen credits are roles in A Clever Dummy (1917), The Summer Girls (1918), East Lynne with Variations (1919), When Love Is Blind (1919), A Lightweight Lover (1920), The Simp (1920), and For Land's Sake (1920). Her death certificate lists her as an actress with the Fox Film Corporation up until 1932.

Three young men kidnaped Rea, threw her into a large red truck, and transported her to a eucalyptus grove at 120th Street and Compton Avenue, South Los Angeles on September 2, 1936. She was then assaulted by the three.

Rae committed suicide by ingesting ant paste. She died on June 17, 1937 in Los Angeles.

George Reeves

(January 5, 1914 – June 16, 1959) American actor.

Reeves was born George Keefer Brewer in Woolstock, Iowa

Following a divorce from his father, Reeves' mother moved to California to stay with her sister. There, Helen met and married Frank Bessolo

In 1927, Frank Bessolo adopted George, and the boy became George Bessolo. Frank and Helen Bessolo's marriage lasted 15 years and ended in divorce while Reeves was away visiting relatives. His mother told Reeves that Frank had committed suicide.

George began acting and singing in high school and continued performing on stage as a student at Pasadena Junior College.

Reeves's film career began in 1939 when he was cast as one of Scarlett O'Hara's suitors in Gone with the Wind. It was a minor role.

He starred in a number of two-reel short subjects and appeared in several B-pictures, including two with Ronald Reagan and three with James Cagney (Torrid Zone, The Fighting 69th, and The Strawberry Blonde).. Released from his Warners contract, he signed a contract at Twentieth Century-Fox but was released after only a handful of films, one of which was the Charlie Chan movie Dead Men Tell. He freelanced, appearing in five Hopalong Cassidy westerns before director Mark Sandrich cast Reeves as Lieutenant John Summers opposite Claudette Colbert in So Proudly We Hail! (1942.

Reeves was drafted into the U.S. Army in early 1943. He was assigned to the U.S. Army Air Forces and performed in the USAAF's Broadway show Winged Victory. The long Broadway run was followed by a national tour and a movie version. Reeves was then transferred to the Army Air Forces' First Motion Picture Unit, where he made training films.

At the war's end, Reeves returned to Hollywood to find that many studios were cutting down their production schedules. He appeared in a Sam Katzman-produced serial, The Adventures of Sir Galahad. He was able to play against type and starred as a villainous gold hunter in a Johnny Weissmuller Jungle Jim film.

In 1953, Reeves played a minor character, Sergeant Maylon Stark, in the motion picture From Here To Eternity.

In June 1951, Reeves was offered the role of Superman in a new television series entitled Adventures of Superman.

Reeves's career as Superman began with Superman and the Mole . Immediately after completing it, Reeves and the crew began production of the first season's episodes, all shot over 13 weeks in the summer of 1951. The series went on the air the following year, and Reeves was amazed at becoming a national celebrity.

After two seasons, Reeves was dissatisfied with the one-dimensional role and low salary.

By mid-1959, contracts were signed, costumes refitted, and new teleplay writers assigned.. Producers reportedly promised Reeves that the new programs would be as serious and action-packed as the first season, guaranteed him creative input, and slated him to direct several of the new shows as he had done with the final three episodes of the 1957 season

In between the first and second seasons of Superman, Reeves got acting assignments in two feature films, Forever Female (1953) and Fritz Lang's The Blue Gardenia (1953). But by the time the series was airing nationwide, Reeves found himself so associated with Superman and Clark Kent that it was difficult for him to find other roles

Attempting to showcase his versatility, Reeves sang on the Tony Bennett show in August 1956. He appeared on I Love Lucy (Episode #165, Lucy Meets Superman") in 1956 as Superman

His good friend Bill Walsh, a producer at Disney Studios, gave Reeves a prominent role in Westward Ho, the Wagons! (1956), in which Reeves wore a beard and mustache. It was to be his final feature film appearance.

According to the Los Angeles Police Department report, between approximately 1:30 and 2:00 a.m. on June 16, 1959, George Reeves died of a gunshot wound to his head in the upstairs bedroom of his Benedict Canyon home.

* **Wallace Reid**

(April 15, 1891 – January 18, 1923) American actor.

Born in St. Louis, Missouri, his mother was an actress and his father, Hal Reid (actor) (1860–1920), worked successfully in a variety of theatrical jobs.

Reid was drawn to the growing motion picture industry by his father, who would shift from the theatre to acting, writing, and directing films. In 1910, Reid appeared in his first film, The Phoenix.

Wallace Reid was featured in both Birth of a Nation (1915) and Intolerance (1916) both directed by D.W. Griffith.

Already involved with the creation of more than 100 motion picture shorts, Reid was signed by producer Jesse L. Lasky and would star in another sixty plus films for Lasky's Famous Players film company, later Paramount Pictures. While working on The Valley of the Giants (1919), Reid was injured. He was prescribed morphine for his pain. Reid became addicted. Reid's morphine addiction came at a time when drug rehabilitation programs were non-existent, and he died in a sanitarium while attempting recovery.

Brad Renfro (July 25, 1982 – January 15, 2008) American actor

Renfro was born in Knoxville, Tennessee. He was raised from the age of five by his paternal grandmother.

When he was ten, Renfro was discovered by a casting director for Joel Schumacher. Cast as the lead in 'The Client', Renfro starred alongside Susan Sarandon and Tommy Lee Jones. In 1995, he won Hollywood Reporter's "Young Star" award, and was nominated as one of People's "Top 30 Under 30." That year, he played Huckleberry "Huck" Finn in 1995's Tom and Huck with Jonathan Taylor Thomas. He also won a second "Young Star" award, as well as the "Young Artist" award, for his performance in The Cure.

In 1996, Renfro was cast in Sleepers. The film co-starred Robert De Niro, Kevin Bacon, Dustin Hoffman and Brad Pitt.

In 1998, he starred in Apt Pupil. Renfro went on to act in other films, including 2001's Ghost World and Bully, 2002's Confessions of an American Girl, and 2005's The Jacket. He also appeared in two episodes of Law & Order: Criminal Intent and completed filming on the film The Informers, co-starring Mickey Rourke, Winona Ryder and Billy Bob Thornton.

On June 3, 1998, Renfro, then 15, and his 19-year-old cousin were arrested and charged with drug possession. He was carrying two small bags of cocaine in a cigarette box and a bag of marijuana in his sock. He avoided trial by agreeing to be screened randomly for drugs and evaluated for any substance abuse problems in his plea bargain.

On August 28, 2000, Renfro and his friend tried to steal a 45-foot yacht from Fort Lauderdale harbour. They were arrested on the same night and Renfro was charged with grand theft and criminal mischief. In January 2001, Renfro was sentenced to probation .

On January 14, 2002, Renfro violated his probation and was arrested on charges of public intoxication in Knoxville. He was put into a three-month substance abuse treatment program as a result.

In December 2005, Renfro was arrested by LAPD officers during an undercover drug sweep of skid row and was charged with attempted possession of heroin. In 2006, he spent 10 days in jail for convictions of driving while under the influence and attempted heroin possession.

Renfro was found dead on January 15, 2008 in his Los Angeles apartment. He was 25 years old. On February 8, 2008, the Los Angeles County Coroner's office ruled that Renfro's death was accidental, attributing it to acute heroin/morphine intoxication.

Rachel Roberts

(20 September 1927 – 26 November 1980) a Welsh actress.

Roberts is best remembered for her forthright screen performances in two key films of the 1960s, Saturday Night and Sunday Morning and This Sporting

Life, in both of which she played the older mistress of the central male character. In Australia, she is remembered for her performance as 'Mrs Appleyard in Peter Weir's Picnic at Hanging Rock.

She appeared in supporting roles in several American films such as Foul Play (1978) after relocating to Los Angeles in the early 1970s, her final British film being Yanks (1979, directed by John Schlesinger.

She married Alan Dobie (1955–1961), then Rex Harrison (1962–1971). Both marriages ended in divorce. Her alcoholism and depression increased after her divorce from Harrison in 1971. Devastated over their divorce, she moved to Hollywood in 1975.

She committed suicide by taking an overdose of barbiturates and alcohol on November 26, 1980 at her home in Los Angeles.

It was reported that her suicide was a result of swallowing lye, alkali, or another unidentified caustic substance on top of the barbiturates which were ingested as detailed in her posthumously published journals. The acidic effect of the poisonous agent was an immediate cause of death which propelled her body smashing through a decorative glass screen divide between two rooms. She was found by her gardener, her body cut to ribbons in a negligee on her kitchen floor amongst the shards of glass on November 26, 1980. She was 53 years old.

Charles Rocket

(August 24, 1949 – October 7, 2005) American film and television actor

Rocket was born Charles Adams Claverie in Bangor, Maine.

He appeared from time to time with his friend Dan Gosch as superheroes "Captain Packard" and his faithful sidekick "Lobo". Rocket made several short films and fronted his band, the Fabulous Motels, on accordion. He later anchored the local news at Channel 12 WPRI and at KOAA-TV in Colorado Springs, Colorado under his own name, and WTVF Nashville under the name Charles Kennedy. He made his network debut on Saturday Night Live in 1980, using the name Charles Rocket. Later in his career Rocket would lend his accordion talents to the David Byrne-produced B-52's album Mesopotamia.

Rocket was cast for the 1980–81 season of Saturday Night Live, which followed the departure of the remaining members of the show's original cast and executive producer Lorne Michaels. Singled out by new executive producer Jean Doumanian, he was promoted as a cross between Bill Murray and Chevy Chase.

Rocket worked steadily in film, with roles in such movies as Earth Girls Are Easy, It's Pat, Steal Big Steal Little, How I Got into College, Dances with Wolves and Dumb and Dumber, often playing comedic foils.

A guest role as a murderer on Law & Order: Criminal Intent marked his final appearance on network television. He also lent his voice to the popular video games Star Wars: Starfighter, Star Wars: Jedi Starfighter (as the character "Nym" in both games), Descent 3, and Age of Mythology.

His final film role came in the 2003 movie Shade, which starred Sylvester Stallone and Melanie Griffith.

Rocket was found dead in a field near his Connecticut home on October 7, 2005; his throat had been cut. The state medical examiner later ruled the death a suicide.

 **Will Rogers**, generally
known as Will Rogers, Jr. (October 20, 1911–July 9,
1993), was a son of legendary humorist Will Rogers
(1879–1935) and his wife, the former Betty Blake
(1879–1944). He was a Democratic U. S. Representative
from California from January 3, 1943 until May 23,
1944, when he resigned to return to the United States
Army. Rogers had several other careers, notably as a
newspaper owner/publisher, an actor, writer, and a
political commentator.

Rogers was born in New York City, where his
father was performing. He grew up in Beverly Hills,
California and attended school there. He received a
Bachelor of Arts degree from Stanford University in
1935. On completing his studies, he served as publisher
of the Beverly Hills Citizen newspaper, a role in which
he continued until 1953. He had been commissioned a
second lieutenant through the Reserve Officers'
Training Corps, but did not go on active duty. With
U.S. entry into World War II, however, he enlisted as a
private in June 1942, and was commissioned in the field

artillery the following month and assigned to the 893rd Tank Destroyer Battalion.

While on active duty, Rogers was elected to the House of Representatives from California, and was sworn into office on January 3, 1943. He served in the 78th Congress. He did not complete his term, however, returning to active duty in the Army after resigning from Congress on May 23, 1944. He was then assigned to the 814th Tank Destroyer Battalion and served in the European Campaign in George Patton's Third United States Army. Rogers was wounded in action and also received a Bronze Star. He was released from active duty on March 1, 1946.

Rogers had a minor career as an actor and was most noted for playing his father (whom he closely resembled), particularly in The Story of Will Rogers (1952). He also appeared frequently in the 1950s television anthology, Schlitz Playhouse of Stars. Rogers starred as "Tom Brewster" in The Boy from Oklahoma, a 1954 Western movie directed by Michael Curtiz, the basis for the 1957 television series Sugarfoot, but the studio cast Will Hutchins in Rogers' part for the TV version. He also starred "Rogers of the Gazette," a CBS Radio series in 1953-54 that lasted one season, playing the role of a small-town newspaper owner. Rogers was one of several actors to host reruns of Death Valley Days (a job later performed by Ronald Reagan), with the episodes he hosted airing under the title The

Pioneers. For one season in 1958 he was host of the CBS morning show and was replaced by Jimmy Dean.

In his later years Rogers retired to his ranch at Tubac, Arizona. In poor health after suffering several strokes, having heart problems, and having had hip replacements, Rogers committed suicide in 1993 at the age of 81.

Michael Roof

(November 24, 1976 - June 9, 2009) was an American television and film actor.

Roof was born at an Air Force hospital in Tampa, Florida to Michael Roof, Sr. and his wife, Jean Tillet.

Roof toured the nation's comedy clubs with a stage name of "Chicken." He was especially popular in college town comedy.

In 2000, he had a central part in the WB Network sketch comedy TV series Hype, but it was canceled after its first season. After Hype, Roof moved to Hollywood, California to pursue a film career.

He landed a number of film roles in big-budget Hollywood productions. Some of these include the role of Private Mike Maddox of the US Rangers in Black Hawk Down, the comedic character of Dil Driscoll in The Dukes of Hazzard.

On the early morning of June 9, Roof's wife contacted police, and reported him missing. Several hours later, his body was found hanged from a tree in a wooded area near a Snellville, Georgia, elementary school parking lot. Roof reportedly suffered from bipolar disorder, and had been despondent about family finances. He is buried in Dunnellon Memorial Gardens, Dunnellon, Florida.

*

Andre René

Roussimoff ((19 May 1946 – 27 January 1993),
best known as André the Giant, a French professional
wrestler and actor. He is also known as Fezzik in the
classic movie The Princess Bride. His great size was a
result of gigantism.

André René Roussimoff was born in France, of
Bulgarian and Polish descent.

His last U.S. television appearance was in a brief
interview on World Championship Wrestling's Clash of
the Champions XX special that aired on TBS on 2
September 1992.

André branched out into acting in the 1970s
and 1980s, making his acting debut playing a Sasquatch
("Bigfoot") on the 1970s television series The Six
Million Dollar Man. He went on to appear in other
television shows, including The Greatest American
Hero, B.J. and the Bear, and The Fall Guy. He also
participated in an episode of Zorro.

Towards the end of his career, André also found work in several movies. He had an unaccredited appearance in the 1984 film Conan the Destroyer, as Dagoth, the resurrected horned giant god who is killed by Conan. But his most noted appearance was as Fezzik in the 1987 film The Princess Bride. In his final film, he appeared in a cameo role as a circus giant in the comedy Trading Mom.

The disease that granted him his immense size eventually began to take its toll on his body. By the late 1980s, André was in constant, near-crippling pain, and his heart struggled to pump blood through his body.

He has been unofficially crowned "The Greatest Drunk on Earth" for once consuming 119 12-ounce beers in 6 hours. In her autobiography, The Fabulous Moolah alleges that André drank 127 beers in a Reading, Pennsylvania hotel bar and later passed out in the lobby. Because the staff could not move him, they had to leave him there until he regained consciousness.

André died in his sleep due to congestive heart failure aggravated by alcoholism on the night of January 27, 1993, in a Paris hotel room.

 **Alma Rubens**

(February 19, 1897 – January 22, 1931) American silent film actress.

Born in San Francisco, California, Alma's first stage opportunity came in 1917, when a chorus girl in a comedy became ill; the young woman was asked to replace her. Soon the stock company came to Los Angeles, California. After a short time, Rubens left the troupe to go into movies.

Her breakthrough performance was in 1916 in Reggie Mixes In. She made six more films in that same year. In 1917 she starred in The Firefly of Tough Luck. She gained notoriety when she became Douglas Fairbanks's leading lady in The Half Breed (1916) and supported

She continued to work successfully until 1924. In that year she starred in The Price She Paid and Cytherea. She retired from the screen in 1926.

Rubens played Julie in the 1929 part-talkie film version of Show Boat--her next-to-last film and one of her few sound films.

She found it hard to get work because of her addiction to cocaine. At Marion Davies's request,

William Randolph Hearst helped with her support. Because of her addiction, she was in and out of mental institutions.

Her final stage appearance was in January 1930. She had a role in a play at the Writer's Club in Hollywood. Following her parole from the Patton hospital in December 1930, Rubens traveled to New York but returned to Los Angeles the same month. She was there less than two weeks when she was arrested by Federal officers in San Diego, California, on a narcotics charge.

Rubens claimed she was a victim of a frame-up, and physicians attested to her statements that she was not taking drugs. She was bound over to Federal district court and released on bail, and appeared for a preliminary hearing the second week of January 1931.

Rubens died of pneumonia the following week. She contracted a cold that quickly developed into pneumonia. Her doctor described her fatal illness as typhoid asthenic pneumonia, one of the most lethal strains.

Gail   Russell

(September 21, 1924 – August 26, 1961) American film and television actress.

She was born Elizabeth L. Russell to George and Gladys Russell in Chicago, Illinois, and then moved to the Los Angeles, California area when she was a teenager. Russell's extraordinary beauty brought her to the attention of Paramount Pictures in 1942. Although she was almost clinically shy and had no acting experience, Paramount had great expectations for her and employed an acting coach to work with her.

At the age of 19 she appeared in Henry Aldrich Gets Glamour (1943). Russell appeared in several films in the early and mid 1940s, including The Uninvited (1944), and Our Hearts Were Young and Gay (1944. Russell later appeared in Calcutta (1947), and two films with John Wayne, Angel and the Badman (1947) and Wake of the Red Witch (1948).

She married actor Guy Madison in 1949, but by 1950, it was known that she had become a victim of alcoholism. Paramount did not renew her contract. She drank on the set of The Uninvited to ease her paralyzing stage fright and lack of self-confidence. Alcohol ruined her career and personal life. She was divorced from Madison in 1954 and after a five-year absence, returned to work with Randolph Scott in the western Seven Men from Now (1956), produced by her friend John Wayne.

On July 5, 1957, she drove her convertible into the front of Jan's coffee shop at 8424 Beverly Blvd while driving under the influence.

She appeared in two more films after that.

On August 26, 1961, Russell was found dead in her apartment in Brentwood, Los Angeles, California at the age of 36. She died from liver damage attributed to alcohol. She was found to have been suffering from malnutrition at the time of her death.

Albert Salmi

(March 11, 1928 – April 22, 1990) American actor.

Albert Salmi was born in Brooklyn, New York, to Finnish immigrant parents, and following a stint in the Army, took up acting as a career, studying Method acting with Lee Strasberg. In 1955, Salmi starred in Bus Stop on Broadway. He volunteered to go on the road with the show, where he fell in love with and married his leading lady, former child star, Peggy Ann Garner, on May 16, 1956. Their only child, Catherine Ann Salmi, died in 1995 of premature heart disease at the age of thirty-eight.

He made his film debut as Smerdjakov in the 1958 movie version of The Brothers Karamazov. Salmi's next film was The Bravados.

He had several memorable roles on The Twilight Zone including "Of Late I Think of Cliffordville", "A Quality of Mercy" and "Execution" and also appeared twice as the incorrigible pirate, Alonzo P. Tucker on Lost in Space.

Salmi and Garner divorced on March 13, 1963. About the same time, he began playing Yadkin on TV's Daniel Boone opposite Fess Parker. He then remarried. They had two daughters.

A high point of Salmi's career came in 1968, when he was cast in the Arthur Miller play The Price. He played the lead on Broadway and in London.

In 1990, Albert and Roberta Salmi were found shot to death in their home in Spokane, Washington. According to police, Salmi, who was separated from Roberta at the time and was suffering from severe clinical depression, shot his wife and then himself.

George   Henry

Sanders (3 July 1906 – 25 April 1972) Russian-born English film, and television actor, singer, and music composer.

Sanders was born in Saint Petersburg, Imperial Russia. His English parents were Henry and Margaret Sanders . His elder brother was actor Tom Conway (1904–1967). Sanders was 11 when, in 1917 at the outbreak of the Russian Revolution, the family went back to England. Like his brother he attended Brighton College. After graduation he worked at an advertising agency where the company secretary, aspiring actress Greer Garson, suggested he take up a career in acting.

Sanders made his British film debut in 1929. Seven years later, after a series of British films his first role in an American production was Lloyd's of London (1936). His smooth, English accent and British manner put him in demand for American films throughout the next decade. He played a supporting role in Rebecca.

He was the lead in both The Falcon and The Saint film series. In 1942 Sanders handed off the Falcon role to his brother Tom, in The Falcon's Brother. The only other film in which the two brothers appeared together was Death of a Scoundrel (1956), in which they also played brothers.

Sanders played Lord Henry Wotton in the 1945 film version of The Picture of Dorian Gray. In 1947 he co-starred with Gene Tierney and Rex Harrison in The Ghost and Mrs. Muir.

In 1950 Sanders drew his greatest success as the theatre critic Addison DeWitt in All About Eve, for which he won an Academy Award for Best Supporting Actor. He then in the 1952

On 27 October 1940 Sanders married Susan Larson. They divorced in 1949. From later that year until 1954 Sanders was married to actress Zsa Zsa Gabor.

Sanders' last marriage was on 4 December 1970 to Magda Gabor, the elder sister of his second wife. This marriage lasted only six weeks, after which he began drinking heavily.

In his later years Sanders suffered from bewilderment, bouts of anger, and poor health. He can be seen teetering in his last films, owing to a loss of balance. At about this time, Sanders found he could no longer play his grand piano, which he dragged outside and smashed with an axe.

On 23 April 1972, Sanders checked into a hotel in Castelldefels, a coastal town near Barcelona. He was found dead two days later, having taken five bottles of Nembutal. Sanders was 65 years old. He left behind a suicide note which read:

Dear World, I am leaving because I am bored. I feel I have lived long enough. I am leaving you with your worries in this sweet cesspool. Good luck.

* **Rebecca**

Schaeffer (November 6, 1967 – July 18, 1989)
American actress.

Schaeffer, the only child of a child psychologist and a writer, was raised in Portland, Oregon. As a teen, she began modeling, appeared in television commercials, and as an extra in a television movie. She then moved to New York to pursue acting. After appearing on the cover of Seventeen magazine, she tested successfully for the part of Patti Russell on the CBS sitcom My Sister Sam. When the series ended in 1988, Schaeffer appeared in Radio Days, Scenes from the Class Struggle in Beverly Hills, The End of Innocence and the television movie Out of Time.

On July 18, 1989, Schaeffer was murdered by Robert John Bardo, an obsessed fan who had been stalking her for three years.

Romy

Schneider (23 September 1938 – 29 May 1982)

German film actress was born Rosemarie Magdalena Albach in Nazi-era Vienna.

She also held French citizenship. Schneider decided to live and to work in France, slowly gaining the interest of film directors such as Orson Welles for The Trial (1962).

A brief stint in Hollywood included appearances in Good Neighbor Sam, a 1964 comedy with Jack Lemmon, and in 1965 'What's New Pussycat?', co-starring Peter O'Toole, Peter Sellers, and Woody Allen, who also wrote the screenplay.

In July 1966 Schneider married Harry Meyen (1924–1979), a German director and actor who committed suicide in Hamburg, Germany in 1979. The couple had a son, David Christopher, born on December 3, 1966. David died at the age of 14 on 5 July, 1981. He had attempted to climb the spiked fence at his stepfather's parents' home when he punctured his femoral artery.

Schneider began drinking alcohol in excess after the death of her son David. When she was found dead in her apartment in Paris on 29 May, 1982, it was suggested that she had committed suicide by taking a lethal cocktail of alcohol and sleeping pills.

Edie

Sedgewick   (April 20, 1943 – November 16, 1971) American actress, socialite, model and heiress.

Edie Sedgwick was born in Santa Barbara, California

Sedgwick's family was long established in Massachusetts history. Her seventh-great grandfather, English-born Robert Sedgwick,was the first Major General of the Massachusetts Bay Colony settling in Charlestown, Massachusetts in 1635.

Despite her family's wealth and high social status, Edie's early life was troubled. All the Sedgwick children had deeply conflicted relationships with their father Fuzzy—they adored him, but by most accounts he was narcissistic, emotionally remote, controlling and frequently abusive. Edie had a very difficult relationship with her father, who openly carried on affairs with other women. On one occasion she walked in on him while he was having sex with one of his paramours. She flew into a rage, but Fuzzy claimed that Edie imagined the whole event. As a result of her emotional problems, Edie developed anorexia by her early teens and settled into a lifelong pattern of binging and purging.

At age 13 Edie began boarding at the Branson School near San Francisco. In 1958 she was enrolled at St. Timothy's School in Maryland. She was taken out the following year. At this point a serious rift developed between Edie's parents, and her mother left the country with Edie, intending to take her to stay with a noble family in Austria. This arrangement was terminated almost immediately, and Edie and her mother returned to the United States within 48 hours.

In the fall of 1962, Edie was admitted to the Silver Hill Hospital in New Canaan, Connecticut. According to fellow patient Virginia Davis, the regime was very lax there, and Edie and her friends often left the hospital after lunch and went into town on shopping sprees, charging up thousands of dollars worth of goods on credit at local stores. Edie easily manipulated the situation at Silver Hill, but her weight kept dropping to just ninety pounds. Consequently, her family had her transferred to a "closed" facility at Bloomingdale, the Westchester County, New York division of the New York Hospital.

In March 1965, Sedgwick met artist Andy Warhol. She began going to The Factory regularly in March 1965. Warhol was filming Vinyl, Despite Vinyl's all-male cast, Warhol put Sedgwick in the movie. She also made a small appearance in another Warhol film, Horse. Although Sedgwick's appearances in both films were brief, they generated so much interest that Warhol decided to create a vehicle in which she could star.

The first of those films, Poor Little Rich Girl, was originally part of a series featuring Sedgwick, called The Poor Little Rich Girl Saga.

On April 30, 1965, Warhol took Sedgwick, to the opening of his exhibit at the Sonnabend Gallery in Paris. Upon returning to New York City, Warhol asked his scriptwriter, Ron Tavel, to write a script for Sedgwick. The result was Kitchen.

Throughout 1965, Sedgwick and Warhol continued making films together, namely, Outer and Inner Space, Prison, Lupe and Chelsea Girls. However, by late 1965, Sedgwick and Warhol's relationship had deteriorated and Sedgwick requested that Warhol no longer show any of her films.

Lupe is often thought to be Sedgwick's last Warhol film, but Sedgwick filmed The Andy Warhol Story in 1966. The Andy Warhol Story was an unreleased film that was only screened once at The Factory.

Following her departure from Warhol's circle, Sedgwick began living at the Chelsea Hotel, where she became close to Bob Dylan. Dylan's friends eventually convinced Sedgwick to sign up with Albert Grossman, Dylan's manager. Sedgwick and Dylan's relationship ended when Sedgwick learned Dylan had married Sara Lownds..

Throughout most of 1966, Sedgwick was with Bob Neuwirth. During this period, she became increasingly dependent on barbiturates. Although she experimented with illegal substances including opiates, there is no evidence that Sedgwick ever became a heroin addict. In early 1967, Neuwirth, unable to cope with Sedgwick's drug abuse and erratic behavior, broke off their relationship.

Sedgwick's rapidly deteriorating health saw her return to her family in California, spending time in several different psychiatric institutions. In August 1969, she was hospitalized in the psychiatric ward of Cottage Hospital after being arrested for drug offenses by the local police.

When Sedgwick married Michael Post on July 24, 1971, she reportedly stopped abusing alcohol and other drugs for a short time. Her sobriety lasted until October, when pain medication was given to her to treat a physical illness.

On the night of November 15, 1971, Sedgwick went to a fashion show at the Santa Barbara Museum. After the fashion show, she attended a party where a drunken guest insulted her. Sedgwick phoned Post, took her back to their apartment.

Before they both fell asleep, Post gave Sedgwick the medication that had been prescribed for her.

When Post awoke the following morning, Edie Sedgwick was dead. The coroner ruled Sedgwick's death as "undetermined/accident/suicide. The death certificate claims the immediate cause was "probable acute barbiturate intoxication" due to ethanol intoxication. She was 28.

* **Tupac Shakur** (June 16, 1971 – September 13, 1996), American rapper and actor.

Tupac Amaru Shakur was born on the East Harlem section of Manhattan in New York City. He was named after Túpac Amaru II, a Peruvian revolutionary who led an indigenous uprising against Spain and was subsequently executed.

His mother, Afeni Shakur, and father, Billy Garland, were members of the Black Panther Party in New York in the late 1960s and early 1970s; he was born just one month after his mother's acquittal on more than 150 charges of "Conspiracy against the

United States government and New York landmarks" in the New York Panther 21 court case.

His godfather, Elmer "Geronimo" Pratt, a high ranking Black Panther, was convicted of murdering a school teacher during a 1968 robbery, although his sentence was later overturned. His stepfather, Mutulu, spent four years at large on the FBI's Ten Most Wanted Fugitives list beginning in 1982. Mutulu was wanted in part for having helped his sister Assata Shakur (also known as Joanne Chesimard) to escape from a penitentiary in New Jersey, where she had been incarcerated for shooting a state trooper to death in 1973. Mutulu was caught in 1986 and imprisoned for the robbery of a Brinks armored truck in which two

Even as he garnered attention as a rapper and actor, Shakur gained notoriety for his conflicts with the law:

In October 1991, he filed a $10 million civil suit against the law enforcement of the Oakland Police Department, alleging they brutally beat him for jaywalking.

In 1992, a Texas state trooper was killed by a teenager who was listening to 2Pacalypse Now which included songs about killing police. This caused a swirl of media controversy. Dan Quayle, the Vice President of the United States at the time, demanded that the album be withdrawn from music stores and media across the country; Interscope refused. Shakur claimed his first album was aimed at the problems facing young black males, but it was criticized for its graphic language and images of violence by and against law enforcement. Quayle publicly denounced the album as having "no place in our society."

On August 22, 1992, in Marin City, California, Shakur rapped at an outdoor festival, and stayed for an hour signing autographs and pictures. Some earlier negative remarks made by Shakur about Marin City had caught up and when arguments started, voices got loud; he pulled a Colt Mustang, cocked it, fumbled and it fell. Someone picked up the gun and a bullet discharged. Though nobody in the crowd was shot, about 100 yards away, 6-year-old Qa'id Walker-Teal rode a bicycle at a schoolyard and was hit in the forehead with a bullet that killed him. (Some sources reported that the child was the victim of a stray bullet in a shootout between Shakur's entourage and a rival group.) Shakur and Mopreme left in their car and were stopped by an angry mob, by chance, in front of a sheriff's substation. The police "rescued" them and took the two into custody, who were soon released without charge. In 1995, a wrongful death suit was brought against Shakur by Qa'id's mother. Ballistics tests proved the bullet that killed the boy was not from Shakur's or any members of his entourage's guns. No criminal charges were brought. Shakur's lawyer said that the festival was a "nasty situation," and Shakur was saddened by the death of the boy. Shakur's record company settled the lawsuit for an undisclosed amount, reportedly between $300,000 and $500,000.

In October 1993, in Atlanta, two brothers and off-duty police officers, Mark and Scott Whitwell, were with their wives celebrating Mrs. Whitwell's recent passing of the state bar examination. As they crossed the street, a car with Shakur inside passed by them or "almost struck them," after which the Whitwells began an altercation with the driver, Shakur and the other passengers, which was then joined by a second passing car. Shakur shot one officer in the buttocks, and the other in the leg, back, or abdomen, according to varying news reports. There were no other injuries, but Mark Whitwell was charged with firing at Shakur's car and later lying to the police during the investigation, and Shakur with the shooting, until prosecutors decided to drop all charges against all parties.

In November 1993, Shakur and others were charged with sexually assaulting a woman in a hotel room. According to the complaint, Shakur sodomized the woman and then encouraged his friends to sexually abuse her. Shakur denied the charges. According to Shakur, he had prior relations days earlier with the woman; she performed oral sex on him on a club dance floor and the two later had consensual sex in his hotel room. The complainant claimed sexual assault after her second visit to Shakur's hotel room; she alleged that

Shakur and his entourage gang banged her, and she said to Shakur when she left, "Why you let them do this to me?" Shakur claimed that he fell asleep shortly after the woman arrived and later awoke to her accusations and legal threats. In the ensuing trial, Shakur was convicted of sexual abuse. In sentencing Shakur to 1½–4½ years in prison, the judge described the crime as "an act of brutal violence against a helpless woman." After serving part of his sentence, Shakur was released on bail pending appeal. On April 5, 1996, a judge sentenced him to serve 120 days in jail for violating terms of his release on bail.

On the night of November 30, 1994, the day before the verdict in his sexual abuse trial was to be announced, Shakur was shot five times and robbed after entering the lobby of Quad Recording Studios in Manhattan by two armed men in army fatigues. He would later accuse Sean Combs, Andre Harrell, and Biggie Smalls—whom he saw after the shooting—of setting him up. Shakur also suspected his close friend and associate, Randy "Stretch" Walker, of being involved in the attempt. According to the doctors at Bellevue Hospital, where he was admitted immediately following the incident, Shakur had received five bullet wounds; twice in the head, twice in the groin and once through the arm and thigh. He checked out of the hospital, against doctor's orders, three hours after surgery. In the day that followed, Shakur entered the courthouse in a wheelchair and was found guilty of three counts of molestation, but innocent of six others, including sodomy. On February 6, 1995, he was sentenced to one-and-a-half to four-and-a-half years in prison on a sexual assault charge. A year later on November 30, 1995, Stretch was killed after being shot twice in the back by three men who pulled up alongside his green minivan at 112th Ave. and 209th St. in Queens Village, while he was driving. His minivan smashed into a tree and hit a parked car before flipping over. On March 27, 2008, the Los Angeles Times issued an apology to Combs for blaming him for having a role in the November 1994 shooting. The article stated that Shakur was led to the studio by Biggie's associates to gun him down to make favor with Biggie. The newspaper relied on forged documents that The Smoking Gun proved to be faked. Combs stated that he was disgusted with the LA Times for printing the story.

On June 15, 2011, an inmate admitted to this shooting and robbery, claiming to have been hired to do so by James Rosemond, owner of Czar Entertainment.

Shakur began serving his prison sentence at Clinton Correctional Facility on February 14, 1995. Shortly afterwards, he released his multi-platinum album Me Against the World. Shakur became the first artist ever to have an album at number one on the Billboard 200 while serving a prison sentence: the only other artist to have achieved this feat is fellow rapper Lil Wayne, whose album I Am Not a Human Being reached number one in 2010 whilst he was serving a nine-month prison term for criminal possession of a weapon. Me Against the World made its debut on the Billboard 200 and stayed at the top of the charts for four weeks. The album sold 240,000 copies in its first week, setting a record for highest first week sales for a solo male rap artist at the time. While serving his sentence, he married his long-time girlfriend, Keisha Morris, on April 4, 1995; the couple later divorced in 1996. While imprisoned, Shakur read many books by Niccolò Machiavelli, Sun Tzu's The Art of War and other works of political philosophy and strategy. He also wrote a screenplay titled Live 2 Tell while incarcerated, a story about an adolescent who becomes a drug baron.

In October 1995, Shakur's case was on appeal but due to all of his legal fees he could not raise the $1.4 million bail. After serving eleven months of his one-and-a-half year to four-and-a-half year sentence, Shakur was released from the Attica Correctional Facility due in large part to the help and influence of Suge Knight, the CEO of Death Row Records, who

On the night of September 7, 1996, Shakur attended the Mike Tyson–Bruce Seldon boxing match at the MGM Grand in Las Vegas. After leaving the match, one of Suge's associates spotted 21-year-old

Orlando "Baby Lane" Anderson, a member of the Southside Crips, in the MGM Grand lobby and informed Shakur, who then attacked Anderson. Shakur's entourage, as well as Suge and his followers, assisted in assaulting Anderson. The fight was captured on the hotel's video surveillance. Earlier that year, Anderson and a group of Crips had robbed a member of Death Row's entourage in a Foot Locker store, precipitating Shakur's attack. After the brawl, Shakur went to rendezvous with Suge to go to Death Row-owned Club 662 (now known as restaurant/club Seven). He rode in Suge's 1996 black BMW 750iL sedan as part of a larger convoy including many in Shakur's entourage.

At 10:55 pm, while paused at a red light, Shakur rolled down his window and a photographer took his photograph. At around 11:00–11:05 pm, they were halted on Las Vegas Blvd. by Metro bicycle police for playing the car stereo too loud and not having license plates. The plates were then found in the trunk of Suge's car; they were released without being fined a few minutes later. At approximately 11:15 pm, a white, four-door, late-model Cadillac with an unknown number of occupants pulled up to the sedan's right side, rolled down one of the windows, and rapidly fired a volley of gunshots at Shakur; bullets hit him in the chest, pelvis, and his right hand and thigh. One of the rounds apparently ricocheted into Shakur's right lung

On the afternoon of September 13, 1996, Shakur died of internal bleeding. Shakur's body was cremated and some of his ashes were later mixed with marijuana and smoked by members of the Outlawz.

* **Elizabeth Short** (July 29, 1924 – January 15, 1947) American murder victim known as **"The Black Dahlia"**.

Elizabeth Short was born in Boston, Massachusetts, the third of five daughters of Cleo Short and Phoebe Mae Sawyer. Her father built miniature golf courses until the 1929 stock market crash, in which he lost much of the family's assets. In 1930, he parked his car on a bridge and vanished, leading some to believe he had committed suicide. Troubled by asthma and bronchitis, at the age of 16, Short was sent to live in Miami, Florida. She spent the next three years there during the cold months and in Medford the remainder of the year. Having learned of her father's whereabouts, at age 19, Short travelled to Vallejo, California to live with him. The two moved to Los Angeles in early 1943, but an altercation resulted in her leaving there and finding work in the post exchange at Camp Cooke, near Lompoc, California. Short next moved to Santa Barbara, where she was arrested on September 23, 1943, for underage drinking. Following her arrest, she was sent back to Medford by the juvenile authorities in Santa Barbara. Short then returned to Florida to live, with occasional visits back to Massachusetts.

In Florida, Short met Major Matthew Michael Gordon Jr., a decorated United States Army Air Forces officer who was assigned to the 2nd Air Commando Group and in training for deployment to China Burma India Theater of Operations. Short told friends Gordon wrote her a letter from India proposing marriage while he was recovering from injuries sustained from an airplane crash. She accepted his proposal, but Gordon died in a second airplane crash on August 10, 1945 before he could return to the United States. She later exaggerated this story, saying that they were married and had a child who died.

Elizabeth returned to Los Angeles in July 1946 to visit Army Air Corps Lieutenant Joseph Gordon Fickling, an old boyfriend she had met in Florida during the war. At the time Short returned to Los Angeles, Fickling was stationed at NARB, Long Beach.

The body of Elizabeth Short was found in the Leimert Park district of Los Angeles on January 15, 1947. Her remains had been left on a vacant lot on the west side of South Norton Avenue midway between Coliseum Street and West 39th Street. Short's severely mutilated body was found nude and severed at the waist, completely drained of blood. Her face had been slashed from the corners of her mouth toward her ears, creating an effect called the Glasgow smile. The body had been washed and cleaned and she had been "posed" with her hands over her head and elbows bent at right angles.

William Randolph Hearst's papers, the Los Angeles Herald-Express and the Los Angeles Examiner, sensationalized the case; the black tailored suit Short was last seen wearing became "a tight skirt and a sheer blouse" and Elizabeth Short became the "Black Dahlia," an "adventuress" who "prowled Hollywood Boulevard". As time passed, the media coverage became more outrageous with claims her lifestyle "made her victim material."

On January 23, 1947, the killer rang the editor of the Los Angeles Examiner, expressing concern that news of the murder was tailing off in the newspapers and offering to mail items belonging to Short to the editor. The following day a packet arrived at the Los Angeles newspaper containing Short's birth certificate, business cards, photographs, names written on pieces of paper and an address book with the name Mark Hansen embossed on the cover. Hansen, the last person known to have seen Short alive (on January 9), became the prime suspect. The killer would later write more letters to the newspaper, calling himself "the Black Dahlia Avenger," after the name given to Short by the newspapers.

Short was buried at the Mountain View Cemetery in Oakland, California.

Don Simpson

(October 29, 1943 – January 19, 1996) American film producer, screenwriter, and actor.

Simpson was born in Seattle, Washington, grew up in Anchorage, Alaska and attended West Anchorage High School. He then went on to attend the University of Oregon, where he was a member of the Phi Delta Theta fraternity.

According to High Concept, a Simpson biography by reporter Charles Fleming, Simpson's prescription drug expenses were over $60,000 a month at the time of his death. His job as an executive at Paramount Pictures came to an end when he allegedly passed out in the middle of a meeting.

Simpson's unusual personal life has been documented in a number of sources. A chapter in the book You'll Never Make Love in This Town Again (which describes four prostitutes' stories about their sexual encounters with Hollywood celebrities) discusses his preferences for S & M and videotaping of their sessions. He is also known to have had several plastic surgery operations.

On Friday, January 19, 1996, Simpson was found dead in his home in Los Angeles. The cause of death was a cardiac arrest from combined drug intoxication.

*

Elliott Smith (August 6, 1969 – October 21, 2003) American singer-songwriter and musician.

Smith was born in Omaha, Nebraska, raised in Texas, and resided for a significant portion of his life in Portland, Oregon, where he first gained popularity. His primary instrument was the guitar, but he was also proficient at piano, clarinet, bass guitar, drums, and harmonica. Smith had a distinctive vocal style characterized by his "whispery, spiderweb-thin delivery" and use of digital multi-tracking to create vocal layers, textures, and harmonies.

After playing in the rock band Heatmiser for several years, Smith began his solo career in 1994 with releases on the independent record labels Cavity Search and Kill Rock Stars. In 1997 he signed a contract with DreamWorks Records, for which he recorded two albums. Smith rose to mainstream prominence when his song "Miss Misery"—included in the soundtrack for the film 'Good Will Hunting', and was nominated for an Oscar in the Best Original Song category in 1998.

Smith suffered from depression, alcoholism, and drug addiction, and these topics often appear in his lyrics. At age 34, he died in Los Angeles, California from two stab wounds to the chest. The autopsy evidence was inconclusive as to whether the wounds were self-inflicted. At the time of his death, Smith was working on his sixth studio album, From a Basement on the Hill, which was posthumously released.

Phillip Harvey "Phil"

Spector (December 26, 1939-) American record producer and songwriter.The originator of the "Wall of Sound" production technique, Spector was a pioneer of the 1960s girl-group sound and produced over 25 Top 40 hits between 1960 and1965. After this initial success, Spector later worked with artists including Ike and Tina Turner, John Lennon, George Harrison, and the Ramones with similar acclaim. He produced The Beatles' Academy Award winning album Let It Be, and the Grammy Award–winning Concert for Bangladesh by former Beatle George Harrison. In 1989, Spector was inducted into the Rock and Roll Hall of Fame as a non-performer. The 1965 song "You've Lost That Lovin' Feelin'", produced and co-written by Spector for The Righteous Brothers, is listed by BMI as the song with the most U.S. airplay in the 20th century.

On February 3, 2003, actress Lana Clarkson was found dead, killed by a firearm, in Spector's mansion in Alhambra, California. Spector stated that Clarkson's death was an "accidental suicide" and that she "kissed the gun". The emergency call from Spector's home, made by Spector's driver Adriano De Souza, quotes Spector as saying, "I think I've killed someone." According to some women who were said to have met Spector, there would come a point when they wanted to leave Spector's home, whereupon he would hold them at gunpoint. The prosecution argued that the testimony of the other women was important in order to demonstrate a "common plan or scheme". The defense sought to prevent the women from providing such testimony. Though the law in California and other states generally forbids the introduction of evidence showing a defendant's previous transgressions, the judge sided with the prosecutors and ruled that the testimony of the other women "can be used to show lack of accident or mistake". Prior to and during the first trial, Spector went through at least three sets of attorneys. Defense attorney Robert Shapiro represented Spector at the arraignment and early pretrial hearings and achieved his release on $1 million bail. Bruce Cutler represented him during the 2007 trial, but withdrew on August 27, 2007, claiming "a difference of opinion between Mr. Spector and me on strategy." Attorney Linda Kenney Baden then became lead lawyer for closing arguments.

Spector remained free on $1 million bail while awaiting trial. The trial began on March 19, 2007. Presiding judge Larry Paul Fidler allowed the trial to be televised. At the start of the trial, the defense's forensic expert Henry Lee was accused of hiding crucial evidence which the District Attorney's office claimed could prove Spector's guilt. On September 26, 2007,

Judge Fidler declared a mistrial because of a hung jury (10 to 2 for conviction).

The retrial of Spector for murder in the second degree began on October 20, 2008, with Judge Fidler again presiding; this time it was not televised. The case went to the jury on March 26, 2009, and nineteen days later, on April 13, the jury returned a guilty verdict. In addition, he was found guilty of using a firearm in the commission of a crime. Spector was immediately taken into custody and was formally sentenced on May 29, 2009, to 19 years to life in the California state prison system.

The California Court of Appeal affirmed Spector's conviction in May 2011 and denied his request for a rehearing of the appeal shortly thereafter. On August 17, 2011 the California Supreme Court refused to review the Court of Appeal's decision to affirm his conviction. (S193961 Petition for review denied). Spector is serving his sentence at the California Substance Abuse Treatment Facility and State Prison (SATF) in Corcoran, California. Although it is in Corcoran, it is a separate facility from California State Prison, Corcoran. Spector will be 88 years old before becoming eligible for parole.

Inger Stevens

(October 18, 1934 – April 30, 1970) Swedish-American movie and TV actress.

Inger Stevens was born Inger Stensland in Stockholm, Sweden. She was an insecure child and was ill often. When she was nine, her parents divorced and she moved with her father to New York City. At age 13 she and her father moved to Manhattan, Kansas, where she attended Manhattan High School. At 16 she worked in burlesque shows in Kansas City. At 18 she left Kansas for New York City where she worked as a chorus girl, and in the Garment District while taking classes at the Actors Studio.

Stevens appeared on television series, commercials and in plays, until she got her big break in the movie Man on Fire starring Bing Crosby.

Roles in major films followed, but she achieved her greatest success in the ABC television series The Farmer's Daughter, with William Windom. Previously, Stevens appeared in episodes of Bonanza, Route 66, The Alfred Hitchcock Hour, The Eleventh Hour, Sam Benedict and The Twilight Zone.

Following the cancellation of The Farmer's Daughter in 1966, Stevens appeared in several movies:

A Guide for the Married Man (1967) with Walter Matthau, Hang 'Em High with Clint Eastwood, 5 Card Stud with Dean Martin, and Madigan with Henry Fonda and Richard Widmark, all in 1968. Stevens was attempting to make a comeback on television with the detective drama series, The Most Deadly Game, when she died.

Among her many films were Man on Fire (1957),m Cry Terror! (1958), The Buccaneer (1958), The World, the Flesh and the Devil (1959), The New Interns (1964), The Borgia Stick (1967, Guide for the Married Man (1967), A Time for Killing (1967), Firecreek (1968), Madigan (1968), 5 Card Stud (1968), Hang 'Em High (1968), House of Cards (1968), A Dream of Kings (1969)

Her first husband was her agent, Anthony Soglio, to whom she was married from 1955 to 1957. From 1961 until her death she secretly was married to Ike Jones, an African-American actor. In addition to these marriages she also had been romantically linked with Bing Crosby, Anthony Quinn, Dean Martin, Clint Eastwood, Harry Belafonte, Mario Lanza, and Burt Reynolds.

On the morning of April 30, 1970, a house guest found Stevens lying face down on her kitchen floor, having overdosed on Tedral (a combination drug of theophylline, ephedrine and phenobarbital), washed down with alcohol.

Stevens had attempted suicide in 1959 when her reported romance with Bing Crosby ended.

* **Dorothy Stratten**

(February 28, 1960 – August 14, 1980) was a Canadian model and actress.

Stratten was born Dorothy Ruth Hoogstraten in a Salvation Army hospital in Vancouver, British. In 1977 she was attending Centennial High School in Coquitlam when, while working part-time at a local Dairy Queen she met twenty-six year old Vancouver-area club promoter and pimp Paul Snider, who romanced her. Snider later had professional nude photos taken of her which were sent to Playboy magazine. She was underage and when her mother refused to sign the model release, her signature was forged.

\In 1979 the two moved to Los Angeles. With her surname shortened to Stratten, she became Playboy's Miss August and began working as a bunny at the Century City Playboy Club. She guest starred in episodes of the television series Buck Rogers and Fantasy Island, along with a small role in the 1979 roller disco comedy Skatetown, U.S.A..

In 1980 she became Playboy's Playmate of the. Stratten also played the title role in the sci-fi parody Galaxina.

Stratten began an affair with Peter Bogdanovich while he was directing They All Laughed, her first and only major film. Stratten moved in with Bogdanovich, planning to file for a divorce from Snider.

Shortly after noon on August 14, 1980 Snider and Stratten met at Snider's house. Stratten had come to talk about an amicable divorce and brought along $1,000 to give Snider.

At about 11:00 PM Snider's private investigator called Cushner on his private line, saying he had been trying to telephone Snider for several hours, but Snider would not answer his phone. Cushner broke into Snider's room and found them dead from shotgun blasts, both bodies nude and swarmed by ants.

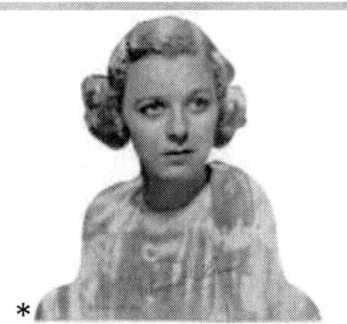

* **Margaret**

Sullivan (May 16, 1909 – January 1, 1960;) American stage and film actor.

Sullavan was born in Norfolk, Virginia. She moved to Boston and lived with her half-sister, Weedie, where she studied dance at the Boston Denishawn studio and drama at the Copley Theatre.

Sullavan succeeded in getting a chorus part in the Harvard Dramatic Society 1929 spring production Close Up. Another member of the University Players and one who had the comic lead in Close Up was Henry Fonda.

In the summer 1929 Sullivan appeared opposite Fonda in The Devil in the Cheese, her debut on the professional stage.

In 1930 she played the lead in Strictly Dishonorable by Preston Sturges A Shubert scout saw her in that play as well and eventually she met Lee Shubert himself. At that moment Sullavan suffered from a bad case of laryngitis. Consequently, her voice was huskier than usual. Shubert loved it. In subsequent years Sullavan would joke that she cultivated that "laryngitis" into a permanent hoarseness by standing in every available draft.

Sullavan made her debut on Broadway in A Modern on May 20, 1931. At one point in 1932 she starred in four Broadway flops in a row (If Love Were All, Happy Landing, Chrysalis (with Humphrey Bogart) and Bad Manners.

In March 1933, Sullavan replaced another actor in Dinner at Eight in New York. Movie director John M. Stahl happened to be watching the play and offered her a three-year, two-pictures-a-year contract at $1,200 a week. She accepted it and had a clause put in her contract that allowed her to return to the stage on occasion.

Sullavan arrived in Hollywood on May 16, 1933. Her film debut came that same year in Only Yesterday. She followed that role with one in Little Man, What Now? (1934), which tells the story of a couple struggling to survive in the poverty of post–World War I Germany.

The Good Fairy (1935) was a comedy that Sullavan, although not a natural comedienne, had insisted on doing to demonstrate her "wide-ranging versatility". Her then-husband William Wyler was the director.[1]

King Vidor's So Red the Rose (1935) dealt with the Civil War effects on the South and preceded Gone With the Wind by four years and Margaret Mitchell's novel by one year.

In Next Time We Love (1936), Sullavan plays opposite James Stewart

In the comedy The Moon is Our Home (1936), Sullavan plays opposite her ex-husband Henry Fonda.

Sullavan reunited with Stewart in The Shopworn Angel (1938). Her ninth film was the rather soapy The Shining Hour (1938

In The Shop Around the Corner (1940), Sullavan and Stewart worked together again, playing colleagues who do not get along at work, but have both responded to a lonely-hearts ad and are (without knowing it) exchanging letters with each other.

The Mortal Storm (1940) was the last movie Sullavan and Stewart ever did together. Sullavan is a young German girl engaged to a confirmed Nazi (Robert Young) in 1933. When she realizes the true nature of his political views, she breaks the engagement and turns her attention to anti-Nazi Stewart.

Back Street (1941) was lauded as one of the best performances of Sullavan's Hollywood career. She wanted Charles Boyer to play opposite her so much that she agreed to surrender top billing to him. So Ends Our Night (1941) is yet another wartime drama.

Cry 'Havoc' (1943) is another war drama (World War II) but one of the rare all-female pictures.

Sullavan retired from films from 1943 to 1950 and concentrated on her family and the stage. She came back to the screen in 1950 to do one last picture, No Sad Songs for Me.

In 1955-56 Sullavan appeared in Janus, a comedy by playwright Carolyn Green. The play ran for 251 performances from November 1955 to June 1956. In the late fifties Sullavan's hearing and depression were getting worse. However, in 1959 she agreed to do Sweet Love Remembered by playwright Ruth Goetz. Rehearsals began on December 1, 1959. Sullavan had mixed emotions about a return to acting and her depression soon became clear to everyone: "I loathe acting", she said on the very day she started rehearsals. "I loathe what it does to my life. It cancels you out. You cannot live while you are working. You are a person surrounded by an unbreachable wall". That was the last interview she gave. The play was to open on February 4, 1960.

On January 1, 1960, at about 5:30 p.m., Sullavan was found in bed, barely alive but unconscious, in a hotel room in New Haven, Connecticut. Her copy of the script to Sweet Love Remembered, was found open beside her. Sullavan was rushed to Grace New Haven Hospital, but shortly after 6:00 p.m. she was pronounced dead. No note had been found to indicate suicide, and no conclusion was reached as to whether her death was the result of a deliberate or an accidental overdose. The death was later identified as apparent suicide.

Sullavan's troubled daughter Bridget was found dead in her apartment only 8 months after her mother had died; she died at the age of 21 (of an overdose).

Sullavan's son Bill committed suicide in 2008 at the age of 66.

Carl Switzer

(August 7, 1927 – January 21, 1959) American child actor, professional dog breeder and hunting guide

Switzer was born in Paris, Illinois. He and his older brother, Harold Switzer, became famous around their hometown for their musical talent and performances; both sang and played a number of instruments.

The Switzers took a trip to California in 1934 to visit with family members. They eventually wound up at Hal Roach Studios. 8-year-old Harold and 6-year-old Carl entered the Hal Roach Studio's cafeteria, the Our Gang Café, and began an impromptu performance. Producer Hal Roach was and was impressed by the performance. He signed both Switzers to appear in Our Gang.

The Switzer brothers first appeared in the 1935 Our Gang short, Beginner's Luck. By the end of the year, Alfalfa was one of the main characters in the series, while Harold had more or less been relegated to the role of a background player.

Although Carl Switzer was an experienced singer and musician, his character Alfalfa was often called upon to sing off-key.

After Hal Roach sold Our Gang to Metro-Goldwyn Mayer (MGM) in 1938, Switzer's behavior was extreme, and he often sabotaged the production of the Our Gang films. Once, during a break in filming The Big Premiere, Switzer urinated on the set's lights. When filming resumed, the lights heated up and filled the set with such a stench that filming had to be halted for the rest of the day

Switzer's work on Our Gang ended in 1940, when Carl was twelve. Carl continued to appear in, including I Love You Again, Going My Way, Courage of Lassie, and It's a Wonderful Life .

Switzer had a fleeting cameo in the 1946 Christmas film It's A Wonderful Life as Mary Hatch's date at the high school.

His final film role was in 1958's The Defiant Ones and on the television series The Roy Rogers Show.

In the early 1950s, Switzer moved to Kansas. He lived and worked on a farm at Pretty Prairie, west of Wichita. There he met and married Diane Collingwood, the heiress of grain elevator empire Collingwood Grain. The marriage only lasted four months.

Prior to a hunting guide job, Switzer had borrowed a hunting dog from Moses Stiltz. The dog was lost, and Switzer offered a $50 reward. A man found the dog and brought it to the bar where Switzer was working. Switzer paid the man $35 and bought him $15 worth of drinks from the bar. Several days later Switzer Stiltz owed him the $50 paid to the man who found the dog. allegedly arrived drunk at Stiltz's home to collect the money.

When Stiltz refused to hand over the money, the two engaged in a fight. Stiltz retreated to his bedroom and returned with a .38-caliber revolver. Switzer immediately took the gun away from him. Switzer then forced Stiltz into a closet, despite the fact that Stiltz had gotten the gun back. Switzer allegedly pulled a switchblade but just as Switzer was about to charge Stiltz, Stiltz shot Switzer in the groin. Switzer suffered massive internal bleeding and was pronounced dead on arrival at the hospital.

The killing was held to be a justifiable homicide. Switzer had allegedly pulled a knife; therefore, the shooting was judged to be self-defense. During the inquest regarding Switzer's death, it was revealed that what was originally reported as a hunting knife was a penknife. It had been found by crime scene investigators under his body, but with no blade exposed.

*

Sharon Tate

(January 24, 1943 – August 9, 1969) was an American actress

Sharon Tate was born in Dallas, Texas, At six months of age, Sharon Tate won the "Miss Tiny Tot of Dallas Pageant. By age 16, Sharon Tate had lived in six different American cities.

She began entering beauty pageants, winning the title of "Miss Richland" in 1959. Paul Tate was then transferred to Italy, taking his family with him.

Tate became interested in the filming of Adventures of a Young Man, which was being made nearby with Paul Newman, Susan Strasberg and Richard Beymer, and obtained a part as an extra. Beymer noticed Tate in the crowd and introduced himself. Beymer encouraged Tate to pursue a film career. In 1961, Tate was employed by the singer Pat Boone, and appeared with him in a television special he made in Venice.

Later that year, when Barabbas was being filmed near Verona, Tate was once again hired as an extra. Actor Jack Palance was impressed by her. He arranged a screen test for her in Rome. Tate returned to the United States alone, saying she wanted to further her studies, but tried to find film work. After a few months, Doris Tate, who feared for her daughter's safety, suffered a nervous breakdown and, after much coercion from her family, Tate returned to Italy.

The Tate family returned to the United States in 1962, and Sharon Tate moved to Los Angeles, where she contacted Richard Beymer's agent. Gefsky agreed to represent her, and secured work for her in television and magazine advertisements. In 1963 he introduced her to Martin Ransohoff, director of Filmways, Inc., who signed her to a seven-year contract. He gave her small parts in Mr. Ed and The Beverly Hillbillies to help her gain experience.

In 1964, she met Jay Sebring, a former sailor who had established himself as a leading hair stylist in Hollywood.

She continued to gain experience with minor television appearances. Ransohoff gave her roles in two motion pictures in which he was producer: The Americanization of Emily and The Sandpiper. In late 1965, Ransohoff finally gave Tate her first major role in a motion picture in, Eye of the Devil, co-starring David Niven, Deborah Kerr, Donald Pleasence, and David Hemmings.

Tate and Sebring traveled to London to prepare for filming. After filming, Tate remained in London where she immersed herself in the fashion world and nightclubs. Around this time she met Roman Polanski.

Polanski was planning The Fearless Vampire Killers, Ransohoff insisted that Polanski cast Tate, and after meeting with her, he agreed that she would be suitable on the condition that she wore a red wig during filming.

The company traveled to Italy for filming. As filming progressed, Polanski praised her performances and her confidence grew. They began a relationship, and Tate moved into Polanski's London apartment after filming ended.

Tate returned to the United States to film Don't Make Waves with Tony Curtis. Tate played the part of Malibu.

Polanski returned to the United States, and was contracted by the head of Paramount Pictures to direct and write the screenplay for Rosemary's Baby

During the shooting of Valley of the Dolls, Tate confided to Parkins that she was "madly in love" with Polanski.

In late 1967, Tate and Polanski returned to London. They were married in Chelsea, London on January 20, 1968. The couple returned to Los Angeles and quickly became part of a social group that included some of the most successful young people in the film industry. Jay Sebring remained one of the couple's most frequent companions. They arranged to lease Patty Duke's home on in Beverly Hills during the latter part of 1968.

In the summer of 1968, Tate began her next film, The Wrecking Crew (1969.

Tate became pregnant near the end of 1968, and on February 15, 1969 she and Polanski moved Benedict Canyon. Tate chose the comedy The Thirteen Chairs as her next project, as she later explained, largely for the opportunity to co-star with Orson Welles. In March 1969, she traveled to Italy to begin filming, while Polanski went to London to work on The Day of the Dolphin.

After completing The Thirteen Chairs, Tate joined Polanski in London. She returned from London to Los Angeles, on July 20, 1969. Polanski was due to return on August 12 in time for the birth, and he asked Frykowski and Folger to stay in the house with Tate until then.

On August 8, 1969, Tate was two weeks from giving birth. She entertained two friends, actresses Joanna Pettet and Barbara Lewis, for lunch at her home. In the evening she went to her favorite restaurant, El Coyote, with Sebring, Frykowski and Folger, returning about 10:30 p.m.

During the night they were murdered by members of Charles Manson's "Family" and their bodies discovered the following morning by Tate's housekeeper, Winifred Chapman. Police arrived at the scene to find the body of a young man, later identified as Steven Parent, shot to death in his car, which was in the driveway. Inside the house, the bodies of Tate and Sebring were found in the living room; a long rope tied around each of their necks connected them. On the front lawn lay the bodies of Frykowski and Folger. All of the victims, except Parent, had been stabbed numerous times. The coroner's report for Tate noted that she had been stabbed sixteen times.

In November 1969, while in prison in connection with a car theft, Susan Atkins boasted to an inmate that she was responsible for the murder of Sharon Tate. This led to her indictment, along with the accomplices she named, Charles Manson, Charles "Tex" Watson, Patricia Krenwinkel and Linda Kasabian. Atkins also revealed that the murders of Leno and Rosemary LaBianca in Los Feliz, Los Angeles, the night after the Tate murders, were also committed by "Family" members, and incriminated Leslie Van Houten as a participant in the second murder.

William Desmond Taylor (April 26, 1872 – February 1, 1922) Irish-born American actor

He was born William Cunningham Deane-Tanner. He sailed for America in 1890, when he was 18 years old.

He briefly pursued an acting career in New York City before marrying Ethel May Hamilton on December 7, 1901. Though she appeared as a member of the Florodora sextette as Ethel May Harrison, she was the daughter of a wealthy Wall Street broker who provided Taylor with the money to set up the English Antiques Shop. The Tanners were well-known in New York society until he abruptly vanished on October 23, 1908 at the age of 36, following an affair with a married woman, deserting his wife and daughter. Taylor had suffered "mental lapses" before, and the family thought he had perhaps wandered off during an episode of aphasia.

Changing his name to William Desmond Taylor, he was in Hollywood by December 1912 and worked successfully as an actor before making his first film as a director, The Awakening (1914). Over the next few years, he directed more than fifty films.

In July 1918, towards the end of World War I, Taylor enlisted in the British Army as a private at the age of 46. He was assigned to the Royal Army Service Corps of the Expeditionary Forces Canteen Service. Returning to Los Angeles, Taylor became president of the Motion Picture Directors Association.

At 7:30 a.m. on the morning of February 2, 1922, the body of William Desmond Taylor was found inside his bungalow in the Westlake Park area of downtown Los Angeles. It was determined that the 49-year-old film director had been shot in the back.

Lou   Tellegen

(November 26, 1881 – October 29, 1934) Dutch born
silent film and stage actor.

Born   Isidore   Louis   Bernard   Edmon   van
Dommelen.

He was the illegitimate child of army lieutenant
Isidore Louis Bernard Edmon Tellegen (1836–1902)
and Anna Maria van Dommelen.

He left his birth town Sint Oedenrode to make
his stage debut in Amsterdam in 1903, and was invited
to perform in Paris, co-starring in several roles with
Sarah Bernhardt.

In 1910, he made his first motion picture
appearance in La dame aux camélias, a silent film, and
he and Bernhardt then travelled to the United States.
Back in France in 1912, they made their second film
together, Les Amours de la reine Élisabeth.

In the summer of 1913, Tellegen went to
London where he produced and starred in the Oscar
Wilde play, The Picture of Dorian Gray. Invited back to

the United States, Tellegen worked in theatre and made his first American film in 1915, titled The Explorer, followed by The Unknown.

Tellegen had appeared in many films before his face was damaged in a fire. One of his memorable roles was as the villain in John Ford's 1926 western 3 Bad Men.

Then, employment not forthcoming, and debt-ridden, he went bankrupt. He was diagnosed with cancer, and he became despondent. In 1931, he wrote his autobiography Women Have Been Kind.

On October 29, 1934, while a guest in a Cudahy mansion, Tellegen locked front of a full-length mirror, he committed suicide by stabbing himself with a pair of sewing scissors.

The Real Housewives of Beverly Hills

At least 10 failed marriages, two bankruptcies, a foreclosure, and two deaths have occurred to cast members and family since the series began in 2006.

Russell Armstrong, cast member of Real Housewives, and ex-husband of Taylor Armstrong was discovered by Taylor at his Los Angeles home on August 17, 2011. Armstrong, 47, reportedly hanged himself. Armstrong was more than $1.5 million in debt as a result of trying to keep up with expectations for the lavish lifestyle portrayed on the show, his lawyer told ABCNews.com. "He wasn't a really wonderful guy," said Howard Bragman, a Hollywood publicist who represents two "Real Housewives of Beverly Hills" cast members. "And what the reality situation does is shine a lot of light on that and, if you have skeletons in your closet, they're going to come out and that's exactly what happened to him," Bragman said.

"These couples join these shows, and then they keep trying to outdo each other and they end up spending all their money trying to sustain a lifestyle that's unrealistic and wasn't there prior to the show," said Ronald Richards, Armstrong's attorney. "The weekly social events, the dinners and all the BS, trying to pretend you have unlimited resources in Beverly Hills is tough. When every night is a potential sound bite or posting on a website, you end up getting addicted to it, you go out all the time."

The $11 million bankruptcy filing of New Jersey housewife Teresa Guidice, another example, made headlines around the country as the shopping-obsessed star and her husband headed to court to try and keep their lavish mansion in one of the most exclusive towns in New Jersey. Now, the two are being prosecuted for bankruptcy fraud in New Jersey courts.

In 2009, Real Housewives cast member Kandi Burress lost her fiancé, A.J. Jewel, when he was struck in the head and killed by people fighting outside of an Atlanta nightclub.

* **Thelma Todd** (July 29, 1906 – December 16, 1935) American actress

Todd was born in Lawrence, Massachusetts. In her late teens, she began entering beauty pageants, and won the title of Miss Massachusetts in 1925. While representing her home state, she was spotted by a Hollywood talent scout and began her career in film.

Thelma Todd became highly regarded as a comedian, and she played opposite Wheeler & Woolsey, Buster Keaton, Joe E. Brown, and the Marx Brothers. She also appeared in such films as the 1931 film version of The Maltese Falcon. During her career she appeared in 119 movies."

In August 1934, she opened a successful cafe at Pacific Palisades, called Thelma Todd's Sidewalk Cafe

Todd continued her work in short-subject films through 1935, and was featured in the full-length Laurel and Hardy comedy The Bohemian Girl. This was her last film; she died after completing all of her scenes, but most of them were re-shot.

On the morning of Monday, December 16, 1935, Thelma Todd was found dead in her car inside the garage of Jewel Carmen, a former actress and former wife of Todd's lover and business partner, Roland West. Her death was determined to have been caused by carbon monoxide poisoning. The Grand Jury ruled her death as suicide. It was believed that she was the target of extortion, but refused to pay. It is also possible that she was locked in the garage by her assailant after she started the car. Blood from a wound was found on her face and dress, leading some to believe that she was knocked unconscious and placed in the car so that she would succumb to carbon monoxide poisoning.

Olive Thomas

(October 20, 1894 – September 10, 1920) American silent film actress

Thomas was born into a working class Irish American family in the Pittsburgh-area. Her father died in 1906 and she was forced to leave school at age 15 to help support her mother and two younger brothers

In 1914, after answering a newspaper ad, she won "The Most Beautiful Girl in New York City", a contest run by commercial artist Howard Chandler Christy. She then modeled for artist Harrison Fisher and landed on the cover of Saturday Evening Post.

Fisher wrote a letter of recommendation to Flo Ziegfeld resulting in Thomas being hired. She subsequently performed in the more risqué Midnight Frolic, a show staged after hours in the roof garden of the New Amsterdam Theatre. Before long, the attractive Thomas was the center of attention of the in-crowd. She soon found herself pursued by a number of wealthy men. She received expensive gifts from her admirers. It was said that the German Ambassador gave her a $10,000 string of pearls.

She posed nude for Peruvian artist Alberto Vargas, and signed with International Film Company as the leading lady in the Harry Fox movies. Thomas went on to appear in more than twenty Hollywood films over the next four years. In October 1916, Thomas moved to Triangle Pictures where she worked with Thomas Ince. Shortly after, news broke of her engagement to Jack Pickford, whom she had actually married a year prior

In December 1918, Thomas was persuaded by Myron Selznick to sign with Selznick Pictures Company. In 1920, Thomas once again played a teenager in the Frances Marion movie The Flapper.

Thomas was the first actress to be described by the term flapper, preceding the likes of Clara Bow, Louise Brooks, and Joan Crawford. She would go on to play the flapper role in her final film Everybody's Sweetheart.

On the night of September 5, 1920, the Pickfords went out for a night of entertainment and partying at the famous bistros in the Montparnasse Quarter of Paris. Returning to their room in the Hotel Ritz around 3:00 a.m., Pickford either fell asleep or was outside the room for a final round of drugs. It was rumored that Thomas may have taken cocaine that night though it was never proven. An intoxicated and tired Thomas accidentally ingested a large dose of a mercury bichloride liquid solution, which had been prescribed for her husband's chronic syphilis. Being liquid it was supposed to be applied topically, not ingested.

She had either thought the flask contained drinking water or sleeping pills; accounts vary. The label was in French which may have added to the confusion. She was taken to the American Hospital in the Paris suburb of Neuilly-sur-Seine, where Pickford remained at her side until she succumbed to the poison a few days later.

 **Hunter**

Stockton Thompson (July 18, 1937 –

February 20, 2005) American journalist and author.

Thompson was born in Louisville, Kentucky, to Jack Robert Thompson, and Virginia Ray Davison. On July 3, 1952, when Thompson was 14 years old, his father, aged 58, died of myasthenia gravis. Hunter and his brothers were raised by their mother. Virginia worked as a librarian to support her children, and is described as having become a "heavy drinker"

Charged as an accessory to robbery after being in a car with the robber, Thompson was sentenced to 60 days in Kentucky's Jefferson County Jail. He served 31 days and, a week after his release, enlisted in the United States Air Force.

Thompson completed basic training at Lackland Air Force Base in San Antonio, Texas, and transferred to Scott Air Force Base in Belleville, Illinois to study electronics. He applied to become an aviator, but was rejected by the Air Force's aviation-cadet program. In 1956, he transferred to Eglin Air Force Base near Fort Walton Beach, Florida. There he landed his first professional writing job as sports editor of the The Command Courier by lying about his job experience. Thompson traveled with the team around the United States, covering its games. In 1957, he also wrote a sports column anonymously for The Playground News, a local newspaper in Fort Walton Beach, Florida.

Thompson was discharged from the Air Force in June 1958 as an Airman First Class, having been recommended for an early honorable discharge by his commanding officer. "In summary, this airman, although talented, will not be guided by policy", Col. William S. Evans, chief of information services wrote to the Eglin personnel office. "Sometimes his rebel and superior attitude seems to rub off on other airmen staff members

After the Air Force, he worked as sports editor for a newspaper in Jersey Shore, Pennsylvania before relocating to New York City. There he attended the Columbia University School of General Studies part-time on the G.I. Bill, taking classes in creative writing.

During this time he worked briefly for Time, as a copy boy. While working, he used a typewriter to copy F. Scott Fitzgerald's The Great Gatsby and Ernest Hemingway's A Farewell to Arms in order to learn about the writing styles of the authors. In 1959, Time fired him for insubordination. Later that year, he worked as a reporter for The Middletown Daily Record in Middletown, New York. He was fired from this job after damaging an office candy machine and arguing with the owner of a local restaurant who happened to be an advertiser with the paper.

In 1960 Thompson moved to San Juan, Puerto Rico, to take a job with the sporting magazine El Sportivo, which folded soon after his arrival. After the demise of El Sportivo, Thompson worked as a stringer for the New York Herald Tribune and a few stateside papers. After returning to the States, Hunter hitchhiked across the United States along U.S. Hwy 40, eventually ending up in Big Sur, California working as a security guard and caretaker at the Big Sur hot springs for an eight-month period in 1961, just before it became the Esalen Institute. While there, he was able to publish his first magazine feature in the nationally distributed Rogue magazine on the artisan and bohemian culture of Big Sur. Thompson had had a rocky tenure as caretaker of the hot springs, and the unwanted publicity generated from the article finally got him fired.

During this period, Thompson wrote two novels, Prince Jellyfish and The Rum Diary, and submitted many short stories to publishers with little success. The Rum Diary, which fictionalized Thompson's experiences in Puerto Rico, was eventually published in 1998, long after Thompson had become famous.

From May 1962 to May 1963, Thompson traveled to South America as a correspondent for a Dow Jones-owned weekly newspaper, the National Observer. In Brazil, he spent several months working also as a reporter on the Brazil Herald, the country's only English-language daily, published in Rio de Janeiro. His longtime girlfriend Sandra Dawn Conklin (aka Sandy Conklin Thompson, now Sondi Wright) later joined him in Rio.

Thompson and Conklin were married on May 19, 1963, shortly after they returned to the United States. They briefly relocated to Aspen, Colorado, and had one son. Hunter and Sandy divorced in 1980 but remained close friends until Thompson's death.

In 1964 the Thompson family then moved to Glen Ellen, California, where Thompson continued to write for the National Observer on an array of domestic subjects, including a story about his 1964 visit to Ketchum, Idaho, in order to investigate the reasons for Ernest Hemingway's suicide. While working on the story, Thompson symbolically stole a pair of elk antlers hanging above the front door of Hemingway's cabin. Thompson and the editors at the Observer eventually had a falling out after the paper refused to print Thompson's review of Tom Wolfe's 1965 essay collection The Kandy-Kolored Tangerine-Flake Streamline Baby, and he moved to San Francisco, immersing himself in the drug and hippie culture that was taking root in the area. About this time he began writing for the Berkeley underground paper The Spyder.

In 1965, Carey McWilliams, editor of The Nation, offered Thompson the opportunity to write a story based on his experience with the California-based Hells Angels motorcycle club. After The Nation published the article, Thompson received several book offers and spent the next year living and riding with the Hell's Angels. The relationship broke down when the bikers concluded that Thompson was exploiting them for his personal gain. The gang demanded a share of the profits from his writings and after an argument at a party Thompson ended up with a savage beating, or "stomping" as the Angels referred to it. Random House published the hard cover Hell's Angels: The Strange and Terrible Saga of the Outlaw Motorcycle Gangs in 1966. A reviewer for The New York Times praised it as an "angry, knowledgeable, fascinating and excitedly written book", that shows the Hells Angels "not so much as dropouts from society but as total misfits, or unfits — emotionally, intellectually and educationally unfit to achieve the rewards, such as they are, that the contemporary social order offers." The reviewer also praised Thompson as a "spirited, witty, observant and original writer; his prose crackles like motorcycle exhaust."

Following the success of Hells Angels, Thompson was able to publish articles in a number of well-known magazines during the late 1960s, including The New York Times Magazine, Esquire, Pageant, and others. In the Times Magazine article, published in 1967, shortly before the "Summer of Love", and entitled "The Hashbury is the Capital of the Hippies", Thompson wrote in-depth about the Hippies of San Francisco, deriding a culture that began to lack the political convictions of the New Left and the artistic core of the Beats, instead becoming overrun with newcomers lacking any purpose other than obtaining drugs. It was an observation on the 1960s' counterculture that Thompson would further examine in Fear and Loathing in Las Vegas and other articles.

In late 1967, Thompson and his family moved back to Colorado and rented a house in Woody Creek, a small mountain hamlet outside Aspen. In early 1969, Thompson finally received a $15,000 royalty check for the paperback sales of Hells Angels and used two-thirds of the money for a down payment on a modest home and property where he would live for the rest of his life. He named the house Owl Farm and often described it as his "fortified compound."

In 1970, Thompson ran for sheriff of Pitkin County, Colorado, as part of a group of citizens running for local offices on the "Freak Power" ticket. The platform included promoting the decriminalization of drugs (for personal use only, not trafficking, as he disapproved of profiteering), tearing up the streets and turning them into grassy pedestrian malls, banning any building so tall as to obscure the view of the mountains, and renaming Aspen "Fat City" to deter investors. With polls showing him with a slight lead in a three-way race, Thompson appeared at Rolling Stone magazine headquarters in San Francisco with a six-pack of beer in hand and declared to editor Jann Wenner that he was about to be elected the next sheriff of Aspen, Colorado, and wished to write about the Freak Power movement. Thus, Thompson's first article in Rolling Stone was published as The Battle of Aspen with the byline "By: Dr. Hunter S. Thompson (Candidate for Sheriff)." Despite the publicity, Thompson ended up narrowly losing the election.

Thompson's first published use of the word Gonzo appears in a passage in Fear and Loathing in Las Vegas: "Free Enterprise. The American Dream. Horatio Alger gone mad on drugs in Las Vegas. Do it now: pure Gonzo journalism."

The book for which Thompson gained most of his fame had its genesis during the research for Strange Rumblings in Aztlan, an exposé for Rolling Stone on the 1970 killing of the Mexican-American television journalist Rubén Salazar. Salazar had been shot in the head at close range with a tear gas canister fired by officers of the Los Angeles County Sheriff's Department during the National Chicano Moratorium March against the Vietnam War. One of Thompson's sources for the story was Oscar Zeta Acosta, a prominent Mexican-American activist and attorney. Finding it difficult to talk in the racially tense atmosphere of Los Angeles, Thompson and Acosta decided to travel to Las Vegas, Nevada, and take advantage of an assignment by Sports Illustrated to write a 250-word photograph caption on the Mint 400 motorcycle race held there.

Thompson first submitted to Sports Illustrated a manuscript of 2,500 words, which was, as he later wrote, "aggressively rejected." Rolling Stone publisher Jann Wenner was said to have liked "the first 20 or so jangled pages enough to take it seriously on its own terms and tentatively scheduled it for publication — which gave me the push I needed to keep working on it", Thompson later wrote.

The result of the trip to Las Vegas became the 1971 book Fear and Loathing in Las Vegas which first appeared in the November 1971 issues of Rolling Stone as a two-part series. It is written as a first-person account by a journalist named Raoul Duke on a trip to Las Vegas with Dr. Gonzo, his "300-pound Samoan attorney", to cover a narcotics officers' convention and the "fabulous Mint 400". During the trip, Duke and his companion (always referred to as "my attorney") become sidetracked by a search for the American Dream, with "...two bags of grass, seventy-five pellets of mescaline, five sheets of high-powered blotter acid, a salt shaker half full of cocaine, and a whole galaxy of multi-colored uppers, downers, screamers, laughers [...] and also a quart of tequila, a quart of rum, a case of Budweiser, a pint of raw ether, and two dozen amyls." Duke i.e.Thompson soaked the floor mat on the driver's side with ether. He told his attorney, "There is nothing more helpless and irresponsible, and depraved than a man in the depths of an ether binge." Then they proceeded on their way.

Coming to terms with the failure of the 1960s countercultural movement is a major theme of the novel, and the book was greeted with considerable critical acclaim, including being heralded by The New York Times as "by far the best book yet written on the decade of dope". "The Vegas Book", as Thompson referred to it, was a mainstream success and introduced his Gonzo journalism techniques to a wide public.

Thompson went on to become a fierce critic of Nixon, both during and after his presidency. After Nixon's death in 1994, Thompson famously described him in Rolling Stone as a man who "could shake your hand and stab you in the back at the same time" and said "his casket [should] have been launched into one of those open-sewage canals that empty into the ocean just south of Los Angeles. He was a swine of a man and a jabbering dupe of a president. [He] was an evil man—evil in a way that only those who believe in the physical reality of the Devil can understand it." Following Nixon's pardon by Gerald Ford in 1974, Hunter ruminated on the approximately $400,000 pension Nixon maneuvered his way into by resigning before being formally indicted. While the Washington Post was lamenting Nixon's "lonely and depressed" state after being forced from the White House, Hunter wrote that '[i]f there were any such thing as true justice in this world, his [Nixon's] rancid carcass would be somewhere down around Easter Island right now, in the belly of a hammerhead shark.

Wenner then asked Thompson to travel to Vietnam to report on what appeared to be the closing of the Vietnam War. Thompson accepted, and left for Saigon immediately. He arrived with the country in chaos, just as the United States was preparing to evacuate and other journalists were scrambling to find transportation out of the region. While there, Thompson learned that Wenner had pulled the plug on this excursion, and Thompson found himself in Vietnam without health insurance or additional financial support. Thompson's story about the fall of Saigon would not be published in Rolling Stone until ten years later.

These two incidents severely strained the relationship between the author and the magazine, and Thompson contributed far less to the publication in later years.

The year 1980 marked both his divorce from Sandra Conklin and the release of Where the Buffalo Roam, a loose film adaptation of situations from Thompson's early 1970s work, with Bill Murray starring as the author. Murray would go on to become one of Thompson's trusted friends.

Thompson was named a Kentucky Colonel by the Governor of Kentucky in a December

Thompson's work was popularized again with the 1998 release of the film Fear and Loathing in Las Vegas, which opened to considerable fanfare. The book was reprinted to coincide with the film, and Thompson's work was introduced to a new generation of readers.

Soon thereafter, Thompson's "long lost" novel The Rum Diary was published, as were the first two volumes of his collected letters, which were greeted with critical acclaim.

Hunter married his longtime assistant, Anita Bejmuk, on April 23, 2003.

Thompson died at his "fortified compound" known as "Owl Farm" in Woody Creek, Colorado, at 5:42 p.m. on February 20, 2005, from a self-inflicted gunshot wound to the head.

On August 20, 2005, in a private ceremony, Thompson's ashes were fired from a cannon atop a 153-foot tower of his own design (in the shape of a double-thumbed fist clutching a peyote button - originally used in Hunter S. Thompson's 1970 campaign for sheriff of Aspen, Colorado. It has become a symbol of Thompson and gonzo journalism as a whole) to the tune of Norman Greenbaum's "Spirit in the Sky" and Bob Dylan's "Mr. Tambourine Man." Red, white, blue, and green fireworks were launched along with his ashes. As the city of Aspen would not allow the cannon to remain for more than a month, the cannon has been dismantled and put into storage until a suitable permanent location can be found. According to his widow Anita, Thompson's funeral was financed by actor Johnny Depp, a close friend of Thompson. Depp told the Associated Press, "All I'm doing is trying to make sure his last wish comes true. I just want to send my pal out the way he wants to go out."

Other famous attendees at the funeral included U.S. Senator John Kerry and former U.S. Senator George McGovern; 60 Minutes correspondents Ed Bradley and Charlie Rose; actors Jack Nicholson, Bill Murray, Benicio del Toro, Sean Penn, and Josh Hartnett; singers Lyle Lovett, John Oates and numerous other friends. An estimated 280 people attended the funeral.

Sammee Tong

(April 21, 1901 — October 27, 1964) American film and television character actor.

He appeared in more than thirty films and some forty television programs between 1935 and 1965. He first appeared as a waiter in Charlie Chan in Shanghai (1934), and later in Think Fast, Mr. Moto (1937). In 1956, Tong appeared in "Ah Sid, Cowboy", and in Edgar Buchanan's, Judge Roy Bean.

From 1957-1962, he appeared in Bachelor Father. At the time of his suicide, he had appeared in the Mickey sitcom on ABC starring Mickey Rooney. His final appearance was as Cook in the 1965 film Fluffy. He also appeared the Slaughter on Tenth Avenue (1957), and It's a Mad, Mad, Mad, Mad World (1963).

He committed suicide by drug overdose in 1964, aged 63.

Helen

Twelvetrees (December 25, 1908 - February 13, 1958) American stage and screen performer,

Born Helen Marie Jurgens in Brooklyn, New York, she was a graduate of the American Academy of Dramatic Arts, where she met her first husband, actor Clark Twelvetrees. She went to Hollywood to help replace the silent stars that could not or would not make the transition to talkies. Her first job was with Fox Film Corporation and she appeared in The Ghost Talks (1929).

After a mere three films with Fox, she was released from her contract. However, she was signed by Pathé shortly thereafter, and along with Constance Bennett and Ann Harding, Twelvetrees starred in several dramas.

She played opposite Spencer Tracy in 1934's Now I'll Tell; opposite Donald Cook in The Spanish Cape Mystery; and costarred in Paramount's A Bedtime Story with Maurice Chevalier. She also starred in two Metro-Goldwyn-Mayer films.

Twelvetrees left films in favor of summer stock in 1939 and made her Broadway debut in Jacques

Deval's Boudoir in 1941. The play folded after only eleven performances and she semi-retired to Middletown, Pennsylvania. She occasionally continued to act and successfully played the role of Blanche DuBois in A Streetcar Named Desire in summer stock in Sea Cliff, New.

On February 13, 1958, Twelvetrees committed suicide in Harrisburg, Pennsylvania by overdosing on drugs. She was 49 years old.

Woodbridge Strong Van Dyke, Jr. March 21, 1889 – February 5, 1943) American actor

Born in San Diego, California, Van Dyke was a child actor on the vaudeville circuit.. His first movie assignment in Hollywood was as an assistant director on the D. W. Griffith feature motion picture Intolerance (1916).

He received Academy Award for Best Director nominations for The Thin Man (1934) and San Francisco (1936).

His other films include White Shadows in the South Seas (1928) Trader Horn (1931), Tarzan the Ape Man (1932), Manhattan Melodrama (1934), and Marie Antoinette (1938). He is remembered for directing Myrna Loy and William Powell in four Thin Man films: The Thin Man (1934), After the Thin Man (1936), Another Thin Man (1939) and Shadow of the Thin Man (1941); and Jeanette MacDonald and Nelson Eddy in six of their greatest hits, Naughty Marietta (1935), Rose-Marie (1936), Sweethearts (1938), New Moon (1940), Bitter Sweet (1940) and I Married an Angel (1942).

Prior to World War II, Van Dyke set up a Marines recruiting center in his MGM office. He was one of the first Hollywood bigwigs to advocate early U.S. involvement, and he convinced stars like Clark Gable, James Stewart, Robert Taylor and Nelson Eddy to become involved in the war effort.

Ill with cancer and a bad heart, he directed one last film: Journey for Margaret, it was a heart-rending movie that made five-year old Margaret O'Brien an overnight star.

After finishing his last film he said his goodbyes to his wife, children and studio boss Louis B. Mayer, and committed suicide on February 5, 1943. in Brentwood, Los Angeles, California

Lupe Velez (July 18, 1908 – December 14, 1944) a Mexican film actress.

Vélez was born María Guadalupe Villalobos Vélez in the city of San Luis Potosí in Mexico. Lupe was educated at a convent school in Texas. From an early age, she had a strong temper and an explosive personality. She took dancing lessons and in 1924, made her performing debut at the Teatro Principal in Mexico City. In 1923 she moved to Texas, where she began dancing in vaudeville shows and finding work as a sales assistant. She moved to California, where she met the comedienne Fanny Brice, who promoted her career as a dancer. In 1924 she was first cast in movies by Hal Roach.

Vélez's first feature-length film was The Gaucho (1927) starring Douglas Fairbanks. She worked under film directors like Victor Fleming in The Wolf Song (1929) opposite Gary Cooper; D.W Griffith in Lady of the Pavements (1928); Tod Browning in Where East is East and Cecil B. de Mille in The Squaw Man in 1931.

Within a few years Vélez found her niche in comedies, playing beautiful but volatile foils to comedy stars. Her slapstick battle with Laurel and Hardy in Hollywood Party and her dynamic presence opposite Jimmy Durante in Palooka (both 1934) are typically enthusiastic Vélez performances.

Vélez was now nearing 30 and she left Hollywood for Broadway. In New York, she landed a role in You Never Know. After the run of You Never Know, Vélez returned to Hollywood in 1939, where she landed the lead in, The Girl from Mexico.

She established such a rapport with co-star Leon Errol that RKO made a quick sequel, Mexican Spitfire.

The Spitfire films rejuvenated Lupe Vélez's career, and for the next few years she starred in musical and comedy features for RKO, Universal Pictures, and Columbia Pictures. In one of her last films, Columbia's Redhead from Manhattan, she played a dual role: one in her exaggerated comic dialect, and the other in her actual speaking voice, which was surprisingly fluid and had only traces of a Mexican accent.

In the mid-1940s, she had a relationship with the young actor Harald Maresch, and became pregnant with his child. Unable to face the shame of giving birth to an illegitimate child, she decided to take her own life. Her alleged suicide note read, "To Harald: May God forgive you and forgive me, too; but I prefer to take my life away and our baby's, before I bring him with shame, or killing him. Lupe." She retired to bed after taking an overdose of sleeping pills. According to newspaper accounts, her body was found by her secretary and companion of ten years, Beulah Kinder, on her bed surrounded by flowers, as she had wished.

Herve Villechaize

(April 23, 1942 – September 4, 1993) French actor.

Villechaize was born in Paris, France. He also had Filipino ancestry. After studying art at Beaux-Arts college, he left for the USA in 1964. He settled in a Bohemian section in New York, taught himself English by watching television, and continued his career as an artist, painter, and photographer. He began acting in Off Broadway productions, including The Young Master and a play by Sam Shepard, and he also did some modeling for National Lampoon, before moving on to film. Villechaize suffered from dwarfism due to a thyroid dysfunction. His first movie appearance was in Chappaqua, which was followed by Crazy Joe, Oliver Stone's first film, Seizure, The Gang That Couldn't Shoot Straight, and The Forbidden Zone. He was so poor he was living out of his car in Los Angeles when he was cast in The Man with the Golden Gun in 1974.

Prior to being signed up he made ends meet by working as a rat catcher's assistant.

Villechaize was a difficult actor on Fantasy Island. He continually propositioned women and quarrelled with the producers. He was fired after demanding a salary equal to that of co-star Ricardo Montalbán. The show's popularity waned after this move, and it was soon cancelled. According to his former butler, Villechaize never got over losing his job, and for the remainder of his life practiced an often nightly ritual of drinking in a darkened room while screaming obscenities at an episode of Fantasy Island playing on his television.

He starred in the 1980 cult classic movie Forbidden Zone.

He made his final appearance in a cameo as himself in an episode of The Ben Stiller Show.

Villechaize began to abuse alcohol and suffered from clinical depression in the last few years of his life. This led to erratic and sometimes violent behavior, including an incident in which he allegedly held his agent at gunpoint in a booth at a restaurant in Los Angeles.

In the early morning hours of September 4, 1993, Villechaize shot himself at his home. Villechaize left a suicide note saying he was despondent over longtime health problems.

Gary Vinson

(October 22, 1936 – October 15, 1984) American actor

Born in Los Angeles, Vinson began acting in 1957, working as a. guest star on various television series including Perry Mason, Gunsmoke, ,The Adventures of Ozzie and Harriet, Bat Masterson, Harbor Command, and The Rough Riders. In 1960, Vinson was cast as copy-boy Chris Higbee in thirty-nine episodes of ABC's The Roaring 20's.

That same year, Vinson appeared on McHale's Navy, starring Ernest Borgnine. Vinson worked in seventy-nine episodes from 1962 to 1966, when the series ended. After McHale's Navy, Vinson was cast as Sheriff Harold Sikes in CBS's Pistols 'n' Petticoats.

In 1968, he starred in the film Nobody's Perfect. The following year he guest starred on The Virginian, and The F.B.I..

During the 1970s and 1980s, Vinson continued with guest roles in various shows. He made his last on-screen appearance in a 1982 episode of The Incredible Hulk.

On October 15, 1984, Vinson committed suicide in Redondo Beach. He was 47 years old.

Marie Walcamp

(July 27, 1894 — November 17, 1936) was an American actress of the silent movie era.

Born in Dennison, Ohio, Walcamp headed to the East Coast in search of acting jobs on the stage after she finished her formal education. After landing various roles in New York, she eventually landed a role in 1913's The Werewolf when she was 19 years old. Walcamp would not appear in another picture until Coral in 1915.

The following year would be the busiest of her film career when she appeared in four productions including a role in Liberty (1916). By the mid 1920s, Walcamp appeared in only five features, her final film being In a Moment of Temptation in 1927. She had appeared in 107 films between 1913 and 1927.

On November 17, 1936, Walcamp committed suicide from an overdose of medication. She was 42 years old.

* # Robert Walker

(actor) (October 13, 1918) – (August 28, 1951)

Born in Salt Lake City, Utah, to Zella and Horace Walker, he was the youngest of four sons. Emotionally scarred by his parents' divorce when he was still a child, he subsequently developed an interest in acting .

While attending the AADA, Walker met fellow aspiring actress Phylis Isley, who later became the film star Jennifer Jones. After a brief courtship, the couple were married in Tulsa, Oklahoma on January 2, 1939 and moved to Hollywood to find work in films. Their prospects proved to be poor and they returned to New York. Walker soon found work in radio while Phylis stayed home and gave birth to two sons in quick succession, actor Robert Walker, Jr., born April 15, 1940, and Michael Walker, born March 13, 1941. Phylis then returned to auditioning where her luck changed when she was discovered in 1941 by producer David O. Selznick, who changed her name to Jennifer Jones. During their initial meetings Selznick was highly attracted to Jones and they began an affair. She eventually landed the plum role of Bernadette Soubirous in the Twentieth Century Fox production The Song of Bernadette (1943).

The couple returned to Hollywood, and Selznick's connections helped Walker secure a contract with Metro-Goldwyn-Mayer, where he started work on the war drama Bataan (1943). Walker's charming demeanor and boyish good looks caught on with audiences, and he worked steadily. He also appeared in Selznick's Since You Went Away (1944) in which he and his wife portrayed doomed young lovers. By that time Selznick and Jones' affair was common knowledge, and Jones and Walker separated in November 1943, in the midst of production. The filming of their love scenes was torturous as Selznick insisted that Walker perform take after take of each love scene with Jones. She filed for divorce in April 1945.

That year, Walker starred in the film The Clock opposite Judy Garland in her first straight dramatic film. Although Walker continued to work steadily in Hollywood, he was distraught over the divorce and was soon prone to drinking, emotional outbursts and eventually, a nervous breakdown. He spent time at the Menninger Clinic in 1949 where he was treated for a psychiatric disorder.

Following his discharge from the Menninger Clinic, he was cast by Alfred Hitchcock for Strangers on a Train (1951). His performance as the psychopathic homosexual Bruno Anthony was considered to be his finest role.

His final film role was in the title role of anti-Communist film, My Son John (1952).

On the night of August 28, 1951, Walker's housekeeper found him in an emotional state. She called his psychiatrist, who arrived and administered sodium amytal to Walker in an effort to calm him down. Walker suffered an acute allergic reaction to the drug, and stopped breathing. All efforts to resuscitate him failed. Walker was 32 years old.

Keith Wayne

(January 16, 1945 — September 9, 1995), born Ronald Keith Hartman American actor.

Known for his (only) role as Tom in the George A. Romero film Night of the Living Dead (1968). Following the completion of the film, he worked as a singer for a number of years with The Bill Roberts Show, and others, and then became a chiropractor.

Wayne was born in Washington, Pennsylvania. He graduated from Mansfield University in Mansfield, PA, where he majored in music and was a fixture in university theatrical productions. During his college career he led an extremely popular dance band, Ronnie and the Jestors.

He committed suicide on September 9, 1995, in Cary, North Carolina.

Doodles Weaver

(May 11, 1912 – Jan 13, 1983 American actor

Weaver began his career in the 1940s as a comedian on radio and touring with the Spike Jones Music Revue. In 1951, he broke into television with NBC's "The Doodles Weaver Show" going on to appear in on TV shows Batman, Land of the Giants, Dragnet, The Andy Griffith Show and The Monkees. He appeared in more than 90 films, including The Great Imposter (1961), The Birds (1963), The Nutty Professor (1963) and Under the Rainbow (1981). He was the uncle of actress Sigourney Weaver.

The older he got, the bitterer he became. 1948, when he issued his novelty tunes with Spike, was probably his' best year. 1983 would be his worst...in fact, despite of or because of alcohol and pills, be couldn't stand to live more than a few weeks into 1983.

Weaver committed suicide on Jan 13, 1983.

Richard Webb

(September 9, 1915 – June 19, 1993) film, television and radio actor.

He appeared in more than fifty films, including Out of the Past (1947), Night Has a Thousand Eyes (1948), I Was a Communist for the FBI (1951) and Carson City (1952). Today, he may be best remembered as the star of the 1950s TV series Captain Midnight. In 1954, Webb played the notorious gunfighter John Wesley Hardin in an episode of Jim Davis's Stories of the Century. Webb played Lieutenant Commander Ben Finney on Star Trek: The Original Series — "Court Martial"

In 1958, he guest starred as agent James Foster in Bruce Gordon's Behind Closed Doors.

In 1959, he appeared as the fictitious Don Jagger, the deputy chief of the United States Border Patrol in the Border Patrol.

He committed suicide in Van Nuys, California.

Deborah "Debbie" Weems (February 3, 1951 - February 22, 1978) was

an American actress and singer.

Weems was born in Houston, Texas. During childhood her parents separated and each remarried. The family later relocated to Marlin, a town northwest of Houston.

During the 1960s, Weems attended the Interlochen Arts Academy in Michigan. She played a lead role in productions such as Annie Get Your Gun, The King and I, and The Miracle Worker, as well as smaller roles in many other productions. She also attended the Boston Conservatory of Music for two years ('68/'70) where she captured leading roles in two major productions - Carnival and Once Upon A Mattress. Weems later moved to New York City, where she appeared in an Off Broadway musical, Godspell. Weems was also a regular stock player at the Lakewood Theatre in Barnesville, Pennsylvania during 1970. Weems also appeared in various commercials.

From 1973 to 1977, Weems appeared as a regular on Captain Kangaroo. In 1976, songs from the television series sung by Weems were released on an album, Debbie Weems Sings Songs from Captain Kangaroo, published by Wonderland Records.

Weems' only other role during this time was in the 1977 movie, Between the Lines where she played a small role of "Annie One". Shortly before her death, Weems was admitted to a residential treatment facility.

Weems died on February 22, 1978, falling from the 16th floor of her apartment building. Her death has been considered a suicide.

Dick Wesson

(February 20, 1919-January 27, 1979) was an American movie and television announcer.

Wesson started in radio and worked as an announcer on early television shows like Space Patrol. On the live television special covering the opening of Disneyland, Wesson appeared as the captain of the Rocket To The Moon ride and was interviewed by Art Linkletter and Danny Thomas. He occasionally did some acting, including appearances in the Golden Horseshoe Revue show at Disneyland.

Wesson did the narration for many movie trailers, Disney and non-Disney, as well as the opening announcements for such television series as Hawaiian Eye, The Fugitive, and The Invaders.

Dick Wesson committed suicide on January 27, 1979, aged 59. He had been battling cancer.

*

James Whale (22

July 1889 – 29 May 1957) English film director, theatre director and actor.

Whale was born in Dudley, England. He attended Kates Hill Board School, followed by Bayliss Charity School and finally Dudley Blue Coat School.

World War I broke out in 1914. Although Whale had little interest in the politics behind the war, he realized that conscription was inevitable so he enlisted in the Army. Considered because of his age a good candidate for officer training, Whale joined the "Inns of Court" cadet corps in October 1915 and was stationed in Bristol. He was commissioned as a second lieutenant in the Worcestershire Regiment in July 1916.[5] He was taken a prisoner of war during the course of the Flanders Campaign in August 1917 and was housed at the Holzminden prison camp.[6] Whale was held for two years.

In 1919 Whale embarked on a professional stage career. Under the tutelage of actor-manager Nigel Playfair, Whale worked as an actor, set designer and builder, and director.

In 1922, while with Playfair, Whale met Doris Zinkeisen. The two were considered a couple for some two years, despite Whale's living as an openly gay man. The couple was reportedly engaged in 1924 but by 1925 the engagement was off.

Whale traveled to Hollywood in 1929 and signed a contract with Paramount Pictures. He was assigned as "dialogue director" for a film called The Love Doctor (1929). Whale completed work on the film in 15 days and his contract was allowed to expire. It was at around this time that Whale met David Lewis.

Whale next went to work for independent film producer and aviation pioneer Howard Hughes, who planned to turn the previously-silent production Hell's Angels (1930) into a talkie. Hughes hired Whale to direct the dialogue sequences. With work completed, Whale headed to Chicago to direct another company of Journey's End.

Universal Studios signed Whale to a five-year contract in 1931 and his first project was Waterloo Bridge

In 1931, Universal chief Carl Laemmle, Jr. offered Whale his choice of any property the studio owned. Whale chose Frankenstein. Casting Colin Clive as Henry Frankenstein and Mae Clarke as his fiancée Elizabeth, Whale turned to an unknown actor named Boris Karloff to play the Monster. Shooting began on 24 August 1931 and wrapped on 3 October. Reviews were held 29 October with wide release on 21 November. Frankenstein was an instant hit with critics and the public. It is one of only a few of Whale's films that has remained in the public eye and is regarded as a classic of the horror genre.

Next from Whale were Impatient Maiden and The Old Dark House, both in 1932. The Old Dark House is credited with reinventing the "dark house" subgenre of horror films.

Whale's next film was The Kiss Before the Mirror (1933), a critical success but a box office failure. Whale next turned his attention to The Invisible Man (1933). Shot from a script approved by H. G. Wells the film was a blend of horror, humor and confounding visual effects. The film was critically acclaimed, with The New York Times listing it as one of the

Bride of Frankenstein was Whale's next project. Whale had long resisted doing a sequel to Frankenstein as he feared being pigeonholed as a horror director. Bride hearkened back to an episode from Mary Shelley's original novel in which the Monster promises to leave Frankenstein and humanity alone if Frankenstein makes him a mate. He does, but then destroys the female without bringing it to life. The film was a critical success and a box office sensation, having earned some $2 million for Universal by 1943. Lauded as "the finest of all gothic horror movies", Bride is frequently hailed as Whale's masterpiece.

Whale immediately went to work on Show Boat (1936). Whale gathered as many of those as he could who had been involved in one production or another of the musical, including Helen Morgan, Paul Robeson and a reluctant Irene Dunne, who believed that Whale was the wrong director for the piece. The 1936 Show Boat is considered the definitive film version of the musical, but became unavailable following the 1951 remake

Whale's career went into sharp decline following the release of his next film, The Road Back (1937). The sequel to Erich Maria Remarque's All Quiet on the Western Front, which Universal had filmed in 1930, the novel and film follow the lives of several young German men who have returned from the trenches of World War I and their struggles to re-integrate into society.

With the outbreak of World War II, Whale volunteered his services to make a training film for the United States Army. Whale shot the film, called Personnel Placement in the Army, in February 1942.

Whale directed his final film in 1950, a short subject based on the William Saroyan one-act play Hello Out There. The film, financed by supermarket heir Huntington Hartford, was the story of a man in a Texas jail falsely accused of rape and the woman who cleans the jail. Hartford intended for the short to be part of an anthology film along the lines of Quartet.[74] However, attempts to find appropriate short fiction companion pieces to adapt were unsuccessful and Hello Out There was never commercially released.[75]

Whale's last professional engagement was directing Pagan in the Parlour, a farce about two New England spinster sisters who are visited by a Polynesian whom their father, when shipwrecked years earlier, had married. The production was mounted in Pasadena for two weeks in 1951. Plans were made to take it to New York, but Whale suggested taking the play to London first. While visiting Harrington in Paris, Whale went to some gay bars. At one he met a 25-year-old bartender named Pierre Foegel, who Harrington believed was nothing but "a hustler out for what he could get". The 62-year-old Whale was smitten with the younger man and hired him as his chauffeur.

Whale returned to California in November 1952 and advised David Lewis that he planned to bring Foegel over early the following year. Appalled, Lewis moved out of their home. While this ended their 23-year romantic relationship, the two men remained friends. Lewis bought a small house and dug a swimming pool, prompting Whale to have his own pool dug, although he did not himself swim in it. Whale began throwing all-male swim parties and would watch the young men cavort in and around the pool. Foegel moved in with Whale in early 1953 and remained there for several months before returning to France. He returned in 1954 permanently and Whale installed him as manager of a gas station that he owned. Whale and Foegel settled into a quiet routine until the spring of 1956, when Whale suffered a small stroke. A few months later he suffered a larger stroke and was hospitalized. While in the hospital he was treated for depression with shock treatments.

Upon his release, Whale hired one of the male nurses from the hospital to be his personal live-in nurse. A jealous Foegel maneuvered the nurse out of the house and hired a female nurse as a non live-in replacement. Whale suffered from mood swings and grew increasingly and frustratingly more dependent on others and his mental faculties were diminishing. Whale committed suicide by drowning himself in his swimming pool on 29 May 1957 at the age of 67.[86] He left a suicide note, which Lewis withheld until shortly before his own death decades later. Because the note was suppressed, the death was initially ruled accidental.

James Whale lived as an openly gay man throughout his career in the British theatre and in Hollywood, something that was unheard of in the 1920s and 1930s. He and David Lewis lived together as a couple from around 1930 to 1952.

Sue   Williams

(November 14, 1945 – September 2, 1969) was an American actress

Born Karen Susan Hamilton in Glendale, California, she began her career in modeling shortly after graduating from high school. After a photographer sent in pictures he had taken of her to Playboy, she was chosen for a layout in the magazine, posing under the name Sue Williams.

At 4'11, she was one of the shortest women to appear as a Playmate in Playboy.

After appearing in Playboy, she began acting in various films and television. She appeared in several Beach Party films, including How to Stuff a Wild Bikini under the name Sue Hamilton.

Williams committed suicide on September 2, 1969.

De'Angelo Wilson

(March 29, 1979 — November 26, 2008) was an American film and television actor; he was also a hip-hop artist.

He was born De'Angelo Ke'Shine Hill Wilson in Dayton, Ohio. He attended Kent State University, in Kent, Ohio, where he studied acting.

Wilson appeared in four films including 8 Mile (2002) and Antwone Fisher (2002).

Wilson was found hanged in the back room of a commercial building in Los Angeles, California; his death was ruled a suicide. His mother stated that her son became depressed, believing that his career was failing.

* **Dennis Carl Wilson** (December 4, 1944 – December 28, 1983) was an American rock and roll musician.

In 1974 concurrent with the success of the '60s hits compilation Endless Summer, Wilson returned to his role behind the drums. According to Dennis's biographer, Jon Stebbins, it was this year that he co-wrote the lyrics and modified part of the melody of "You Are So Beautiful" at a party with Billy Preston.

In 1968 Dennis Wilson was driving through Malibu when he noticed two female hitchhikers. He picked them up and dropped them off at their destination.[2] Later on Wilson noticed the same two girls hitchhiking again. This time he took them to his home at 14400 Sunset Boulevard near Will Rogers Park. Wilson then went to a recording session. When he returned at around 3 a.m., he was met in his driveway by a stranger, Charles Manson. When he walked into his home, there were about a dozen people occupying the premises, most of them female. Wilson became fascinated by Manson and his followers; the "Manson Family" lived with Wilson for a period of time afterwards at his expense.

Initially impressed by Manson's songwriting talent, Wilson introduced him to a few friends in the music business, including Terry Melcher, whose home on Cielo Drive would later be rented by director Roman Polanski and his wife, actress Sharon Tate. Tate and several others would later be murdered at the home by Manson "family members." Recording sessions for Manson were held at Brian Wilson's home studio. Those recordings, if they exist, have never been released. The Beach Boys released a Manson song, originally titled "Cease To Exist" but reworked as "Never Learn Not To Love," as a single B-side and on the album 20/20.

As Wilson became increasingly aware of Manson's volatile nature and growing tendency to violence, he finally made a break from the friendship by simply moving out of the house and leaving Manson there. When Manson subsequently sought further contact (and money), he left a bullet with Wilson's housekeeper to be delivered with a cryptic message, which was perceived by Wilson as a threat.

In August 1969 the Tate/LaBianca murders occurred. He rarely discussed his involvement with the Manson Family, and he usually became upset when the subject was broached. He was upset in regard to Charles Manson and his "family" and did mention that he felt it was his "fault" for introducing him to the music world.

Dennis Wilson starred alongside James Taylor and Warren Oates in the critically acclaimed film Two-Lane Blacktop (1971) as "The Mechanic." It depicts "The Driver" (Taylor) and "The Mechanic" driving aimlessly across the United States in their '55 Chevy surviving on money made by street drag-racing.

On December 4, 1970, Wilson released his first piece of solo material, a little known single released under the name "Dennis Wilson & Rumbo." The single featured "Sound of Free" on the A-side with "Lady" (also known as "Fallin' In Love") on the B-side. The song was later covered by American Spring and released as the B-side to their single "Shyin' Away."

Wilson released his debut solo album Pacific Ocean Blue in 1977. His collaborators on the album included (the 'Captain' of Captain & Tennille) and. The album peaked at #96 in the U.S. and sold around 300,000 copies, matching that year's Beach Boys album Love You. Dates were booked for a Dennis Wilson solo tour but these were ultimately cancelled. However, Wilson did occasionally perform his solo material on the 1977 Beach Boys tour. Despite Wilson himself claiming the album had "no substance," Pacific Ocean Blue performed well critically and continues to maintain a cult following. Wilson's trademark gravelly and melancholy vocals resonate throughout the work. The album was out of print and difficult to obtain for more than a decade, but it has been reissued as of June 2008. The expanded Sony Legacy edition of Pacific Ocean Blue was voted the 2008 Reissue of the Year in both Rolling Stone and Mojo magazines and made #16 on the British LP charts and #8 and both the Billboard Catalog chart and the Billboard Internet Sales chart.

Pacific Ocean Blue's follow-up, Bambu, began production in the year 1978 at Brother Studios in Santa Monica with the collaboration of then Beach Boys keyboardist and Dennis's close friend Carli Muñoz as songwriter and producer. The first four songs that were officially recorded for Bambu were Muñoz's compositions: "It's Not Too Late," "Constant Companion," "All Alone," and "Under The Moonlight"; they appear on the final 2008 release. The project was initially scuttled by lack of financing and the distractions of simultaneous Beach Boys projects. Bambu was officially released in 2008 along with the Pacific Ocean Blue reissue.

Two songs from the Bambu sessions, "Love Surrounds Me" and "Baby Blue," were lifted for the Beach Boys' 1979 L.A. (Light Album). Wilson and brother Brian also recorded together apart from the Beach Boys in 1980 and 1981. These sessions remain unreleased though widely bootlegged.

At the time of his death, he was married to Shawn Marie Love (allegedly an illegitimate child of cousin and fellow Beach Boy Mike Love), with whom he had a son, Gage Dennis Wilson (born September 3, 1982). Shawn Wilson died after a 15-year battle with cancer shortly after Gage's 21st birthday. The relationship had caused a rift between the two Beach Boys.

Wilson's previous marriages were to Carole Freedman, with whom he had a daughter, Jennifer (born December 21, 1966) and whose son, Scott, he adopted, and Barbara Charren, with whom he had two sons, Michael (born February 19, 1971) and Carl (born December 31, 1972). Wilson also was married twice to Karen Lamm, the ex-wife of Chicago keyboardist Robert Lamm, once in 1976 and again in 1978. Wilson was quoted in the sleeve notes for the album All Summer Long: They say I live a fast life. Maybe I just like a fast life. I wouldn't give it up for anything in the world. It won't last forever, either. But the memories will.

Dennis also had a significant relationship with Christine McVie from 1979 to 1981. Christine ended the relationship after she could no longer cope with his alcohol addiction.

Succeeding years saw Wilson battling alcohol abuse. Smoking and drugs also had taken a toll on his vocal cords, although the resultant gravelly effect helped define him as a singer. On December 28, 1983, shortly after his 39th birthday, Wilson drowned at Marina Del Rey, Los Angeles, after drinking all day.

On January 4, 1984, he was buried at sea off the California coast by the U.S. Coast Guard. His song "Farewell My Friend" was played at the funeral.

Grant Withers

(January 17, 1905 – March 27, 1959) American actor

He worked as an oil company salesman and newspaper reporter before breaking into movies near the end of the silent era. His more than 30-year acting career took off in the late 1920s, Taller than John Wayne and just as tough, it was his early roles for Warner Bros. that brought him his greatest fame.

Starring roles in major pictures later dwindled to supporting parts, mainly as villains in B-movies and serials. Notable exceptions included a 12-part Jungle Jim movie serial (1937), starring Withers and released by Universal Pictures, and the recurring role of the brash police Captain Bill Street in the Monogram Pictures series Mr. Wong.

Withers' film credits at Republic total about 60 films from 1937 to 1957. All told he appeared in more than two hundred films.

In 1930, at twenty-six, his elopement to Yuma, Arizona, with a 17-year-old Loretta Young was widely reported and ended in annulment in 1931, just as their second movie together, ironically titled Too Young to Marry, was released. Some of Withers' later screen appearances were arranged through the help of his friends John Ford and John Wayne. He appeared in nine movies with John Wayne, including Fort Apache (1948) and Rio Grande (1950).

Withers worked up until his suicide in 1959, at the age of 54, when he died from an overdose of barbiturates

Kim Winona (October 10, 1930 — June 23, 1978) was a Native American actress

A Sioux Native American, Winona appeared in the CBS western television series Brave Eagle during 1955-1956 season.

Born in Nebraska as Constance Elaine Mackey, Winona was 25 years old when she landed the role of Morning Star. A Roy Rogers production, Brave Eagle was the first series to present events from the view of the Native Indian.

Winona died in June 1978 at the age of 47, reportedly at her own hand.

 **Walter Wolff** (May 11, 1928 —December 12, 1971)

A native of San Francisco, Frank Wolff was the son of a Bay area physician. The elder Wolff, a political and social maverick, encouraged young Frank to follow an unconventional path. Frank attended UCLA, where he studied acting and stagecraft, wrote and directed. Between 1957 and 1961, he appeared in twenty episodes of TV series and feature films.

Frank Wolff had bit roles in his first two films, Roger Corman's I Mobster and The Wasp Woman. Later in the year, Wolff's billing increased to co-lead status in his next two Corman productions. The first of the two, Beast, remains a well-remembered low-budget horror title. In contrast, the equally poverty-budgeted Attack, on which Corman himself took over the directorial reins, turned out to be a little-noticed World War II quickie in which a quartet of GIs on skis slog through a snowbound landscape. On Corman's advice, Frank Wolff remained in Europe and became a well-known character actor in over fifty, mostly Italian-made, films of the 1960s, including crime/suspense "gialli" and spaghetti westerns.

Frank Wolff killed himself in his Rome hotel room at the age of 43. His final two Italian-made films, Milan Caliber 9 and When Women Lost Their Tails were released posthumously in 1972.

Natalie Wood (July 20, 1938 – November 29, 1981) American actress.

Born Natalia Nikolaevna Zakharenko in San Francisco, to Russian immigrant parents. Her father was born in Vladivostok and he immigrated to Montreal, Canada and later to San Francisco where he worked as a day laborer and carpenter. Her paternal grandfather Stepan worked in a chocolate factory in Russia and was killed in street fighting between Red and White Russian soldiers in 1918. Natalie's mother originally came from Siberia, but grew up in China.

Her mother would take Natalie to the movies as often as she could. Her only professional training was watching Hollywood child stars.

Natalie said her mother used to tell her that the cameraman who pointed his lens out at the audience at the end of the Paramount newsreel was taking my picture. I'd pose and smile like he was going to make me famous or something. I believed everything my mother told me.

Shortly after her birth in San Francisco, her family moved to nearby Sonoma County, and lived in Santa Rosa, California, where Wood was noticed during a film shoot in downtown Santa Rosa. Her mother then moved the family to Los Angeles and pursued a career for her daughter. Wood made her film debut a few weeks before turning five, in a fifteen-second scene in the film Happy Land (1943). Wood, at seven years old, got the part of a German orphan opposite Orson Welles and Claudette Colbert in Tomorrow Is Forever. Welles later said that Wood was a born professional, "so good, she was terrifying". Her mother signed her to a role with 20th Century Fox studio for her first major role, the Christmas classic Miracle on 34th Street (1947), which made her one of the top child stars in Hollywood. She would eventually appear in over 20 films as a child, appearing opposite such stars as Gene Tierney, James Stewart, Maureen O'Hara, Bette Davis and Bing Crosby.

Wood successfully made the transition from child star to ingénue at age 16 when she co-starred with James Dean and Sal Mineo in Rebel Without a Cause. She followed this with a small but crucial role in John Ford's western The Searchers which starred John Wayne and also featured Wood's sister, Lana, who played a younger version of her character in the film's earlier scenes. Although many of Wood's films were commercially profitable, her acting was criticized at times. In 1966 she won the Harvard Lampoon Worst Actress of the Year Award. She was the first performer in the award's history to accept it in person and the Harvard Crimson wrote she was "quite a good sport." Other notable films she starred in were Inside Daisy Clover (1965) and This Property Is Condemned (1966).

After three years away from acting, Wood played a swinger in Bob & Carol & Ted & Alice (1969). After becoming pregnant with her first child in 1970, she went into semi-retirement and only acted in four more theatrical films during the remainder of her life. She appeared as herself in The Candidate (1972. She also reunited on the screen with Robert Wagner in The Affair (1973), a television adaptation of Cat on a Hot Tin Roof (1976) and made cameo appearances on his shows Switch in 1978 as "Bubble Bath Girl" and Hart to Hart in 1979 as "Movie Star". At the time of her death, Wood was filming the sci-fi film Brainstorm

(1983), co-starring Christopher Walken. Due to her untimely death, the ending of Brainstorm had to be re-written.

Natalie Wood's two marriages to actor Robert Wagner were highly publicized. Wood said she had a crush on Wagner since she was a child and on her 18th birthday she went on a studio-arranged date with the 26-year old actor. They married a year later on December 28, 1957.

Wood and Wagner separated in June 1961 and divorced in April 1962.

On May 30, 1969, Wood married British producer Richard Gregson. The couple dated for two and a half years prior to their marriage, while Gregson waited for his divorce to be finalized. They separated in August 1971 after Wood overheard an inappropriate telephone conversation between her secretary and Gregson. She filed for divorce, and it was finalized in April 1972.

In early 1972, Wood resumed her relationship with Wagner. The couple remarried on July 16, 1972, just five months after reconciling and only three months after she divorced Gregson. Their daughter, Courtney Wagner, was born on March 9, 1974. They remained married until Wood's death seven years later on November 29, 1981.

Biographer Suzanne Finstad writes that Wood had a relationship with director Nicholas Ray, director of Rebel Without a Cause, when she was 16 and he was 43. During her teens, Wood went on studio-arranged dates with older men, including actors Tab Hunter and Nick Adams, and dated actor Raymond Burr, when she was 17 and he was 38. Wood also dated actors Michael Caine, Steve McQueen, Warren Beatty and Dennis Hopper, singer Elvis Presley, director Henry Jaglom, and politician Jerry Brown.

The day after Thanksgiving, Wood, Wagner and Walken went to Catalina Island for the weekend. On Saturday night, November 28, the Wagners' yacht was anchored in Isthmus Cove. Also on board was the boat's skipper, Dennis Davern, who had worked for the couple for many years. The official theory is that Wood either tried to leave the yacht or to secure a dinghy from banging against the hull when she accidentally slipped and fell overboard. When her body was found, she was wearing a down jacket, nightgown, and socks. A woman on a nearby yacht said she heard calls for help at around midnight. The cries lasted for about 15 minutes and were answered by someone else who said, "Take it easy. We'll be over to get you". "It was laid back", the witness recalled. "There was no urgency or immediacy in their shouts". There was much partying going on in the area, though, and while it has never been proven that the woman calling for help was, indeed, Natalie Wood, no other person ever has been identified or come forward as having called out for help on that night. An investigation by Los Angeles County coroner Thomas Noguchi resulted in an official verdict of accidental drowning. Noguchi concluded Wood had drunk "seven or eight" glasses of wine and was intoxicated when she died. Noguchi also wrote that he found Wood's fingernail scratches on the side of the rubber dinghy indicating she was trying to get in. Wood was 43 at the time of her death.

Ralph Yearsley

(October 6, 1896 - December 4, 1928) English/American actor

Born in London, England, he attended medical school, and then went to the United States to pursue a career in the film industry. He made his motion picture debut in 1921 in a secondary but good role in the Samuel Goldwyn Productions silent film comedy 'Pardon My French'. That same year he appeared as Saul "Little Buzzard" Hatburn in 'Tol'able David' directed by Henry King. Over the next eight years, Yearsley appeared in another twenty films, in secondary or minor roles. One of his more notable roles was in Harold Lloyd's 1927 film 'The Kid Brother'.

In 1928, Ralph Yearsley committed suicide.

Gig Young

(November 4, 1913 – October 19, 1978) American actor.

Was born Byron Elsworth Barr in St. Cloud, Minnesota, and grew up in Washington D.C. He received a scholarship to the Pasadena Community Playhouse. While acting in Pancho he was spotted by a Warner Brothers talent scout, and signed to a supporting player contract with the studio. Young appeared in supporting roles in many films during the 1940s, and came to be regarded as a popular second lead. Young enlisted in the United States Coast Guard in 1941 where he served as a pharmacist's mate until the end of World War II. After Young's return from the war he began freelancing at various studios. Young won the Academy Award for his role as Rocky, the dance marathon emcee and promoter in the 1969 film. For Young, the Oscar was literally the kiss of death.

Alcoholism plagued his later years, causing him to lose roles. He was fired on the first day of shooting the comedy film Blazing Saddles after collapsing on the set due to withdrawals from alcohol. Young's last role was in the 1978 film Game of Death (1979).

Young was married five times. On September 27, 1978, Young married his fifth wife, a 21-year-old German woman named Kim Schmidt

On October 19, 1978, three weeks after his marriage to Schmidt, the couple was found dead at home in their Manhattan apartment. Police theorized that Young shot his wife and then turned the gun on himself in a murder-suicide.

About the author

Willard C Phillips is a disabled 78 year old USMC combat veteran living on a cattle ranch in Central Texas. Other works include 'The Curse', a mystery set in Hollywood, and 'Lenore and Other Stolen Titles', a collection of short stories and poetry. He can be reached at ppater11@gmail.com. Any complaints regarding this book will be immediately addressed by correction and/or refund. Please give the author a chance to correct errors before posting damning reviews. Please take the time to post a good review if you feel one is justified. Believe it or not, the small income realized from book royalties, are important to the author.

CPSIA information can be obtained at www.ICGtesting.com
Printed in the USA
BVOW031213240212

283759BV00011B/13/P